Creating Powerful Brands

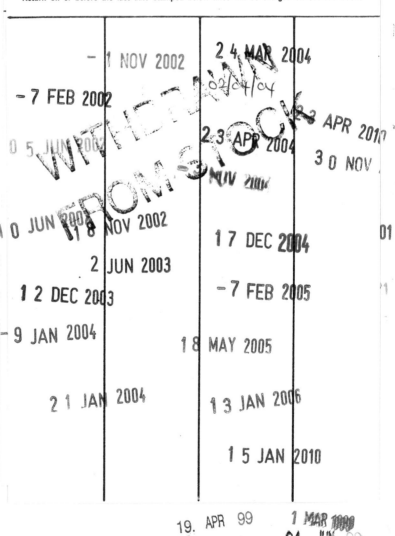

Creating Powerful Brands

The strategic route to success in consumer, industrial and service markets

Leslie de Chernatony
and
Malcolm H. B. McDonald

BUTTERWORTH
HEINEMANN

Butterworth-Heinemann Ltd
Linacre House, Jordan Hill, Oxford OX2 8DP

℞ A member of the Reed Elsevier plc group

OXFORD   LONDON   BOSTON
MUNICH   NEW DELHI   SINGAPORE   SYDNEY
TOKYO   TORONTO   WELLINGTON

First published 1992
Reprinted 1993
Reprinted 1994

British Library Cataloguing in Publication Data
A catalogue record for this book is available from the British Library

ISBN 0 7506 0660 6

Composition by Genesis Typesetting, Laser Quay, Rochester, Kent
Printed in Great Britain by Redwood Books, Trowbridge, Wiltshire

Contents

Preface

The purpose of this book is to cut through the mystique shrouding branding. It aims to clarify what a brand is and to help plan for brands, ensuring a better return on investment. It is not a book on advertising or packaging or about naming procedures. It is a book about planning for successful brands. Nor does it focus on a particular aspect of the marketing mix. Rather it takes a broad perspective, considering how marketing resources have to be blended together, as a consequence of analysing the organization's internal capabilities and the external environment. We believe this approach makes our book unique.

Chapter 1 lays the foundations for this book. It summarizes the latest thinking in the domain of marketing and takes a fresh look at the real nature of an organization's assets, such as market share and supplier and customer relationships, all of which are represented by brands. It also questions traditional thinking and practice in asset accounting and suggests alternative approaches designed to focus attention on the core purpose of this book – how to create powerful brands.

Chapter 2 overviews the roles played by brands and their evolving characteristics. It considers the way that different managers place differing emphasis on the roles they expect their brands to play. These ideas are encapsulated in an eight-category brand typology: brand as a sign of ownership; as a differentiating device; as a functional device; as a symbolic device; as a risk reducer; as a shorthand device; as a legal device, and as a strategic device. These different brand types are expanded on in subsequent chapters. To assess how the resources supporting brands need to be blended, it is important to evaluate the forces influencing brand potential. We present a model of the forces influencing brands which addresses issues affecting the manufacturer, consumers, distributors, competitors and the wider marketing environment. This model and the brand typology helped structure the text.

Chapter 3 focuses on appreciating the way consumers choose brands. It considers the need to trade off quality against quantity of information and reviews the issues involved in naming brands. The concept of perceived risk is described when looking at ways of presenting brands as risk-reducing devices.

Chapter 4 concentrates on the increasing importance of brands in business to business marketing. It considers branding as being more than differentiation. By looking at organizational buying, it discusses the ways in which rational and emotional aspects of buying reduce the need for brands to be presented solely as functional devices.

Chapter 5 follows through the emotional element of branding and discusses the symbolic role brands play. Drawing on self-concept theory, it shows how consumers choose brands to express something about themselves.

Chapter 6 focuses on the added-value element of brands, making the point that added values only help in the branding process if they are relevant to buyers and are noticeably different from those offered by competitors. A four-level model of brands is presented as one way of identifying added values. The problems of relying on the brand as a legal device against counterfeits are reviewed, along with a discussion of other challenges facing brands.

Chapter 7 focuses on retailer issues in branding. It shows how brands have moved from the split, manufacturers' brand versus own label. A review is presented of the own label metamorphosis. The impact of the balance of power shifting from manufacturer to retailer is considered. The issues that retailers and manufacturers have to take into account when cooperating with each other to market brands are discussed.

Chapter 8 looks at planning issues in branding and stresses the need for long-term consistency when positioning brands. A planning model which focuses on the two dimensions of functionality and representationality is described. Consideration is given to the planning of brands over their life cycle.

Chapter 9 concentrates on brands as strategic devices. It reviews the strategies that can be used to position brands in terms of their competitive advantages and the breadth of market they appeal to. The benefits of value chain analysis are presented. The strategic implications from brand share are considered. Characteristics associated with winning brands are described and issues are raised about buying brands and extending brands.

Managers and academics have been forced to think much more clearly about brands as a result of the recent trend towards putting the value of brands on balance sheets in order that they can be managed in the same way as tangible assets. Our aim in this book is not to help managers and academics congratulate themselves on their historical achievements in getting the highest possible goodwill value. Instead, we are concerned with helping current managers and potential managers (some of whom may well be studying at business school), to consider how they can fully capitalize on their brands' assets and sustain accelerated growth. To do this, we have pooled our respective research expertise in branding and marketing planning and presented, in a straightforward style, a synthesis of the key issues involved in planning for successful brands. At the end of each chapter, we have designed a series of questions to help managers test their current brand strategies and help them consider more appropriate routes.

The idea for this book started in the early days of the brand valuation arguments, when one of us was undertaking a PhD concerned with identifying different types of brands in an environment of increasing retailer dominance.* In our subsequent research programmes, consultancy projects and management development workshops, it became increasingly apparent that managers and university students were looking for a clear framework to help them better understand the branding process. By drawing on the considerable literature in branding and testing different frameworks in management development workshops, we developed this text. This book also benefited from discussions with our colleagues, in particular Gil McWilliam at the London Business School.

This book is not just aimed at consumer goods firms, but also at those in services and industrial markets. Branding used to be thought appropriate only for the marketing of consumer goods. This has now changed. With the growing importance of the services sector, many service companies are beginning to appreciate the contributions being made from effective brand strategies. Marketers of industrial goods are also taking advantage of the way branding can help them overcome the low margin, commodity battles that have been historically fought.

Finally Leslie de Chernatony would like to thank his family. His wife Carolyn for her support and two new brands, Gemma and Russell, for their gift of time!

Leslie de Chernatony
Malcolm H. B. McDonald
January 1992

---

* Further details of this can be obtained from Dr Leslie de Chernatony, Centre for Research in Marketing, City University Business School, Frobisher Crescent, Barbican Centre, London EC2Y 8HB.

Acknowledgements

The authors would like to thank the following organizations for granting permission for material to be reproduced in this book: Allen & Hanburys Ltd; Amstrad plc; Appletise plc; Association for Payment Clearing Services; Ayer Ltd; Bradford & Bingley Building Society; Campbell Distillers Ltd; Campbell Gordon, Commercial Property Surveyors, Valuers and Marketing Consultants; Cartier Ltd; Chanel Ltd; The Diamond Information Centre; Dunhill Holdings plc; Electricity Association Technology Ltd; Elida Gibbs Ltd; H J Heinz Company Ltd; Halifax Building Society; Hitachi Europe Ltd; Holiday Inns (UK) Ltd; Interflora; The Invergordon Distillers Ltd; J I Case Europe Ltd; J Sainsbury plc; J Walter Thompson; James Burrough Ltd; The Jenks Group; John Deere Ltd; KLM Royal Dutch Airline; Kodak Ltd; Linn Products Ltd; Lufthansa; Marketing Consultants; Mazda Cars (UK) Ltd; Midland Agriculture; PepsiCo Inc; PG Tips; Philips Electronic and Associated Industries Ltd; Pioneer High Fidelity (GB) Ltd; Port Philip Group; The Prestige Group plc; R Twining and Company Ltd; Royal Mail International; Russell & Bromley Ltd; Safeway plc; Seiko UK Ltd; Sun Alliance Life Ltd; Tesco Stores Ltd; United Distillers UK plc; Vax Appliances Ltd; W H Smith Ltd; William Grant & Sons Ltd.

1 Why it is important to create powerful brands

Summary

This introductory chapter lays the foundations for the remaining chapters of this book. It summarizes the latest thinking and best practice in the domain of marketing and takes a fresh look at the real nature of an organization's assets, such as market share and supplier and customer relationships, all of which are represented by the brand. It also questions traditional thinking and practice in asset accounting and suggests alternative approaches designed to focus attention on the core purpose of this book – how to create powerful brands.

Dispelling misunderstanding about product management

In spite of its somewhat histrionic title, this book is a serious, in-depth attempt by two professional teachers, researchers and practitioners, to focus attention on an aspect of marketing that is frequently misunderstood and consequently neglected – **branding**.

Let us begin the process of orientating our minds towards this important subject by asking ourselves 'what is a product?' or 'what is a service?' The central role that the product plays in business management makes it such an important subject, that mismanagement in this area is unlikely to be compensated for by good management in other areas. Misunderstanding in relation to the nature of *product* management is also the root of whatever subsequent misunderstanding there is about *brand* management.

What is a product?

It should hardly be necessary to explain that a product or a service is a *problem solver*, in the sense that it solves the customer's problems and

Exhibit 1.1   *Royal Mail International present their service as a problem solver*

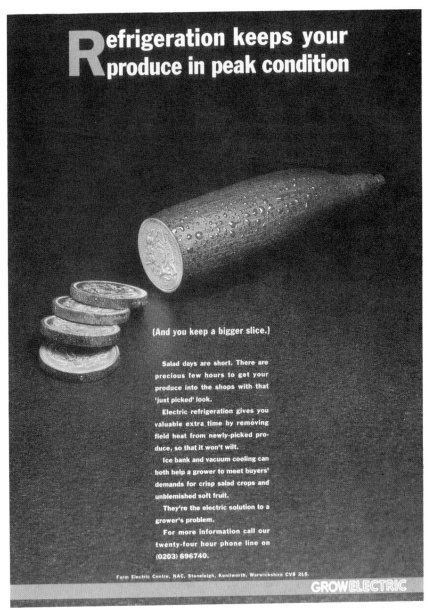

Exhibit 1.2   *As this advertisement exemplifies, the concept of presenting a product or service as a problem solver is not unique to consumer marketing*

is also the means by which the organization achieves its own objectives. And since it is what actually changes hands, it is clearly a subject of great importance.

The clue to what constitutes a product can be found in an examination of what it is that customers appear to buy. For instance, Theodore Levitt, the famous management writer, illustrates that what customers want when they buy ¼-inch drills is ¼-inch holes. In other words the drill itself is only a means to an end. The lesson here for the drill manufacturer is that if he really believes his business is the manufacture of drills rather than, say, the manufacture of the means of making holes in materials, he is in grave danger of going out of business as soon as a better means of making holes is invented, such as, say, a pocket laser.

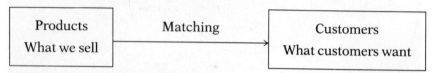

The important point about this is that a company which fails to think of its business in terms of customer benefits rather than in terms of physical products is in danger of losing its competitive position in the market.

We can now begin to see that when a customer buys a product, even if he is an industrial buyer purchasing a piece of equipment for his company, he is still buying a particular bundle of benefits which he perceives as satisfying his own particular needs and wants.

We can all begin to appreciate the danger of leaving product decisions entirely to engineers or R & D people. If we do, engineers will often assume that the only point in product management is the actual technical performance, or the functional features of the product itself. These ideas are incorporated in Figure 1.1.

We can go even further than this and depict two outer circles as the 'product surround'. This product surround can account for as much as 80 per cent of the added values and impact of a product or service. Often, these only account for about 20 per cent of costs, whereas the reverse is often true of the inner circle.

The nature of relationships with customers

Figure 1.1 also begins to throw light on the nature of the confusion surrounding the relationships that organizations enjoy with their customers. It is a sad reflection on the state of marketing that in spite of fifty years of marketing education, ignorance still abounds concerning what marketing is. The following are the major areas of confusion:

1 *Confusion with product management*   The belief that all a company has to do to succeed is to produce a good product still abounds, and

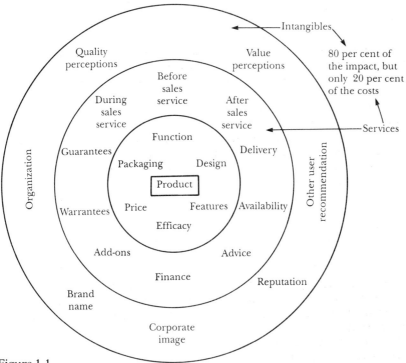

Figure 1.1

neither Concorde, the EMI Scanner, nor the many thousands of brilliant products that have seen their owners or inventors go bankrupt during the past twenty years will convince such people otherwise.

2 *Confusion with advertising*   This is another popular misconception and the annals of business are replete with examples such as Dunlop, Woolworths and British Airways who, before they got professional management in, won awards with their brilliant advertising campaigns, while failing to deliver the goods. Throwing advertising expenditure at the problem is still a very popular way of tackling deep-rooted marketing problems.

3 *Confusion with customer service*   The 'Have a nice day' syndrome is currently having its hey-day in many countries of the world, popularized by Peters and Waterman in *In Search of Excellence*. The banks are amongst those who have spent millions training their staff to be charming to customers while still getting the basic offer fundamentally wrong – for example, many banks are still closed when the public most needs them open! Likewise, in many railway companies around the world, while it helps to be treated nicely, it is actually much more important to get there on time.

Likewise, selling is just one aspect of communication with customers, and to say that it is the only thing that matters is to ignore the importance of product management, pricing, distribution and other forms of communication in achieving profitable sales. Selling is just one part of this process, in which the transaction is actually clinched. It is the culmination of the marketing process, and success will only be possible if all the other elements of the marketing mix have been properly managed. Imagine having a horse that didn't have four legs! The more attention that is paid to finding out what customers want, to developing products to satisfy these wants, to pricing at a level consistent with the benefits offered, to gaining distribution, and to communicating effectively with our target market, the more likely we are to be able to exchange contracts through the personal selling process.

The organization's marketing assets

Textbook definitions of marketing have emphasized the satisfaction of identified customer needs as a fundamental article of faith. Various interpretations exist, but the concept of 'putting the customer at the centre of the business' summarizes these viewpoints.

Philosophically, there is little to argue with in this notion. However, it must be recognized that the ability of the business to produce offerings that meet real needs will generally be limited to very specific areas. More particularly, what we find is that an organization's skills and resources are the limiting factor determining its ability to meet market-place needs. The example of a slide rule manufacturer being unable to compete in the age of electronic calculators underlines this point. The strengths and skills of such a company, whatever they may have been, were quite definitely not in the manufacture of electronic calculators, whereas they may well have had a strength in marketing and distribution in specialized markets – thus possibly providing an opportunity to distribute other manufacturers' products aimed at those markets.

What we are in effect saying is that marketing should really be seen as the process of achieving *the most effective deployment of the firm's assets* to achieve overall corporate objectives. By assets in this context, we refer specifically to those assets which might best be described as 'marketing assets'.

What are marketing assets? Typically when we talk about assets, we think first of financial assets, or more precisely those assets that are recognized in the balance sheet of the business. So, fixed assets, such as plant and machinery, and current assets, such as inventory or cash, would be typical of this view of assets.

In fact, the marketing assets of the business are of far greater importance to the long-run health of the business and yet paradoxically rarely appear in the balance sheet. Ultimately, the only assets that have value are those that contribute directly or indirectly to profitable sales, now or in the future. Included in our categorization of marketing assets would be such things as:

- *Market 'franchise'* Are there certain parts of the market that we can call our own? The loyalty of customers and distributors will be a factor here.
- *Distribution network* Do we have established channels of distribution which enable us to bring products or services to the market in a cost-effective way?
- *Market share* The 'experience effect' and economies of scale mean that for many companies there are substantial advantages to being big. For example, costs will be lower and visibility in the market-place will be higher.
- *Supplier relationships* The ability to have access to raw materials, low-cost components, and so on, can be of substantial advantage. Additionally, close cooperation with suppliers can frequently lead to innovative product developments.
- *Customer reactions* 'Close to the customer' has become the motto of the 1990s, and many organizations can testify to the advantage of strong bonds between the company and its customers.
- *Technology base* Does the company have any unique skills, processes or know-how strengths that can provide a basis for product/market exploitation?

It is only through the effective use of these and any other marketing assets that the company can build successful marketing strategies. There still, of course, remains the crucial task of seeking market-place opportunities for the exploitation of this asset base; however, this is an issue outside the scope of this book.

Nevertheless, if we are to be serious about marketing assets, perhaps managerially we should treat them as we do 'financial' assets. In which case questions such as these arise:

- How do we value market assets?
- How do we protect them?
- How do we grow them?

The question of the valuation of marketing assets is complex and controversial. Traditionally, the only time that an attempt is made to put a financial value on these intangible assets is when a company is bought or sold. It will often be the case that one company, in acquiring another, will pay more than the 'book value' of the acquired company – as represented, that is, in the balance sheet. The accountants' answer to this is to treat the difference between the purchase price and the book value as 'goodwill' and then to write it off against reserves or amortize it through the profit-and-loss account over a number of years.

The importance of the brand

Perceptive readers will already have observed that, so far, we have deliberately chosen not to make any reference to brands as assets. It will also be clear by now that Figure 1.1 depicts not just a physical product, but a *relationship* with the customer. This relationship is personified either by the organization's name, or by the brand name on the product itself. ICI, IBM, BMW, Kodak and Cadburys are excellent examples of company brand names. Persil, Nescafe, Fosters, Dulux and Castrol GTX are excellent examples of product brand names.

First, then, it should be stressed, that when we refer to the term 'brand' in this book, we use it to encompass not only consumer products, but a whole host of offerings, which include people (such as politicians and pop stars), places (such as Bangkok), ships (such as the Queen Elizabeth), companies, industrial products, service products, and so on.

Second, a distinction should be drawn between a 'brand' and a 'commodity'. Commodity markets typically are characterized by the lack of perceived differentiation by customers between competing offerings. In other words, one product offering in a particular category is much like another. Products like milk or potatoes come to mind or tin and iron ore. Whilst there may be quality differences the suggestion is that, within a given specification, this bottle of milk is just the same as that bottle of milk.

In situations such as these, one finds that purchase decisions tend to be taken on the basis of price or availability, and not on the basis of the brand or the manufacturer's name. Thus one could argue that the purchase of petrol falls into the commodity category, and whilst the petrol companies do try and promote 'image', they inevitably end up relying upon promotions such as wine glasses and games to try to generate repeat purchase.

There are examples, however, of taking a commodity and making it a brand. Take, for example, Perrier Water: the contents are naturally occurring spring water which, whilst it has certain distinctive characteristics, at the end of the day is still spring water. Yet through packaging and, more particularly, promotion, an international brand has been created with high brand loyalty and consequently it sells for a price well in excess of the costs of the ingredients.

Conversely, one can also find examples of once-strong brands which have been allowed to decay and in effect become commodities. This process is often brought about because the marketing asset base has been allowed to erode – perhaps through price cutting or through a lack of attention to product improvement in the face of competition. One market where this has happened in the UK is in the fruit-squash drink market. Fifteen or twenty years ago, there were a number of very strong brands – Suncrush, Kia-ora, Jaffa Juice, to name a few. In this market, the quality of the brand had traditionally been stressed, but a switch in promotional emphasis occurred in the 1960s towards promotional offers of one sort or another. Price cutting became prevalent and resources were switched out of advertising which promoted the values of the brand and into so-called 'below the line' promotional activities. The main effect of this, twenty years later, has been to reduce the bottle of orange squash to the level of a commodity to such an extent that the major brands are now retailers' own label products.

Figure 1.2 depicts the process of decay from brand to commodity as, over time, the distinctive values of the brand become less clear and thus the opportunity to demand a premium price reduces. So, today, we find a bottle of Perrier Water selling at a premium over a bottle of orange squash!

Figure 1.2 is referred to again later in the book.

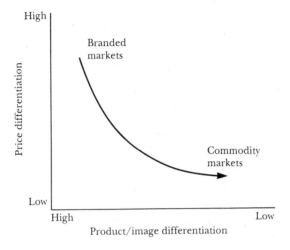

Figure 1.2   *From brand to commodity*

The difference between a brand and a commodity can be summed up in the phrase 'added values'. A brand is more than just the sum of its component parts. It embodies, for the purchaser or user, additional attributes which, whilst they might be considered by some to be 'intangible', are still very real. To illustrate the power of these added values consider the results of a *blind* test (i.e. where the brand identity is concealed) in which Diet Pepsi was compared against Diet Coke by a panel of consumers:

- Prefer Pepsi   51 per cent
- Prefer Coke   44 per cent
- Equal/can't say   5 per cent

When the same two drinks were given to a matched sample in an *open test* (i.e. the true identity of the brands was revealed), the following results were produced:

- Prefer Pepsi   23 per cent
- Prefer Coke   65 per cent
- Equal/can't say   12 per cent

How can this be explained if not in terms of the added values that are aroused in the minds of consumers when they see the familiar Coke logo and pack?

This example is referred to in more detail later in the book.

The same phenomenon is also encountered in industrial marketing. In a commodity market such as fertilizers, the initials 'ICI' printed on a plastic sack have the effect of communicating to the purchaser a statement about quality and reliability, giving ICI a considerable advantage over lesser-known brands.

Often, these added values are emotional values which customers might find difficult to articulate. These values are given to a product quite simply through the marketing mix of product, packaging, promotion, price and distribution. All of these elements of the mix can be used to develop a distinctive *position* in the customers' mental map of the market. As in all the references to brands thus far, the concept of 'positioning' is developed in greater detail in the following chapters, but suffice it to say at this juncture that in commodity markets, competing products, because they are undifferentiated, are seen by the customer as occupying virtually identical positions and thus to all intents and purposes are substitutable. The more distinctive a *brand* position, however, the less likelihood that a customer will accept a substitute.

It is thus the case that the most effective dimensions of competition are the relative added values of competing brands. The 'core' product is purely the tangible features of the offering – usually easy to imitate. The added values that augment the product and where distinctive differences can be created, are to be found in the 'product surround', summarized again in Figure 1.3.

The larger the 'surround' in relation to the core product, the more likely it is that the offering will be strongly differentiated from the competition, and vice versa.

The Coca-Cola example, to which we shall return in the main body of the text, is one of the best indications of the value of what we have

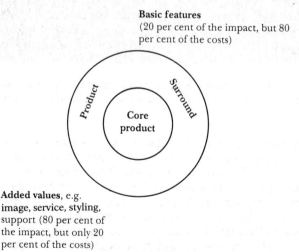

Basic features
(20 per cent of the impact, but 80 per cent of the costs)

Added values, e.g. image, service, styling, support (80 per cent of the impact, but only 20 per cent of the costs)

Figure 1.3   *The importance of added values*

Exhibit 1.3   *Coco Parfum from Chanel is a good example of a brand succeeding by surrounding a core product with the added value of a highly respected brand personality*

called the 'product surround'. That it is a major determinant of commercial success, there can be little doubt. When one company buys another, as in the case of Nestle and Rowntrees, it is abundantly clear that the purpose of the acquisition is not to buy the tangible assets which appear on the balance sheet, such as factories, plant, vehicles and so on, but the brand names owned by the company to be acquired. This is because it is not factories which make profits, but relationships with customers, and it is brand names which secure these relationships.

It might be argued, therefore, that if it is possible to value a company for sale, then surely it should be possible to do so on an on-going basis and specifically to recognize the worth of marketing assets as represented by brands.

The question of asset protection and development is in a sense what marketing is all about. The 'stewardship' of marketing assets is a key responsibility which is recognized in many companies by, for example, the organizational concept of brand management. Here, an executive is given the responsibility for a brand or brands and acts as the product 'champion', competing internally for resources and externally for market position. It is but a short step from this organizational concept to a system of 'brand accounting' which would seek to identify the net present value of a brand based upon the prospect of future cash inflows compared with outgoings.

One advantage of such an approach is that it forces the manager to acknowledge that money spent on developing the market position of a brand is in fact an investment which is made in order to generate future benefits. There is a strong argument for suggesting that, for internal decision making and on questions of resource allocation, a 'shadow' set of management accounts be used, not the traditional approach whereby marketing costs are expensed in the period in which they are incurred, but an approach which recognizes such expenditure as investments.

Buying a major brand nowadays often makes more sense to organizations than launching a new brand, with all the risk and uncertainty that this entails. This is just one of the reasons why brand valuation has emerged as a major issue in recent times and why brands are increasingly sought after as assets.

Some of the more spectacular examples of the value of brands as assets can be seen in acquisitions in which colossal premiums were paid above the balance sheet asset value. Philip Morris, for example, bought Kraft for $12.9 bn, four times the value of Kraft's tangible assets. Grand Metropolitan bought Pillsbury for $5.5 bn, a 50 per cent premium on Pillsbury's pre-bid value. More recently, AT and T paid a massive premium for the NCR brand. RHM, taking its cue from this trend, more than trebled its asset value when it voluntarily valued its own brands and incorporated them on the balance sheet.

Building successful brands

We hope that we have, by now, been able to give some initial signals about increasing importance of brands in business success. Later in this book, we refer to the PIMS data base (Profit Impact of Market Strategies), which, along with other data bases, show conclusively that strong, successful brands enable organizations to build stable, long-term demand and enable them to build and hold better margins than either commodity products or unsuccessful brands. (Brands, of course, can be either successful or unsuccessful. Waterways in the UK is a prime example of an unsuccessful brand.)

Successful brand building helps profitability by adding values that entice customers to buy. They also provide a firm base for expansion into product improvements, variants, added services, new countries, and so on. They also protect the organizations against the growing power of intermediaries. And last, but not least, they help transform organizations from being faceless bureaucracies to ones that are attractive to work for and to deal with.

The following chapters of this book contain an in-depth treatment of every aspect relevant to successful brand building. How to create powerful brands is a major challenge facing all organizations today. It is unlikely that this challenge will be met unless a more rigorous approach is taken to the issues surrounding branding.

We urge you to read on!

Book modus operandi

Each of the following chapters covers a number of vital aspects of brand management and concludes with an action checklist. Finally, for the convenience of our readers, we have included a further reading list on the more important aspects covered in each chapter.

2 Understanding the branding process

Summary

The purpose of this chapter is to provide an overview of the key issues involved in planning for brand success. It begins by explaining that successful branding is more than merely the use of names, then goes on to discuss the concept of the brand, the historical evolution of brands, distributors' brands and generics, brand categorization in the 1990s, the value of brands to manufacturers, distributors and buyers, the importance of brand planning and the issues influencing the potential of a brand.

Brand success through integrating marketing resources

When BMW drivers proudly turn the ignition keys for the first time in 'the ultimate driving machine', they are not only benefiting from a highly engineered car with an excellent performance, but are also taking ownership of a symbol that signifies the core values of exclusivity, performance, quality and technical innovation. Purchasers of a Prudential insurance policy are not just buying the security of knowing that damage to their home through unforseen events can rapidly and inexpensively be rectified. They are also buying the corporate symbol of the face of Prudence reminding them of the added values of heritage, size and public awareness, inspiring confidence and sustained credibility. Likewise the data processing manager buying an IBM computer, is not just buying a device that rapidly computes data into a format that is more managerially useful, but is also buying the security of a back-up facility and commitment to customer satisfaction signified by the three letters of IBM.

While these purchasers in the consumer, service and industrial markets have bought solutions to their individual problems, they have also paid a price premium for the added values provided by buying *brands*. In addition to satisfying their core purchase requirements, they have bought an augmented solution to their problem, for which they perceive sufficient added value to warrant paying a premium over other alternatives that might have satisfied their buying needs.

The added values they sought, however, were not just those provided through the presence of a brand name as a differentiating device, nor through the use of brand names to recall powerful advertising. Instead, they perceived a total entity, the *brand*, which is the result of a coherent marketing approach which uses all elements of the marketing mix. A man does not give a woman a box of branded chocolates because she is hungry. Instead, he selects a brand that communicates something about his relationship with her. This, he hopes, will be recognized through the pack design, her recall of a relevant advertising message, the quality of the contents, her chiding of him for the price he paid and her appreciation of the effort he took to find a retailer specializing in stocking such an exclusive brand. The same goes for a woman buying a man a special box of cigars.

These examples show that thinking of branding as being 'to do with naming products', or 'about getting the right promotion with the name prominently displayed', or 'getting the design right', is too myopic. In the mid 1980s, we came across Scottowels when doing some work in the kitchen towels market. Managers in the company thought that this was a branded kitchen towel, but consumers perceived this as little more than another kitchen towel with a name added – one stage removed from being a commodity. It had a brand name, but because the rest of the marketing mix was neglected, it had to fight for shelf space on the basis of price and was ultimately doomed because of the vicious circle driven by minimum value leading to low price.

There are hundreds of examples of well-known brand names that have failed commercially. There are even some which are reviled by the public. Such unsuccessful brands are examples of a failure to integrate all the elements of marketing in a coherent way.

Thus, branding is a powerful marketing concept that does not just focus on one element of the marketing mix, but represents the result of a carefully conceived array of activities across the whole spectrum of the marketing mix, directed towards making the buyer recognize relevant added values that are unique when compared with competing products and services and which are difficult for competitors to emulate. The purpose of branding is to facilitate the organization's task of getting and maintaining a loyal customer base in a cost-effective manner to achieve the highest possible return on investment. In other words, branding should not be regarded as a tactical tool directed towards one element of the marketing mix, but rather should be seen as the result of strategic thinking, integrating a marketing programme across the complete marketing mix.

Neither is this a concept that should be regarded as more appropriate for consumer markets. Indeed, the concept of branding is increasingly being applied to people and places, such as politicians,

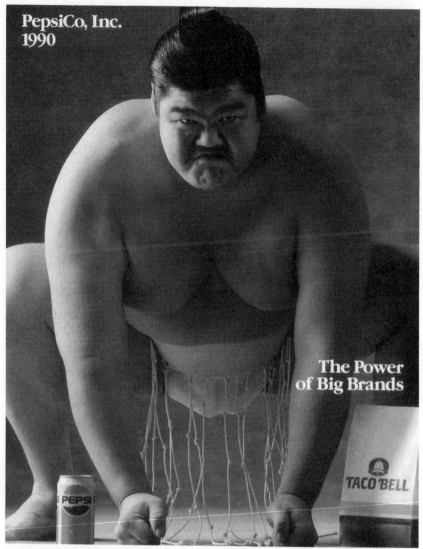

**PepsiCo, Inc.
1990**

**The Power
of Big Brands**

PEPSI

TACO BELL.

Exhibit 2.1   *With a commitment to an integrated and coherent marketing
approach to branding, PepsiCo Inc are proud of their enhanced profitability from
brands. (Reproduced with kind permission of © PepsiCo Inc 1991, Purchase,
New York)*

pop stars, holiday resorts and the like, whilst it has always been
equally relevant to the marketing of products and services. Were this
not so, organizations such as IBM would be unable to charge
significantly higher prices for their computers, which compete so
successfully with technically more advanced machines selling at lower
prices. Strategic branding is concerned with evaluating how to achieve
the highest return on investment from brands, through analysing,

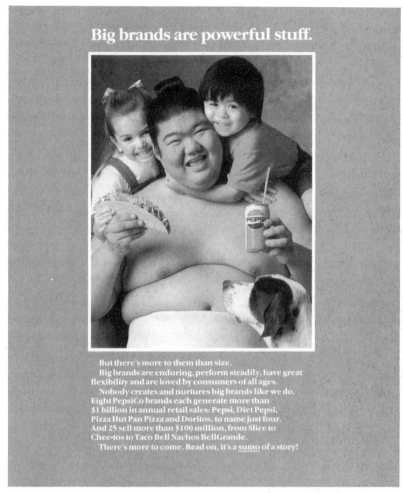

Exhibit 2.1 *(continued)*

formulating and implementing a strategy that best satisfies users, distributors and brand manufacturers. It is only recently that a strategic perspective on branding has emerged, with firms beginning to recognize that they are sitting on valuable assets that need careful attention, as we shall see in the next section.

The concept of the brand

Successful brands, that is those which are the focus of a coherent blending of marketing resources, represent valuable marketing assets. During the 1980s the value of brands was ironically brought to the attention of marketers by the financial community. For example, in 1985 Reckitt and Colman acquired Airwick Industries and put on its balance sheet £127 million as the financial value resulting from the intangible benefits of goodwill, heritage and loyalty conveyed by the newly acquired brand names. While this may have been one of the opening shots to make organizations aware of the financial value of brands, it was Rank Hovis McDougal who really brought the brand debate to life. They announced in 1988 that they had put £678 million on their balance sheet as the valuation of their brand names. In the same year Jacobs Suchard and Nestle fought for the ownership of Rowntree. At the time of the takeover battle it was estimated that Rowntree's tangible net assets were worth around £300 m, yet Nestle won control by paying £2.5 bn. This difference of £2.2 bn represented the value that Nestle saw in the potential earnings of strong brands such as Kit Kat, Polo, Quality Street and After Eight Mints!

Thus, because consumers recognize and appreciate the added values of successful brands, they are able to sustain a higher price premium over equivalent commodity items and generally generate healthy profits.

The ultimate assessor of the real value of a brand, however, is not the manufacturer or the distributor, but the buyer or the user. Marketers are able to develop strategies to convey added values to purchasers, but because of what is called the 'perceptual process', the target audience may well focus on only a part of the available information and 'twist' some of the messages to make them congruent with their prior beliefs. For example should a wallpaper paste manufacturer show an apparently incompetent DIY householder mixing paste in a television commercial in an attempt to communicate the smoothness and ease of application of their brand of wallpaper paste, they run the risk of some consumers interpreting the brand as being 'suitable for idiots'. This is one example of the perceptual process.

It is imperative to recognize that while marketers instigate the branding process (i.e. branding as an input), it is the buyer or the user who forms a mental vision of the brand (i.e. branding as an output), which may be different from the intended marketing thrust. While marketers talk about the branding effort they are undertaking, they should never lose sight of the fact that the final form of the brand is the mental evaluation held by the purchasers or users. Branding, then, needs to be appreciated in terms of both the input and the output process.

Drawing on the points discussed so far, we can better clarify the term 'brand' through our definition:

A successful brand is an identifiable product, service, person or place, augmented in such a way that the buyer or user perceives relevant unique added values which match their needs most closely. Furthermore its success results from being able to sustain these added values in the face of competition.

Later in this chapter we review the plethora of brand definitions, some of which provide a helpful insight for the practitioner, but none of which fully describe the concept. Our definition above recognizes that brands exist in both product (consumer and industrial) and service domains and even relate to people, for example pop stars, and places, for example the marketing of cities as tourist attractions.

Brands are successful when developed with a clear statement of intent about the product's or service's purpose, the specific group of customers the brand is targeted at and a commitment to equipping the brand with the right types of resources to achieve the stated purpose.

Exhibit 2.2   *The travel firm is taking advantage of the brand benefits offered by Queensland Tourist Commission*

For example, Coca-Cola's success is partly attributable to a clear positioning as a refreshing, fun-type drink, targeted at teenagers and backed by a tradition of quality and continual consumer communication.

Brands deliver a variety of benefits, which for ease can be classified as satisfying buyers' rational and emotional needs. Successful brands are those which have the correct balance in terms of their ability to satisfy these two needs. For example, cigarette smokers have a variety of rational needs such as seeking the best value, or best taste, or best quality, or a certain aroma or achieving relaxation, etc. The extent to which different brands satisfy particular rational needs will be assessed by the consumer trying different brands, examining the packaging, looking at the shape of the cigarette, considering its price, etc. Besides these rational needs they will also be seeking to satisfy emotional needs, such as prestige, or distinctiveness, or style, or social reassurance, etc. The extent to which different brands satisfy these emotional needs will be evaluated by consumers recalling promotions, or assessing who smokes different brands, or considering what situations different brands are consumed in, etc. To succeed, the marketer must understand the extent to which their brand satisfies rational and emotional needs and then develop marketing programmes accordingly.

Some may question whether the rational dimension dominates industrial branding and therefore whether there is any need to consider emotional aspects at all. Our work has shown that emotion plays an important role in the industrial brand selection process. For example, some office services managers do not just consider the rational aspects of office furniture brands they are about to buy, but also seek emotional reassurance that the correct brand decision might reaffirm their continual career development or that they have not lost credibility amongst colleagues through the wrong brand choice.

Characteristics of brands

Our definition of a brand adheres to a model which shows the extent to which a product or service can be augmented to provide added value to increasing levels of sophistication. This model, which is expanded on in Chapter 6, views a brand as consisting of four levels:

- generic
- expected
- augmented
- potential

The *generic* level is the commodity form that meets the buyer's or user's basic needs, for example the car satisfying a transportation need. This is the easiest aspect for competitors to copy and consequently successful brands have added values over and above this at the *expected* level.

Within the *expected* level, the commodity is value engineered to satisfy a specific target's minimum purchase conditions, such as functional capabilities, availability, pricing, etc. As more buyers enter the market and as repeat buying occurs, the brand would evolve through a better matching of resources to meet customers' needs (e.g. enhanced customer service).

With increased experience, buyers and users become more sophisticated, so the brand would need to be *augmented* in more refined ways, with added values satisfying non-functional (e.g. emotional) as well as functional needs. For example, promotions might be directed to the user's peer group to reinforce his or her social standing through ownership of the brand.

With even more experience of the brand, and therefore with a greater tendency to be more critical, it is only creativity that limits the extent to which the brand can mature to the *potential* level. For example, grocery retail buyers regarded the Rowntree confectionery brands as having reached the zenith of the *augmented* stage. To counter the threat of their brands slipping back to the *expected* brand level, and therefore having to fight on price, Rowntree shifted their brands to the *potential* level by developing software for retailers to manage confectionery shelf space to maximize profitability. Experienced consumers recognize that competing items are often similar in terms of product formulation and that brand owners are no longer focusing only on rational functional issues, but are addressing the *potential* level of brands by promoting more intangible, emotional factors.

To succeed in the long run, a brand must offer added values over and above the basic product characteristics, if for no other reason than that functional characteristics are so easy to copy by competitors. In the services sector, when all other factors are equal, this could be as simple as a correctly spelt surname on the monthly bank statement. In the industrial market, it could be conveyed by the astute sales engineer presenting the brand as a no-risk purchase (due to the thoroughness of testing, the credibility of the organization, compliance with British Standards, case histories of other users, etc.). It is most important to realize that the added values must be relevant to the customer and not just to the manufacturer or distributor. Car manufacturers who announced that their brands had the added value of electronic circuits emitting 'computer speak' when seat belts were not worn didn't take long to discover that this so-called benefit was intensely disliked by customers. In the retail banking sector, customers perceive added value when a full quota of clerks are present to serve, rather than a teller's cheerful face to greet the customer after a ten-minute wait resulting from inadequate staffing levels.

Buyers perceive added value in a brand because they recognize certain clues which give signals about the offer. In industrial markets, for example, buyers evaluate brands on a wide variety of attributes, rather than just on price. As a consequence, price is rarely the most important variable influencing the purchase decision. So it is not unusual for a buyer to remain loyal to a supplier during a period of price rises. However, if the price of a brand rises and one of the signalling clues is weak (say, poor reliability of delivery) compared with the other signalling clues (say, product quality), the buyer may perceive that the brand's value has diminished and will therefore be more likely to consider competitive brands. A further example of the need to provide consistency of signalling clues about brands is that of an advertising agency which produced an advertisement targeted at businesspeople, to portray the added value of in-flight comfort. Depth interviews amongst businesspeople revealed strong feelings about the poor quality of the advertisement and a concomitant rejection of any belief that such a company could deliver in-flight comfort. Sophisticated consumers recognized the high predictive capability of a clue (poor advertising) and rejected the brand's added value.

If brands are to thrive, their marketing support will have been geared towards providing the user with the maximum satisfaction in a particular context. Buyers often use brands as non-verbal clues to communicate with their peer groups. In other words, it is recognized that people do not use brands only for their functional capabilities, but also for their badge or symbolic value. It has been observed that people take care over their selection of clothes, since according to the situation, their brand of clothes is being used to signal messages of propriety, status or even seduction. Buyers choose brands with which they feel both physical and psychological comfort in specific situations. They are concerned about selecting brands which reinforce their own concept of themselves in specific situations. A very self-conscious young man may well drink a particular brand of lager with his peer group because he believes it will convey an aspect of his lifestyle; whilst at home alone his brand consumption behaviour may well be different, since he is less concerned about the situational context. Chapter 5 considers in more detail the importance of appreciating the situation within which the consumer uses the brand.

It is worth noting that this phenomenon has been recorded by many researchers. For example, it has been found that for cars and clothing, people were more likely to buy brands which they perceived were similar to their own concept of themselves. Where marketers have grounds for believing that their brands are being used by consumers as value-expressive devices, they need to be attuned to the interaction of the marketing mix with the user's environment and provide the appropriate support. In some instances this may involve targeting promotional activity to the user's peer group, to ensure that they recognize the symbolic messages being portrayed by the brand.

Whilst this issue of appreciating the buyer's or user's environment relates to consumer markets, it is also apparent in industrial markets. One researcher found that in a laboratory with a high proportion of well-educated scientists, there was a marked preference for a piece of scientific equipment that had a 'designer label' cabinet, over the same equipment presented in a more utilitarian manner. In a highly rational environment, scientists were partly influenced by a desire to select a brand of equipment which they felt better expressed their own concept of themselves

Finally, our definition of a brand adopts a strategic perspective, recognizing that unless the added value is unique and sustainable against competitive activity, the life time will be very short. Without such a strategic perspective, then, it is questionable whether it is viable to follow a branding route. Chapter 9 reviews the way that the concept of the value chain can be used to identify where in the value-adding process the firm's brand has a unique advantage over competition and also considers whether any of these strengths can be rapidly copied. For example, in the coffee market Nestle have a competitive advantage for their brand through consistently sourcing high-grade coffee beans, Porsche's and Swatch's competitive advantage is excellence of product design, Federal Express in their distribution planning and monitoring systems and the Equitable Life Assurance Company in its low cost sales force. It is our contention that unless brand instigators have a sustainable differential advantage, they should seriously consider the economics of following a manufacturer's brand route and consider becoming a supplier of a distributor's brand. In such situations it is more probable that the firm will follow a more profitable route by becoming a distributor brand supplier (i.e. a supplier of own label products) as discussed in Chapter 8.

Historical evolution of brands

Having clarified the concept of the brand, it is worth appreciating how brands evolved. This historical review shows how different *types* of brands evolved.

There were examples of brands being used in Greek and Roman times. With a high level of illiteracy, shop keepers hung pictures above their shops indicating the types of goods they sold. Symbols were developed to provide an indication of the retailer's speciality and thus the brand logo as a *shorthand device* signalling the brand's capability was born. Use is still made of this aspect of branding, as in the case, for example, of the poised jaguar indicating the power developed by the Jaguar brand.

In the Middle Ages, craftsmen with specialist skills began to stamp their marks on their goods and trademarks. *Distinguishing* between different suppliers became more common. In these early days, branding gradually became a *guarantee* of the source of the product and ultimately as a form of *legal protection* against copying grew. Today, trademarks include words (e.g. Matchbox), symbols (e.g. the distinctive Shell logo) or a unique pack shape (e.g. the Coca-Cola bottle), which have been registered and which purchasers recognize as being unique to a particular brand. However, as the well-travelled reader is no doubt aware, trademark infringement is a source of concern to owners of well-respected brands such as Rolex.

The next landmark in the evolution of brands was associated with the growth of cattle farming in the New World of North America.

Cattle owners wanted to make it clear to other potentially interested parties which animals they owned. By using a red hot iron, with a uniquely shaped end, they left a clear imprint on the skin of each of their animals. This process appears to have been taken by many as the basis for the meaning of the term brand, defined by the *Oxford English Dictionary* as 'to mark indelibly as proof of ownership, as a sign of quality, or for any other purpose'. This view of the purpose of brands as being identifying (*differentiating*) devices has remained with us until today. What is surprising is that in an enlightened era aware of the much broader strategic interpretation of brands, many of today's leading marketing textbooks still adhere to the brand solely as a differentiating device, for example, 'a name, term, sign, symbol, or design, or a combination of them, which is intended to identify the goods or services of one seller or group of sellers and to differentiate them from those of competitors'. Towards the end of the nineteenth century, such a view was justified, as the next few paragraphs clarify. However, as the opening sections of this chapter have explained, to regard brands as little more than differentiating devices is to run the risk of the rapid demise of the product or service in question.

To appreciate why organizations subscribed to brands as *differentiating* devices over 100 years ago and to appreciate why this view held favour until the 1960s, it is necessary to consider the evolving retailing environment, particularly that relating to groceries, where classical brand management developed. In the first half of the nineteenth century, people bought their goods through four channels:

1 retailers;
2 from those who grew and sold their own wares;
3 from markets where farmers displayed produce;
4 from travelling salesmen.

Household groceries were normally produced by small manufacturers supplying a locally confined market. Consequently the quality of similar products varied according to retailer, who in many instances blended several suppliers' produce. With the advent of the Industrial Revolution, several factors influenced the manufacturer–retailer relationship, i.e.:

• the rapid rise of urban growth, reducing manufacturer-consumer contact;
• the widening of markets through improved transportation;
• the increasing number of retail outlets;
• the wider range of products held by retailers;
• increasing demand.

A consequence of this was that manufacturers' production increased, but with their increasing separation from consumers, they came to rely more on wholesalers. Likewise, retailers' dependence on wholesalers increased, from whom they expected greater services. Until the end of the nineteenth century, the situation was one of wholesaler dominance. Manufacturers produced according to wholesalers' stipulations, who, in turn, were able to dictate terms and strongly influence the product range of the retailer. As an indication of the importance of wholesalers, it is estimated that by 1900, wholesalers were the main suppliers of the independent retailers, who accounted for 87–90 per cent of all retail sales.

During this stage, most manufacturers were:

- selling unbranded goods;
- having to meet wholesalers' demands for low prices;
- spending minimal amounts on advertising;
- selling direct to wholesalers, while having little contact with retailers.

In this situation of competitive tender, the manufacturer's profit depended mostly on sheer production efficiency. It was virtually commodity marketing, with little scope for increasing margins by developing and launching new products.

The growing levels of consumer demand and the increasing rate of technological development were regarded by manufacturers as attractive opportunities for profitable growth through investing in large-scale production facilities. Such action, though, would lead to the production of goods in *anticipation*, rather than as a *response*, to demand. Not only were manufacturers perturbed by having to adopt the new techniques of planning, but with such large investments, they were concerned about their reliance on wholesalers. To protect their investment, patents were registered and brand names affixed by the owners. The power of the wholesalers was also bypassed by advertising brands direct to consumers. The role of advertising in this era was to stabilize demand, ensuring predictable large-scale production protected from the whims of wholesalers. In such a situation, the advertising tended to focus on promoting awareness of reliability and guaranteeing that goods with brand names were of a consistent quality. The third way that manufacturers invested in protecting the growth of their brands was through appointing their own salesmen to deal directly with retailers.

By the second half of the nineteenth century, many major manufacturers had embarked on branding, advertising and using a sales force to reduce the dominance of wholesalers. In fact, by 1900, the balance of power had swung to the manufacturer, with whom it remained until the 1960s. With branding and national marketing, manufacturers strove to increase the consistency and quality of their brands, making them more recognizable through attractive packaging that no longer served the sole purpose of protection. Increased advertising was used to promote the growth of brands and with manufacturers exercising legally backed control over prices, more and more manufacturers turned to marketing branded goods.

This review of the changing balance of power from wholesaler to manufacturer by the end of the last century marked another milestone in the evolutionary period of brands. Brand owners were concerned with using their brands as legal registrations of their unique characteristics. Besides this, they directed their efforts towards consumers to make them aware that their brand was different in some way from those of competitors. Furthermore, they wanted their brand names to encourage belief in a consistent quality level that most were prepared to guarantee. Thus, whilst the *differentiating* aspect of the concept was initially regarded as the key issue, this soon also encompassed *legal protection* and *functional communication*.

Throughout this century, manufacturers' interest in branding increased and with more sophisticated buyers and marketers, brands also acquired an *emotional dimension* that reflected buyers' moods, personalities and the messages they wished to convey to others. However, with the greater choice to buyers through the availability of more competing products, the level of information being directed at buyers far exceeded their ability to be attentive to the many competing messages. Because of their limited cognitive capabilities, buyers began to use brand names as *shorthand devices* to recall either their brand experiences or marketing claims and thus saved themselves the effort of having constantly to seek information. Chapter 3 provides more information about the role of the brand as a shorthand device to facilitate buyers' decision processes.

The only other major landmark in the growth of branding was the metamorphosis from manufacturers' brand to distributors' brand that began to occur around the turn of this century. The advent of own labels (or more precisely distributor brands) is explained in the next section, along with the unsuccessful attempt by distributors to turn the wheel of branding back full circle with generics (products which have only their function on the label).

Brand evolution: distributors' brands and generics

To appreciate how further tiers of brands evolved, one must again consider the changing nature of the retailing environment. Around the 1870s, multiple retailers (i.e. those owning ten or more outlets) emerged, each developing their own range of brands, for which they controlled the production and packaging. These distributor brands (usually referred to as own labels or private labels) became common in emergent chains such as Home & Colonial, Lipton and International Stores. The early versions of distributor brands tended to be basic grocery items. Not only did the chains undertake their own production, but they also managed the wholesaling function, with branding being almost an incidental part of the total process.

The reason for the advent of distributor brands was that, due to resale price maintenance, retailers were unable to compete with each other on the price of manufacturers' brands and relied upon service as the main competitive edge to increase store traffic. The multiples circumvented this problem by developing their own distributor brands (own label). The degree of retailer production was limited by the complexity of the items and the significant costs of production facilities. Thus, it became increasingly common for multiple retailers to commission established manufacturers to produce their distributor brands which were packaged to the retailer's specifications. Before World War II, distributor brands accounted for 10–15 per cent of multiples' total sales, but with multiple retailers accounting for only 17 per cent of food sales the overall importance of distributor brands was far exceeded by manufacturer brands. During World War II, distributor brands were withdrawn due to shortages and were not reintroduced until the 1950s.

One of the consequences of the increasing growth of the multiples was the decline of independent retailers (i.e. those owning no more than nine shops). As a means of protecting themselves, some independent retailers joined together during the 1950s and collaborated with specific wholesalers in symbol/voluntary groups (e.g. Mace–Wavey Line, Spar). With a significant element of their purchasing channelled through a central wholesaler, they were able to achieve more favourable terms from manufacturers. A further consequence of this allegiance was the introduction of symbol/voluntary brands, designed to compete against the multiples brands. It should also be recognized that the once powerful retailing force of the Co-op, with its not-insignificant farming and processing plants, also has a long history of marketing its Co-op brands (albeit with a variety of brand names). Unfortunately, due to the Co-op's inability to adapt to the changing retailing environment, this sector's importance has fallen. With only an 11 per cent share of the packaged grocery sector in 1988, the overall importance of the Co-op brands has declined.

Whilst distributor brands have their origin in the grocery sector, however, where in 1988 they accounted for 28 per cent of packaged grocery sales, it should not be thought that this is their sole domain. For example, it is estimated that in 1989, over 50 per cent of footwear sales and almost half of all menswear sales are accounted for by distributor brands. In the DIY goods sector, approximately a quarter of sales are from distributor brands and a fifth of furniture and floor covering sales are distributor brands. In the retail banking sector, where the service 'manufacturer' is also the distributor, distributor brands are common (e.g. Midland's Meridian Multiservice Account). In the industrial sector, it is less common to see distributor brands, due to the considerable investment in production, the need to appreciate the technology and the greater reliance upon direct delivery, with less reliance on distributors. Chapter 7 provides more detail about distributor brands.

In the packaged grocery sector, where the first alternative tier to manufacturer brands appeared, innovative marketing in the late 1970s also led to a further alternative – generics. In fact, the term 'generics' may be a misnomer, since it implies a return to the days when retailers sold commodities rather than brands. This trend was originally started by Carrefour in 1976, when they launched fifty 'produits libres' in France, promoted as brand-free products. Some UK grocery retailers noted the initial success of these lines and thought the time was right to follow in the UK. At the time there was growing consumer

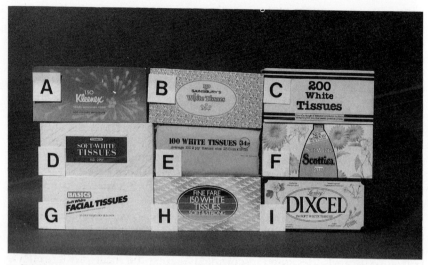

Exhibit 2.3   *A 1985 example of branded (A, F, I), own label (B, D, H) and generic (C, E, G) facial tissues*

scepticism about the price premium being paid for branding and with consumers becoming more confident about selecting what in many cases were better quality distributor brands, it was thought that in a harsh economic environment, generics would be a popular alternative to manufacturer brands, further increasing distributors' control of their product mix.

The thrust behind generics was that of cutting out any superfluous frill surrounding the product. They were distinguishable by their plain packaging, with the marketing emphasis placed on the content, rather than on the promotional or pack features. On average, generics were priced 40 per cent lower than the brand leader and approximately 20 per cent lower that the equivalent distributor brands. Whilst the quality level varied by retailer, they were none the less generally inferior to manufacturers' brands. As Table 2.1 shows, several major grocery retailers launched, and subsequently withdrew, generic ranges.

Table 2.1   *Grocery retailers launching generics*

Retailer	Generic range	Launch	Withdrawn
Argyll	BASICS	October 1981	1987
Carrefour (Gateway)	Brand Free	March 1978	1986
Fine Fare (Gateway)	Yellow Pack	March 1980	1987
International (Gateway)	Plain & Simple	July 1977	1984
Tesco	Value Lines	October 1981	1986

Retailers in the UK who stocked a generic range developed a policy regarding the product, pricing, packaging and merchandizing that only too clearly enabled consumers to associate a particular generic range with a specific store. One retailer went as far as branding their generic range (BASICS). But the withdrawal of generics was not surprising, since consumers perceived generics as similar to distributor brands. They were not perceived as a unique tier and they weakened the image, hence the sales, of the distributor brands of those retailers stocking generics. Furthermore, as they were perceived to be similar to distributor brands, more switching occurred with these, rather than with the less profitable manufacturers' brands.

Chapter 7 considers in more detail the marketing issues associated with generics and the reason for their demise. However, it is worth emphasizing that any organization operating in consumer, services or industrial markets, never has a commodity and is always able to differentiate their offering. Research has shown that marketing a product or service predominantly on the basis of the functional performance of the core product (as was the case with generic groceries), accounts for about 80 per cent of the costs, yet only 20 per cent of the impact. The marketing of generics trims some of the marginal costs away, but leaves the organization having to compete on product dimensions that can be easily copied and which have little impact compared with other attributes (e.g. service, availability, imagery, etc.). Any industrial manufacturers who believe they are marketing a generic product, and therefore have to offer the lowest prices, are deluding themselves. For example, purchasers are not just buying tanker loads of commonly available chemical for their production process. They are also buying a reliable delivery service, a well-administered reordering process, advice from the supplier about the operating characteristics of the chemical, etc. By just considering issues such as these, it is easier to appreciate the fallacy of marketing generics.

Branding in the 1990s: brand categorization

An advertising perspective

This brief historical review has shown how brands evolved and has also briefly introduced the idea of the different *types* of brands. One of the weaknesses with the current views on branding is that the term is used to encompass a very broad range of issues, encouraging the possibility of confusion.

Two well-known researchers recently pointed out that the problem with branding is the surprising number of creative directors, planners, account handlers and clients who have a kindergarten knowledge of branding processes and mechanisms. They are rightly critical of those who regard branding merely as a process to ensure that the name on a product or service is highly visible. Based on a consideration of advertisements, they classified brands into nine categories, each representing a role in advertising, varying from simple through to complex branding. For example, at the simple end of the scale there are those brands which operate through straightforward association with the advertising slogan (e.g. the classic 'Sch . . . you know who'). By contrast, at the most complex end of the spectrum, they identify structural branding, in which for example, objects (scissors, hedge trimmers, etc.) coloured either purple or white are shown in order to ensure a link with Silk Cut cigarettes. Figure 2.1 shows these researchers' (Langmaid and Gordon) interpretation of brand types.

Figure 2.1   *Langmaid and Gordon's (1988) brand typology*

However, whilst their typology is of value to advertisers, its overt advertising bias restricts its value as an aid in evaluating how to employ the other elements of the marketing mix.

An output process

Our research and work with marketing executives have shown that there are other interpretations of the role played by brands, which we will now make explicit, all of which will be addressed in more detail in subsequent chapters. However, a key problem with many of these interpretations, is that they place too much emphasis on branding as something that is done *to* consumers, rather than branding as something consumers do things *with*. It is wrong, in other words, to focus on branding as an *input* process. Clearly we need to consider carefully how marketing resources are being used to support brands, but it is crucial to understand the *output* process as well, since, as mentioned earlier, the final evaluation of the brand is in the buyer's or user's mind. Consumers are not just passive recipients of marketing activity. They consume marketing activity, sometimes with a large subconscious appetite, twisting messages to reinforce prior expectations.

Several highly regarded branding advisers stress the importance of looking at brands as perceptions in consumers' minds, a notion which is comparatively easy to accept and which reinforces the conclusion about the importance of what consumers take out of the process rather than what marketers put into it. Whilst it is clear that marketers design the firm's offer, the ultimate judge about the nature of the brand is the consumer. When buying a new brand, consumers seek clues about the brand's capabilities. They try to evaluate the brand through a variety of perceptual evaluations, such as its reliability, or whether it's the sort of brand they feel right with, or whether it's better than another brand, so that a brand becomes not the producer's, but the consumer's idea of the product. The result of good branding is a perception of the values of a product, or service, interpreted and believed so clearly by the consumer, that the brand adopts a personality. This is so well recognized, that products with little apparent functional differences are regarded as different purely because of the brand personality. For example, while many organizations provide charge cards, American Express is 'the one you don't leave home without'. Parker pens have a personality of their own, as do Singapore Airlines, Fosters lager, and countless other brands around the world.

Thus, recognizing the inherent flaw when marketers focus upon branding as an input process, we have highlighted eight different types of brands that practitioners employ.

An eight-category typology

1 Brand as a sign of ownership
An early theme, given much prominence in marketing circles, was the distinction between brands on the basis of whether the brand was a manufacturers' brand or a distributors' brand ('own label', 'private label'). Branding was seen as being a basis of showing who instigated the marketing for that particular offering and whether the primary activity of the instigator was production (i.e. manufacturers' brand) or distribution (distributors' brand). However, this drew a rather artificial distinction, since nowadays consumers place a far greater reliance on distributor brands – particularly when brands such as Benetton and Marks & Spencer are perceived as superior brands in their own right. In fact, some would argue that with the much greater marketing role played by major retailers and their concentrated buying power, the concept of USP (Unique Selling Proposition) should now be interpreted as 'Universal Supermarket Patronage'! With the much greater marketing activity undertaken by distributors, this typology does little more than clarify who instigated the marketing.

2 Brand as a differentiating device
The historical review earlier in this chapter indicated that, at the turn of the century, a much stronger emphasis was placed on brands purely as differentiating devices between similar products. This perspective is still frequently seen today in many different markets. Yet with more sophisticated marketing and more experienced consumers, brands succeed not only by conveying differentiation, but also by being associated with added values. For example, the brand Cadbury's Dairy

Milk not only differentiates this from other confectionery lines, but is a successful brand since it has been backed by a coherent use of resources that deliver the added value of a high quality offering with a well-defined image. By contrast the one man operation, 'Tom's Taxi Service', is based upon branding as a differentiating device, with little thought to communicating added values.

Small firms seem to be particularly prone to the belief that putting a name on their product or service is all that is needed to set them apart

Exhibit 2.4   *Stressing the functional capability of the brand. (Courtesy NWA)*

from competitors. They erroneously believe that branding is about having a prominent name, more often than not based around the owner's name. Yet there is ample evidence that brands fail if organizations concentrate primarily on developing a symbol or a name as a differentiating device. Chapter 4 gives examples showing the danger of adopting brands solely as differentiating devices. Brands will succeed if they offer unique benefits, satisfying real consumer needs.

Exhibit 2.5   *VAX positioned as a functional brand*

Where an organization has reason to believe that their competitors are marketing brands primarily as differentiating devices, there is an opportunity to develop a strategy which gets buyers to associate relevant added values with their brand name and hence gain a competitive advantage.

3 Brand as a functional device

Another category of brands is that used by marketers to communicate functional capability. This stemmed from the early days of manufacturers' brands when firms wished to protect their large production

If you don't want your burning passion to arrive lukewarm, send it in a Swiftpack.

Whether you want to send your burning passion or the hottest of gossip, Swiftpacks take flight before they have a chance to cool.

The distinctive Swiftpack international express envelopes receive VIP treatment, being handled separately from ordinary mail to enable a speedy arrival.

They're available from your local Post Office from only £2.05p. Isn't someone extra special worth that little extra?

International

By Air, By Land, By Swiftpack, By Hand.

Exhibit 2.6   *Balancing the functional and emotional elements in branding*

investments by using their brands to guarantee consistent quality to consumers.

As consumers began to take for granted the fact that brands represented consistent quality, marketers strove to establish their brands as being associated with specific unique functional benefits.

A brief scan of advertisements today shows the different functional attributes marketers are trying to associate with their brand, for example: VAX, emphasizing the carpet-cleaning features of its less-than-aesthetic vacuum cleaner; SEAT, striving to convey a good value-for-money proposition; Polycell, seeking the association of DIY simplicity; and Castrol GTX, representing 'high technology' engine protection. Firms adopting the view that they are employing brands as functional communicators have the virtue of being customer driven, but clearly run the risk of an excessive reliance on the functional (rational) element of the consumer choice, as all products and services also have some degree of emotional content in the buying process. For example a Post Office campaign run in 1990 for a predominantly functional brand, advertised the emotional dimension using the slogan 'If you don't want your burning passion to arrive lukewarm, send it in a Swiftpack.'

4 Brand as a symbolic device

In certain product fields (e.g. perfume and clothing) buyers perceive significant badge value in the brands, since it enables them to communicate something about themselves (e.g. emotion, status, etc.). In other words, brands are used as symbolic devices, with marketers believing that brands are bought and used primarily because of their ability to help users express something about themselves to their peer groups, with users taking for granted functional capabilities.

Where consumers perceive the brand's value to lie more in terms of the non-verbal communication facility (through the logo or name), they spend time and effort choosing brands, almost with the same care as if choosing a friend. It is now accepted that consumers personify brands and when looking at the symbol values of brands, they seek brands which have very clear personalities and select brands that best match their actual or desired self-concept.

For example, in the beer market, there are only marginal product differences between brands. Comparative consumer trials of competing beer brands without brand names present showed no significant preferences or differences. Yet, when consumers repeated the test with brand names present, significant brand preferences emerged. On the first comparative trial, consumers focused on functional (rational) aspects of the beers and were unable to notice much difference. On repeating the trials with brand names present, consumers were able to use the brand names to recall distinct brand personalities and the symbolic (emotional) aspect of the brands influenced preference.

Through being a member of social groups, people learn the symbolic meaning of brands. As they interpret the actions of their peer group,

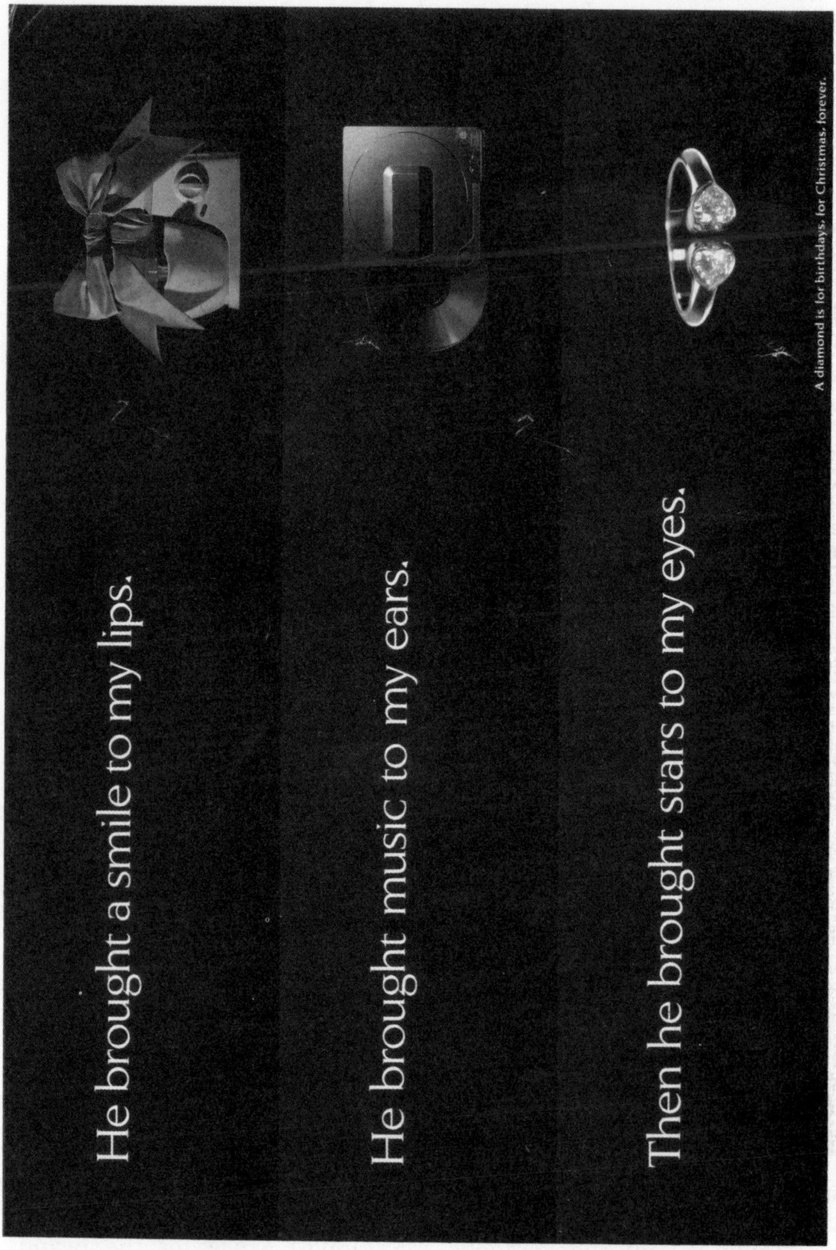

He brought a smile to my lips.

He brought music to my ears.

Then he brought stars to my eyes.

A diamond is for birthdays, for Christmas, forever.

Exhibit 2.7   *The symbolic meaning of diamonds: a sign of eternal love.*
(Courtesy Diamond Information Centre (advertiser) and J. Walter Thompson (agency))

You thought a wedding ring said it all.

But five years later you want to say a little more.

A diamond is forever.

Exhibit 2.7   *(continued)*

they then respond, using brands as non-verbal communication devices (e.g. feelings, status). To capitalize on symbolic brands, therefore, marketers must use promotional activity to communicate the brand's personality and signal how consumers can use it in their daily relationships with others. None the less, whilst there are many product fields where this perspective of brands is useful, it must also be realized that consumers rarely consider just the symbolic aspect of brands. Research by the authors of this book across a wide variety of product fields, ranging from chipboard to watches, showed that consumers often evaluated brands in terms of both a symbolic (emotional) and a functional (rational) dimension. Marketers should, therefore, be wary of subscribing to the belief that a brand acts *solely* as a symbolic device.

5 *Brand as a risk reducer*

Many marketers believe that buying should be regarded as a process whereby buyers attempt to reduce the risk of a purchase decision. When a person is faced with competing brands in a new product field, they feel risk. For example, uncertainty about whether the brand will work, whether they will be wasting money, whether their peer group will disagree with their choice, whether they will feel comfortable with the purchase, etc. Successful brand marketing should therefore be concerned with understanding buyers' perceptions of risk followed by developing and presenting the brand in such a way that buyers feel minimal risk. An example of an industry appreciating perceived risk is the pharmaceutical industry. One company has developed a series of questions which its sales representatives use to evaluate the risk aversion of doctors. When launching a new drug, the company focuses sales presentations initially on doctors with a low risk aversion profile.

To make buying more acceptable, buyers seek methods of reducing risk by, for example, always buying the same brand, searching for more information, only buying the smallest size, etc. Research has shown that one of the more popular methods employed by buyers to reduce risk is reliance upon reputable brands. Some marketers, particularly those selling to organizations rather than to final consumers, succeed with their brands because they find out what dimensions of risk the buyer is most concerned about and then develop a solution through their brand presentation which emphasizes the brand's capabilities along the risk dimension considered most important by the buyer. This interpretation of branding has the virtue of being output driven. Marketers, however, must not loose sight of the need to segment customers by similar risk perception and achieve sufficient numbers of buyers to make risk reduction branding viable.

6 *Brand as a shorthand device*

Glancing through advertisements today, one becomes aware of brands whose promotional platform appears to be based on bombarding consumers with considerable quantities of information (e.g. Guardian Royal Exchange's Choices pension plan). These brands are used as

Exhibit 2.8   *Positioning the brand as a risk reducing device*

shorthand devices by consumers to recall from memory sufficient brand information at a later purchasing time. There is merit in this approach, as people generally have limited memory capabilities. To overcome this, they bundle small bits of information into larger chunks in their memory, and use brand names as handles to recall these larger information chunks. By continuing to increase the size of these few chunks in memory, buyers in consumer, industrial and service sectors can process information more effectively. At the point of purchase, they are able to recall numerous attributes by interrogating their memory.

Exhibit 2.9   *A successfully protected brand*

There is, none the less, the danger of concentrating too heavily on the quantity, rather than the quality of information directed at purchasers. It also ignores the perceptual process which is used by buyers to twist information until it becomes consistent with their prior beliefs – an error fatally overlooked by the short-lived Strand cigarette brand.

7   Brand as a legal device

With the appearance of manufacturers' brands at the turn of this century, consumers began to appreciate their value and started to ask for them by name. Producers of inferior goods realized that to survive they would have to change. A minority, however, changed by illegally packaging their inferior products in packs that were virtually identical to the original brand. To protect themselves against counterfeiting, firms turned to trademark registration as a legal protection. Some firms began to regard the prime benefit of brands as being that of legal protection, with the result that a new category of branding appeared. Within this group of brands, marketers direct their efforts towards effective trademark registration along with consumer education programmes about the danger of buying poor grade brand copies. For example, the pack details on Matchbox products boldly state that 'Matchbox is the trademark of the Matchbox group of companies and is the subject of extensive trademark registrations', while Kodak packs all carry the advice 'It's only Kodak film if it says Kodak'.

Yet again, however, whilst clearly there is a need to protect brands, brand owners also need to adopt a more strategic approach to developing ways of erecting defensive barriers, besides being reliant only on legal redress.

8 Brand as a strategic device

Finally, more enlightened marketers are adopting the view to which we subscribe, which is that brands should be treated as strategic devices. The assets constituting the brand need to be audited, the forces affecting the future of the brand evaluated and by appreciating how the brand achieved its added value, a positioning for the brand needs to be identified such that the brand can be successfully protected and achieve the desired return on investment. To take full advantage of brands as strategic devices, a considerable amount of marketing analysis and brand planning is required, yet many firms are too embroiled in tactical issues and so do not gain the best possible returns from their brands. All the strategic issues associated with capitalizing on strategic branding are covered in this book.

A good example of successful branding through majoring upon a differential advantage and ensuring the sustainability of such an advantage was seen in a colour supplement advertisement by Sharp in 1990. Figure 2.2 shows the main points presented in the advertisement. This organization evaluated the forces that could impede their electronic organizer and developed a unique position for their brand that is difficult for competitors to copy. The technology of the IC card gave the brand a competitive edge. In a true strategic style, the firm had developed a brand which it had differentiated from its competitors and had used its corporate strengths to satisfy customer need better than competitors.

This section has described several different categories of brands and has also highlighted the inherent weaknesses of each type of brand. In Chapter 8, we provide a matrix which enables the marketer to audit what type of brand they have. Based on an appreciation of the brand type, this matrix then enables marketers to consider how resources need to be employed to sustain the brand. The reader may be beginning to wonder, however, why manufacturers undertake the commercial risk of developing manufacturer brands and why distributors extend their activities beyond their area of economic expertise to develop distributor brands. These issues are considered in the next section.

The Sharp IQ leads the field in electronic organizers. A compact way to store and retrieve information, it provides you with complete time and information management at the touch of a button.

Of course it has its imitators. Some limited by their capabilities. Others restricted by their memory. Many requiring computer literacy. Most of them vulnerable to obsolescence.

But what keeps the Sharp IQ a breed apart is its IC card technology: a simple system of integrated circuit software cards which give the IQ infinite expandability. All operated quickly and easily through the IQ's keyboard or an integral touch-sensitive pad.

Figure 2.2   *Advertisement for Sharp IQ*

The value of brands to manufacturers, distributors and consumers

Manufacturers invest effort in branding for a variety of reasons. If the trademark has been effectively registered, the manufacturer has a legally-protected right to an exclusive brand name, enabling it to establish a unique identity, reinforced through its advertising and increasing the opportunity of attracting a large group of repeat purchasers.

With the high costs of developing new brands, the emphasis in the 1990s is on old brand development and line extensions. For example, in the mid part of 1990 it was announced that Lever Brothers planned to launch an entire range of household cleaning products under its leading bleach brand Domestos, rather than following a new brand name route with all its inherent costs. Clearly, good brands keep on building a corporate image and hence reduce the cost of new line additions carrying the family brand name. However, marketers must beware of the dangers of overstretching the brand's core values as Levi did in the early 1980s with their unsuccessful move from jeans into the suit market. This issue of brand extension will be discussed in more detail in Chapter 9.

Manufacturers with a history of strong brands are likely to find distributors more receptive to presentations of brand extensions or even of new brands. Those manufacturers with strong brands maintain greater control over the balance of power between the manufacturer and distributor and indeed, some argue that this is one of the key benefits of strong brands. For example, Kellogg's have been quoted as saying:

> The only discounts available to our customers are those shown on our price list, and all those discounts relate to quantity bought and to prompt payment. There is no possibility of special deals.

In view of the pressures facing brand manufacturers from the powerful multiple retailers, such a comment is indeed a brave statement about a belief in the power of strong manufacturers' brands.

It is also possible for a manufacturer with strong brand names to market different brands in the same product field which appeal to different segments. This is seen in the washing detergents and the soap market, where Unilever and Procter & Gamble market different brands with minimal cannibalization between brands from the same manufacturer. Furthermore, by developing sufficiently differentiated manufacturer brands that consumers desire, higher prices can be charged, as consumers pay less attention to price comparisons between different products because of brand distinctiveness. This clearly enhances profitability. Indeed, Table 2.2 shows the profit impact of powerful brand leaders in the grocery market.

Retailers see strong manufacturer brands as being important, since through manufacturers' marketing activity (e.g. advertising, point of

Table 2.2   *Market share and average net margins for UK grocery brands*

Rank	Net margin (%)
1	17.9
2	2.8
3	−0.9
4	−5.9

sale material, etc.), a fast turnover of stock results. Also, with more sophisticated marketers recognizing the importance of long-term relationships with their customers, many manufacturers and distributors have cause to recognize that their future success depends on each other and therefore strong manufacturer brands are seen as representing profit opportunities both for distributors and manufacturers. Some retailers are interested in stocking strong brands, since they believe that the positive image of a brand can enhance their own image. Recent research has provided clear evidence that a favourable image from a manufacturer's brand can further enhance the image of an already well-regarded store.

Recalling the discussion in the previous section about brand names acting as a means of short circuiting the search for information, consumers appreciate manufacturers' brands since they make shopping a less time-consuming experience. As already noted, manufacturers' brands are recognized as providing a consistent guide to quality, and consistency. They reduce perceived risk and make consumers more confident and in some product fields (e.g. clothing, cars) they also satisfy strong status needs.

Why, then, do so many manufacturers also supply distributors' brands? First, it is important to understand why distributors are so keen on introducing their own brands. Research has shown that they are particularly keen on distributor brands because they enable them to have more control over their product mix. With a strong distributor brand range, retailers have rationalized their product range to take advantage of the resulting cost savings and many stock a manufacturer's brand leader, their own distributor's brand and possibly a second manufacturer's brand. Trade interviews have also shown that distributor brands offered better margins than the equivalent manufacturer's brand, with estimates indicating the extra profit margin to be about 5 per cent more than the equivalent manufacturer's brand. Some of the reasons why manufacturers become suppliers of distributors' brands are:

- economies of scale through raw material purchasing, distribution and production;
- any excess capacity can be utilized;

- it can provide a base for expansion;
- substantial sales may accrue with minimal promotional or selling costs;
- it may be the only way of dealing with some important distributors (e.g. Marks & Spencer);
- if an organization does not supply distributor brands, their competitors will, possibly strengthening the competitors' cost structure and trade goodwill.

Consumers benefit from distributors' brands through the lower prices being charged, but it is interesting to note that our own research found that consumers are becoming increasingly confident about distributors' brands and no longer perceive them as 'cheap and nasty' weak alternatives to manufacturers' brands, but rather as realistic alternatives.

The importance of brand planning

As the previous sections of this chapter have shown, brands play a variety of roles and for a number of reasons satisfy many different needs. They are the end result of much effort and by implication represent a considerable investment by the organization. With the recent interest in the balance sheet value of brands, companies are beginning to question whether their financially valuable assets in the form of brands are being effectively used to achieve high returns on investment. To gain the best return from their brands, firms must adopt a broad vision about their brands and not just focus in isolation on tactical issues of design and promotion. Instead, they need to audit the capabilities of their firm, evaluate the external issues influencing their brand (briefly overviewed in the next section) and then develop a brand plan that specifies realistic brand objectives and the strategy to achieve them (covered in more detail in Chapters 8 and 9).

Brand planning is an important but time-consuming activity, which, if undertaken in a thorough manner involving company-wide discussion, will result in a clear vision about how resources can be employed to sustain the brand's differential advantage. Unfortunately, it is only a minority of organizations who undertake thorough brand planning. Without well-structured brand plans there is the danger of what we call brand 'vandalism'. Junior brand managers are given 'training' by making them responsible for specific brands. Their planning horizons tend to be in terms of a couple of years (i.e. the period before they move on) and their focus tends to be on the tactical issues of advertising, pack design and tailor-made brand promotions for the trade. At best this results in 'fire fighting' and a defensive rather than offensive brand plan. The core values of the brand are in danger of being diluted through excessive brand extensions. For example, one of the key core values of the Ribena brand is vitamin C, yet by extending the brand into other fruits (e.g. Strawberry) this is weakening the brand's proposition and potentially weakening the brand's strength.

Internally, organizations may be oblivious to the fact that they are hindering brand development. Clearly, by not preparing well-documented strategic brand plans, firms are creating their own obstacles to success. Some of the characteristics that internally hinder any chance of brand success are:

- Brand planning is based on little more than extrapolations from the previous few years.
- When it doesn't look as if the annual budget is going to be reached, quarter 4 sees brand investment being cut (i.e. advertising, market research, etc.).
- The marketing manager is unable to delegate responsibility and is too involved in tactical issues.
- Brand managers see their current positions as good training grounds for no more than two years.
- Strategic thinking consists of a retreat once a year, with the advertising agency and sales managers, to a one-day meeting concerned with next year's brand plans.
- A profitability analysis for each major customer is rarely under-taken.
- New product activity consists of different pack sizes and rapidly developing 'me- too' offers.
- The promotions budget is strongly biased towards below-the-line promotional activity, supplemented only occasionally with advertising.
- Marketing documentation is available to the advertising agency on a 'need to know' basis only.

Brand strategy development must involve all levels of marketing management and stands a better chance of success when all the other relevant internal departments and external agencies are actively involved. It must progress on the basis of all parties being kept aware of progress.

British Airways exemplify the notion of brand development as an integrating process, having used this to achieve a greater customer focus. For example, the simple operation of taking a few seats out of an aircraft can be done with confidence, as engineering are consulted about safety implications, finance work out the long-term revenue implication, scheduling explore capacity implications and the cabin crew adjust their in-flight service routines.

The issues influencing brand potential

When auditing the factors affecting the future of brands, it is useful to consider these in terms of the five forces shown in Figure 2.3. The brand strategist can evaluate the intensity and impact of the following brand-impeding issues.

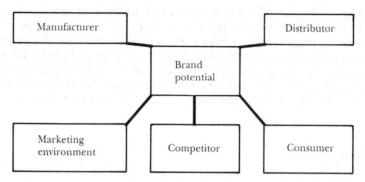

Figure 2.3   *Forces influencing brand potential*

The manufacturer

It is not unusual for an organization to be underutilizing its brand assets through an inability to recognize what is occurring *inside* the organization. Have realistic, quantified objectives been set for each of the brands, and have they been widely disseminated? Aims such as 'to be the brand leader' give some indication of the threshold target, but do little in terms of stretching the use of resources to achieve their full potential. Furthermore, they show every sign of the executive shying away from accepting brand responsibility. Brand leadership may result before the end of the planning horizon, but this may be because of factors that the organization did not incorporate into their marketing audit. But luck also has a habit of working against the player as much as working for the player!

Has the organization made full use of its internal auditing to identify what its *distinctive* brand competences are, and to what extent these match the factors that are critical for brand success? For example, Swatch recognized that amongst fashion-conscious watch owners, its distinctive competences of design and production could satisfy changing consumer demands for novelty watches.

Is the organization plagued by a continual desire to cut costs, without fully appreciating why it is following this route? Has the market reached the maturity stage, with the organization's brand having to compete against competitors' brands on the basis of matching performance, but at a reduced price? If this is so, *all* aspects of the organization's value chain should be geared towards cost minimization (e.g. eliminating production inefficiencies, avoiding marginal customer accounts, having a narrow product mix, working with long production runs, etc.). Alternatively, is the firm's brand unique in some way that competitors find difficult to emulate and for which the firm can charge a price premium (e.g. unique source of high quality raw materials, innovative production process, unparalleled customer service training, acclaimed advertising, etc.)? Where consumers demand a brand which has clear benefits, the manufacturer should ensure all departments work towards maintaining these benefits and signal this to the market (eg by the cleanliness of the lorries, the politeness of the telephonists, the promptness of answering a customer enquiry, etc.). In some instances, particularly in services, the brand planning document can overlook a link in the value chain, resulting in some inherent added value being diminished (e.g. an insurance broker selling reputable quality insurance from a shabby office).

Distributors

The brand strategy of the manufacturer cannot be formulated without regard for the distributor. Both parties rely on each other for their success and even in an era of increasing retailer concentration, notwithstanding all the trade press hype, there is still a recognition amongst manufacturers and distributors that long-term brand profitability evolves through mutual support.

Manufacturers need to identify retailers' objectives and align their brands with those retailers whose aims most closely match their own. With the opening of European markets in 1992, some of the major multiple grocery retailers have already set their sights on growth through market development, involving discussions about pan-European alliances with other retailers. Brand manufacturers who have not fully considered the implications of distributors' longer-term objectives are deluding themselves about the long-term viability of their own brands.

In the UK, there are numerous instances of growing retailer power, with a few major operators controlling a significant proportion of retail sales (e.g. groceries, DIY, jewellery, footwear). The danger of increasing retailer power is that weaker brand manufacturers acquiesce to demands for better discounts, without fully appreciating that the long term well-being of their brands is being undermined. It is crucial for brand manufacturers to analyse regularly what proportion of their brand sales go through each distributor and then for each individual distributor to assess how important a particular manufacturer's brand is to them. For example, Table 2.3 shows a hypothetical analysis for a confectionery manufacturer.

If this hypothetical example were for a Rowntree brand, it is clear that the particular Rowntree brand is more reliant upon Tesco than Tesco is on the particular Rowntree brand. Such an analysis better enables manufacturers to appreciate which retailers are more able to exert pressure on their brand. It indicates that, if the brand manufacturer wants to escape from a position of retailer power, they need to consider ways of growing business for their brands in those sectors other than Tesco *at a faster rate* than is envisaged within this distributor.

When working with a distributor, the brand manufacturer should take into account whether the distributor is striving to offer a good value proposition to the consumer (e.g. Kwik Save, Aldi) or a

Table 2.3   *Power analysis*

Hypothetical Rowntree brand sales to distributors		Hypothetical market share of confectionery brands through Tesco	
Distributor	%	Brand	%
Sainsbury	25	Cadbury	35
Tesco	24	Mars	30
Gateway	19	Rowntree	20
Asda	17	Other	15
Co-op	10		100
Independent	5		
	100		

value-added proposition (e.g. high quality names at Harrods). In view of the loss of control once the manufacturer's brand is in the distributor's domain, the brand manufacturer must annually evaluate the degree of synergy through each particular route and be prepared to consider changes.

Does the manufacturer have an offensive distribution strategy, or is it by default that its brands go through certain channels? What are the ideal characteristics for distributors of its brands and how well do the actual distributors used match these criteria? How do distributors plan to use brands to meet their objectives? The brand manufacturer must have a clear idea of the importance of specific distributors for each brand and in Chapter 7 a matrix is presented which enables the manufacturer to rank the appropriateness of distributors for each of a manufacturer's brands.

Finally manufacturers must recognize that when developing new brands, distributors have a finite shelf space and market research must not solely address consumer issues, but must also take into account the reaction of the trade. One company found that a pyramid pack design researched well amongst consumers, but on trying to sell this into the trade it failed – due to what the trade saw as ineffective use of shelf space!

Consumers

To consumers buying is a process of problem solving. They become aware of a problem (e.g. not yet arranged summer holidays), seek information (e.g. go to travel agent and skim brochures), evaluate the information and then make a decision (e.g. select three possible holidays, then try to book one through the travel agent). The extent of this buying process varies according to purchasers' characteristics, experience and the products being bought. None the less, clearly consumers have to 'work' to make a brand selection. Chapter 3 looks at this in more detail.

Brands offer consumers a means of minimizing information search and evaluation. Through seeing a brand name which has been supported by continual marketing activity, consumers can use this as a rapid means of interrogating memory and if sufficient relevant information can be recalled, only minimal effort is needed to make a purchase decision. As a consequence of this, brand strategists should question whether they are presenting consumers with a few high quality pieces of information, or whether they are bombarding consumers with large quantities of information and ironically causing confusion. Likewise, in business to business markets, it is important to consider how firms make brand selections. This is covered in Chapter 4.

Not only should strategists look at the stages consumers go through in the process of choosing brands, but they also need to consider the role that brands actually play in this process. For example, a businessperson going to an important business presentation may feel social risk in the type of clothes he/she wears and select a respected brand mainly as a risk-reducer. By contrast, in a different situation, they may decide to wear a Gucci watch, because of a need to use the brand as a device to communicate a message (e.g. success, lifestyle) to their peer group. Likewise, one purchasing manager may buy a particular brand, since experience has taught him that delivery is reliable, even though there is a price premium to pay. By contrast, another purchasing manager may be more concerned about rapid career advancement and may choose to order a different brand on the basis that he is rewarded for minimizing unnecessary expenditure on raw materials. Success depends on understanding the way purchasers interact with brands and employing company resources to match these needs.

Competitors

Research has shown that return on investment is related to a product's share of the market. In other words products with a bigger market share yield better returns than those with a smaller market share. Organizations with strong brands fare better in gaining market share than those without strong brands. Thus, firms who are brand leaders will become particularly aggressive if they see their position being eroded by other brands. Furthermore, as larger firms are likely to have a range of brands, backed by large resources, it is always possible for them to use one of their brands as a loss leader to underprice the smaller competitor, and once the smaller brand falls out of the market, the brand leader can then increase prices. Several years ago, Laker took on the major airlines when he launched his Skytrain on the lucrative trans-Atlantic route. The major players recognized the potential danger from this 'no-frills' operation and because they had a wide range of products, they were able to compete at equally low prices, while using their other routes to subsidise this. Without a range of brands, Laker was unable to compete and his brand died.

Brand strategists need to have given some thought to anticipating likely competitor response, as Chapter 9 argues in more detail. Filofax appear to have been taken by surprise by competitive activity. When their time organizer became established in the market, they did not appear to have any short-term retaliatory plans when faced with an increasing number of 'me-too' competitors.

The marketing environment

Brand strategists need to scan their marketing environment continually to identify future opportunities and threats. For example, will the opening of European markets after 1992 result in very powerful grocery retailing chains presenting a considerable threat to weaker brands? Will a shift in the developed countries to a knowledge-based society lead to 'armchair shopping' facilitated by networked personal computers? To draw an analogy with military thinking, good surveillance helps achieve success.

Conclusions

This chapter has provided an overview of the key issues involved in planning for the future of brands. It has shown that brands succeed when marketers regard them as the end result of a well-integrated marketing process. To view branding as naming, design or advertising, is too myopic and such a perspective will shorten the brand's life expectancy. Branding is about the communication of relevant added values for which buyers are prepared to pay a price premium and which competitors find difficult to emulate.

The historical evolution of brands has shown that brands initially served the roles of differentiating between competing items, representing consistency of quality and providing legal protection from copying. With the advent of distributors' brands, more experienced buyers and increasingly sophisticated marketing techniques, eight different types of brands were identified: a sign of ownership of the branding process; a differentiating device; a communicator of functional capability; a device which enables buyers to express something about themselves; a risk-reducing device; a shorthand communication device; a legal device; and a strategic device. To capitalize upon the asset represented by their brand, firms need to adopt strategic brand planning as a way of life. Finally, a model showing the five main factors that influence brand potential was reviewed.

Marketing action checklist

It is recommended that after reading this chapter, marketers undertake the exercises which follow to help clarify the direction of future brand marketing programmes.

1 By either looking through previous market research reports, or by putting yourself in the position of a buyer, write down the four

main reasons, in order of importance, why one of your company brands is being bought. Then show an advertisement for this brand (or a catalogue page describing it) to one of your buyers and ask them to tell you what are the four key points they took from the message.

If the results from the first and second part of this exercise are the same, your brand is correctly majoring upon relevant buyer choice criteria. However, any discrepancy is indicative of inappropriate brand marketing.

2 Write down the core values of one of your brands and ask the other members of your organization to do the same. Compile a summary of the replies (without participants' names) and circulate the findings, asking for comments about: (a) reasons for such varied replies, and (b) which four core values are the key issues your company is trying to major on. Repeat the exercise until a consensus view has been reached.

3 Having identified your team's views about the core values of your brand, ask your team to write down: (a) what your brand communicates about your company's relationship with the purchaser, and (b) how the different resources supporting the brand are satisfying this relationship objective. Collate the replies from all parties and consider how well your team appreciates your brand propositions.

4 Write down what you understand by the term 'brand' and compare your views with those of your colleagues. Where there are a large number of comments relating to 'differentiation', 'logo', or 'unique design', your firm may not be fully capitalizing its brand asset.

5 After making explicit what the added values are of one of your brands, estimate how long it would take a major organization to buy in resources which would help it copy each of these added values. When considering the results of this exercise, also ask yourself: (a) how relevant to the buyer are the added values that this major competitor would find easiest to emulate, and (b) what added values does the buyer not yet have from any brand and how difficult it is to develop these added values.

6 For each of the added value benefits that your brand represents, write down how each element of the marketing mix is to help achieve it. If there are any instances where different elements of the mix are not operating in the same direction, consider why this is so and identify any changes necessary.

7 For each stage of the life cycle of one of your brands (introduction, growth, maturity, saturation, decline) identify how the added values may have to change to adapt to buyer sophistication.

8 Identify what the clues are that buyers use to evaluate the brand's added values and consider how much emphasis is placed on these clues in your marketing activity.

9 Make explicit the main situations within which one of your brands is: (a) bought and (b) consumed. Evaluate the appropriateness of your current brand strategy for each of these situations.

10 If you were to remove the name of your brand from its packaging, is there anything else that would signify the identity of the brand to buyers? How well is this protected against copying?

11 Which of the brand categories outlined in this chapter does each of your company brands reflect (recognize that each of your brands may belong to several of the categories: a sign of ownership; a differentiating device; a functional communicator; a symbolic device; a risk-reducing device; a shorthand information device; a legal device; a strategic device). How are you overcoming the limitations of being in the first seven categories?

12 Rank the importance of the different reasons why those people interested in your brand value it. What are you doing to protect the brand on each of these valued attributes?

13 Does the marketing department annually prepare a brand plan which audits the forces influencing the brand, has quantified brand objectives and well-considered strategies which are able to satisfy the objectives?

14 Using the audit in the section 'The importance of brand planning', what is your view about whether your firm is helping or hindering brand development?

15 How well positioned is each of your brands in relation to the five forces affecting brand potential? (Outlined in the section 'The importance of brand planning'.)

References and further reading

Allan J. (1981). Why Fine Fare believes in private label. Paper presented at Oyez Seminar: Is the Brand Under Pressure Again. London, Sept. 1981.

Allison R., Uhl K. (1964). Influence of beer brand identification on taste perception. *Journal of Marketing Research*, **1**, (3) 36–9.

Assael H. (1987). *Consumer Behavior and Marketing Action*. Boston: Kent Publishing.

Barwise P., Higson C., Likierman A., Marsh P. (1989). *Accounting for Brands*. London: London Business School.

Copeland M. (1923). Relation of consumers' buying habits to marketing methods. *Harvard Business Review*, **1**, (Apr.), 282–9.

de Chernatony L. (1987). Consumers' Perceptions of the Competitive Tiers in Six Grocery Markets. PhD thesis. City University Business School, London.

de Chernatony L. (1988). Products as arrays of cues: how do consumers evaluate company brands? In *Marketing Education Group Proceedings, 1988* (Robinson T. and Clarke-Hill C., eds).Huddersfield: MEG.

de Chernatony L., McWilliam G. (1990). Appreciating brands as assets through using a two dimensional model. *International Journal of Advertising*, **9**, (2), 111–19.

Doyle P. (1989). Building successful brands: the strategic options. *Journal of Marketing Management*, **5**, (1), 77–95.

Economist Intelligence Unit (1968). Own brand marketing. *Retail Business*, No. 128, (October), 12–19.

Euromonitor (1989). *UK Own brands 1989*. London: Euromonitor.

Gordon W., Corr D. (1990). The space between words. *Journal of the Market Research Society*, **32**, (3), 409–34.

Hawes J. (1982). *Retailing Strategies for Generic Grocery Products*. Ann Arbor: UMI Research Press.

Jacoby J., Mazursky D. (1984). Linking brand and retailer images – do the potential risks outweigh the potential benefits? *Journal of Retailing*, **60**, (2), 105–22.

Jacoby J., Speller D., Berning C. (1974). Brand choice behavior as a function of information load: replication and extension. *Journal of Consumer Research*, **1**, (June), 33–42.

Jarrett C. (1981). The cereal market and private label. Paper presented at Oyez Seminar: Is the Brand Under Pressure Again. London, Sept. 1981.

Jefferys J. (1954). *Retail trading in Britain 1850–1950*. Cambridge: University Press.

Jones J. (1986). *What's in a name?* Lexington: Lexington Books.

King S. (1970). *What is a Brand?* London: J. Walter Thompson.

King S. (1984). *Developing New Brands*. London: J. Walter Thompson.

King S. (1985). Another turning point for brands? *ADMAP*, **21**, (Oct.), 480–4, 519.

Kotler P. (1988). *Marketing management*. Englewood Cliffs: Prentice Hall International.

Lamb D. (1979). The ethos of the brand. *ADMAP*, **15**, (Jan), 19–24.

Langmaid R., Gordon W. (1988). 'A great ad – pity they can't remember the brand – true or false'. In *31st MRS Conference Proceedings*. London: MRS, pp. 15–46.

Levitt T. (1970). The morality of advertising. *Harvard Business Review*, (July–Aug.), 84–92.

Levitt T. (1980). Marketing success through differentiation of anything. *Harvard Business Review*, (Jan.–Feb.), 83–91.

McDonald M. (1989). *Marketing Plans*. Oxford: Heinemann.

Meadows R. (1983). They consume advertising too. *ADMAP*, **19**, (July–Aug.), 408–13.

Murphy J. (1990). Brand valuation – not just an accounting issue. *ADMAP*, **26**, (April), 36–41.

Patti C., Fisk R. (1982). National advertising, brands and channel control: an historical perspective with contemporary options. *Journal of the Academy of Marketing Science*, **10**, (1), 90–108.

Pitcher A. (1985). The role of branding in international advertising. *International Journal of Advertising*, **4**, (3), 241–6.

Porter M. (1985). *Competitive Advantage* New York: Free Press.

Room A. (1987). History of branding. In *Branding: A Key Marketing Tool*. Murphy J., ed.) Basingstoke: Macmillan.

Ross I. (1971). Self concept and brand preference. *Journal of Business*, **44**, (1), 38-50.

Schutte T. (1969). The semantics of branding. *Journal of Marketing*, **33**, (2) 5–11.

Simmons M., Meredith B. (1983). Own label profile and purpose. Paper presented at Institute of Grocery Distribution Conference. Radlett: IGD.

Sinclair S., Seward K. (1988). Effectiveness of branding a commodity product. *Industrial Marketing Management*, **17**, 23–33.

Staveley N. (1987). Advertising, marketing and brands. *ADMAP*, **23**, (Jan.), 31–5.

Thermistocli & Associates (1984). *The Secret of the Own Brand*. London: Thermistocli & Associates.

Watkins T. (1986). *The Economics of the Brand*. London: McGraw Hill.

3 How consumers choose brands

Summary

The purpose of this chapter is to show how an understanding of consumers' buying processes can help in developing successful brands. It opens by looking at how consumers process information and shows that, depending on the extent to which consumers perceive competing brands to differ and on their involvement in the brand purchase, so four buying processes can be identified. It then shows how consumers search for information about brands, explains why this search is limited, goes through the arguments for only giving consumers a few pieces of high quality brand information and illustrates how consumers evaluate brands as arrays of clues with the brand name emerging as a very high quality clue. The influence of perception on branding is addressed. Building on earlier concepts in the chapter, brand naming issues are reviewed, along with a consideration of the way that brands can be presented as risk-reducing devices.

Brands and the consumer's buying process

There are many theories about the way consumers buy brands and debate still continues about their respective strengths and weaknesses. For example, some argue that brand choice can be explained by what is known as 'the expectancy-value model'. In this model, it is argued that consumers assign scores to two variables, one being the degree to which they expect a pleasurable outcome, the other being the value they ascribe to a favourable outcome. When faced with competing brands, this model postulates that consumers assign scores to these expectancy-value parameters and, following a mental calculation, make a selection based on the highest overall score.

We find this hard to accept, since people have limited mental processing capabilities and many brands, particularly regularly purchased brands, are bought without much rational consideration.

In reality, consumers face a complex world. They are limited both by economic resources and by their ability to seek, store and process

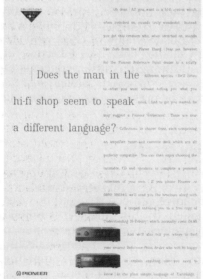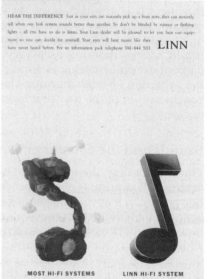

Exhibit 3.1　*Both Pioneer and Linn brands cut through the technical details of hifi. (Courtesy Pioneer High Fidelity (GB) Ltd and Linn Hi-Fi)*

brand information. For this reason, we are also sceptical of the economist's view of consumer behaviour. This hypothesizes that consumers seek information until the marginal value gained is equal to, or less than, the cost of securing that knowledge. Many researchers have shown that consumers do not acquire perfect information – in fact even when presented with the economist's view of 'perfect' information, they are unable to comprehend it! As an example of this, the Pioneer advertisement in Exhibit 3.1 is rightly critical of some hi-fi retailers who cause unnecessary consumer confusion by providing incomprehensible information about competing brands.

It is not our aim to become embroiled in a review of the merits of the different consumer behaviour models which could explain the brand selection process. The interested reader can appreciate this by consulting any of the numerous texts on this subject or by consulting the references at the end of this chapter.

Instead, we subscribe to a more well-accepted model of consumer behaviour. This shows the consumer decision process occurring as a result of consumers seeking and evaluating small amounts of information to make a brand purchase. Consumers rely upon a few pieces of selective information with which they feel confident, to help them decide how the brand might perform. For example, when choosing between different brands of paint, a novice might select Dulux because the name is one that has been around for a long time.

The stages in the buying process when consumers seek information about brands and the extent of the information search, are influenced by an array of factors, such as time pressure; previous experience; advice from friends; and so on. However, two factors are particularly useful in explaining how consumers decide. One is the extent of their involvement in the brand purchase and their perceptions of any differences between competing brands. For example, a housewife may become very *involved* when buying a washing machine, because with her large family it is important that she replaces it quickly. As such, she will show an *active* interest in evaluating different washing machine brands, all of which she can probably evaluate because of her experience. She will be able to evaluate the few brands that broadly appeal and will buy the brand which comes closest to satisfying her needs on one or a number of the key attributes important to her. By contrast, the same housewife is likely to show limited *involvement* when buying a brand of baked beans as they are of little personal importance and evoke little interest in her regular grocery shopping. She may perceive minimal difference between competing brands and because of the low importance of this purchase, does not wish to waste time considering different brands. As such, she is likely to make a rapid decision, based predominantly on previous experience.

With an appreciation of the extent of consumers' *involvement* in a purchase decision and their perception of the degree of *differentiation* between brands, it is possible to categorize the different decision processes using the matrix shown in Figure 3.1.

Significant perceived brand differences	Extended problem solving	Tendency to limited problem solving
Minor perceived brand differences	Dissonance reduction	Limited problem solving
	High consumer involvement	Low consumer involvement

Figure 3.1   *Typology of consumer decision processes. (Adapted from Assael, 1987)*

The strength of this matrix, as will now be shown, is that it illustrates simply the stages through which the consumer is likely to pass when making different types of brand purchases. Each of the quadrants is now considered in more detail.

Extended problem solving

Extended problem solving occurs when consumers are *involved* in the purchase and where they perceive *significant differences* between competing brands in the same product field. This type of decision process is likely for high-priced brands which are generally perceived as a risky purchase due to their complexity (e.g. washing machines, cars, hi-fi, home computers) or brands that reflect the buyer's self-image (e.g. clothing, cosmetics, jewellery). It is characterized by consumers *actively* searching for information to evaluate alternative brands. When making a complex purchase decision, consumers pass through the five stages shown in Figure 3.2.

The decision process starts when the consumer becomes aware of a problem. For example, a young man may have heard his friend's new hi-fi system and become aware of how inferior his own system sounds. This recognition would trigger a need to resolve the problem, and, if he feels particularly strongly, he will embark on a course to replace his system. Depending upon his urgency to act and his situation (e.g. time availability, financial situation, confidence, etc.) he might take action quickly, or, more likely, he will become more attentive to information about hi-fi and buy a brand some time later.

The search for information would start first in his own memory, and if he feels confident that he has sufficient information already, he will be able to evaluate the available brands. Often, though, consumers do not feel sufficiently confident to rely on memory alone (particularly for

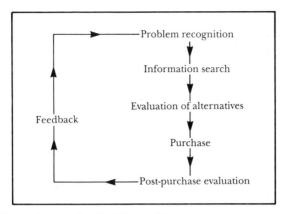

Figure 3.2 *Stages in complex decision making*

infrequently bought brands), so they will begin to scan the external environment (e.g. visit shops, become attentive to certain advertise-ments, talk to friends). As they get more information, the highly involved consumer will start to learn how to interpret the information in their evaluation of competing brands.

Even so, consumers do not single-mindedly search for information about one particular purchase. It has been estimated that in any one day people are bombarded by nearly 500 advertisements, of which they are attentive to about 2 per cent. Consumers' perceptual processes protect them from information overload and help them search and interpret new information. The issue of what these perceptual processes are is dealt with later in this chapter. Should something interest them, their attention will be directed to this new source. Even here, however, of the few advertisements that they take notice of, they are likely to ignore the points that do not conform to their prior expectations and interpret some of the other points within their own frame of reference.

Thus, the brand marketer has to overcome, amongst other issues, three main problems when communicating a brand proposition. First, he has to fight through the considerable 'noise' in the market to get his brand message noticed. If he can achieve this, the next challenge is to develop the content of the message in such a way that there is harmony between what the marketer puts into the message and what the consumer takes out of the message. Having overcome these two hurdles, the next challenge is to make the message powerful enough to be able to reinforce the other marketing activities designed to persuade the consumer to buy the brand.

As the consumer mentally processes messages about competing brands, he would evaluate them against those criteria deemed to be most important. Brand beliefs are then formed (e.g. 'the Sony system has a wide range of features, it's well priced', etc.). In turn, these beliefs begin to mould an attitude and if a sufficiently positive attitude evolves, so there is a greater likelihood of a positive intention to buy that brand.

Having decided which hi-fi brand to buy, the consumer would then make the purchase – assuming he can find a distributor for that particular brand and that the brand is in stock. Once the hi-fi is installed at home, he would discover its capabilities and assess how well his expectations were met by the brand. As can be seen from the model shown in Figure 3.2, he would be undertaking post-purchase evaluation. Satisfaction with different aspects of the brand will strengthen his positive beliefs and attitudes towards the brand. Were this to be so, the consumer would be proud of his purchase and praise its attributes to his peer group. With a high level of satisfaction, the consumer would look favourably at this company's brands in any future purchase.

Should he be dissatisfied though, he would seek further information after the purchase to provide reassurance that the correct choice was made. For example, he may go back to the hi-fi shop, where he bought the brand, and check that he is using the controls properly and that the speakers are correctly connected. If he finds sufficiently reassuring information confirming a wise brand choice, he will become more satisfied. Without such positive support, he will become disenchanted with the brand and over time will become more dissatisfied. He is likely to talk to others about his experience, not only vowing never to buy that brand again, but also convincing others that the brand should not be bought.

In the event that the consumer is satisfied with the brand purchase and repeats it in a relatively short period of time (e.g. buys a hi-fi for his car), he is unlikely to undergo such a detailed search and evaluation process. Instead, he is likely to follow what has now become a more routine problem-solving process. Problem recognition would be followed by memory search, which, with prior satisfaction, would reveal clear intentions, leading to a purchase. Brand loyalty would ensue, which would be reinforced by continued satisfaction (should quality be maintained). This process is shown in Figure 3.3.

When consumers are deeply involved with the brand purchase and when they perceive large differences between brands, they are more likely to seek information actively in order to make a decision about

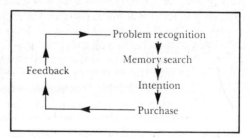

Figure 3.3   *Routine problem-solving behaviour*

which brand to buy. As such, brand advertising may succeed by presenting relatively detailed information explaining the benefits of the brand, as well as reinforcing its unique differential positioning. It is important for the brand marketer to identify those attributes consumers perceive to be important and focus on communicating them as powerfully as possible. In circumstances such as those just

Exhibit 3.2   *Russell & Bromley shoes are backed by both consumer advertising and retailer advice*

described, as the consumer is likely actively to seek information from several different sources, the brand marketer should use a consistent multi-media promotional approach. Also, it is important to ensure that all retail assistants likely to come in contact with our inquisitive consumer are well versed in the capabilities of the product.

Dissonance reduction

This type of brand buying behaviour is seen when there is a high level of consumer *involvement* with the purchase, but the consumer perceives only minor *differences* between competing brands. Such consumers may be confused by the lack of clear brand differences. Without any firm beliefs about the advantages of any particular brand, a choice will most probably be made based on other reasons, such as, for example, a friend's opinion or advice given by a shop assistant.

Following the purchase, the consumer may feel unsure, particularly if they receive information that seems to conflict with their reasons for buying. The consumer would experience mental discomfort, or what is known as 'post-purchase dissonance', and would attempt to reduce this state of mental unbalance. This would be done by either ignoring the dissonant information, for example, by refusing to discuss it with the person giving conflicting views, or by selectively seeking those messages that confirm prior beliefs.

In this type of brand purchase decision, the consumer makes a choice without firm brand beliefs, then changes his attitude *after* the purchase – often on the basis of experience with the chosen brand. Finally, learning occurs on a selective basis to support the original brand choice by the consumer being attentive to positive information and ignoring negative information. This brand buying process is shown in Figure 3.4.

When consumers are involved in a brand purchase, but perceive little brand differentiation or lack the ability to judge between competing brands, the advertising should reduce post-purchase dissonance through providing reassurance after the purchase. For example, in the wallpaper paste market, consumers do not have the ability to evaluate the technical differences between pastes (e.g.

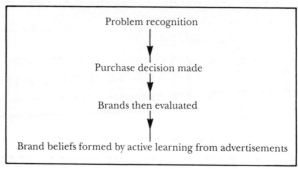

Figure 3.4   *Brand purchasing under dissonance reduction*

adhesion, enabling paper to slip when matching patterns, etc.). However, they are involved in the purchase due to the risk they perceive in ruining the wallpaper decorations. Polycell ran a series of advertisements using the strap line 'You've chosen well' deliberately to reassure consumers after the purchase and to encourage brand loyalty.

Also, close to the point of purchase, as consumers are unsure about which brand to select, promotional material is particularly important in increasing the likelihood of a particular brand being selected. Likewise, any packaging should try to stress a point of difference from competitors and sales staff should be trained to be 'brand reassurers', rather than 'brand pushers'.

Limited problem solving

When consumers do not regard the buying of certain products as important issues, and when they perceive only minor differences between competing brands in these product fields (e.g. packaged groceries, household cleaning materials), then their buying behaviour can be described by the 'limited problem solving process'. The stages that the consumer passes through are shown in Figure 3.5.

Problem recognition is likely to be straightforward. For example, an item in the household may be running low. As the consumer is not particularly interested personally in the purchase, they are not motivated actively to seek information from different sources. Whatever information they have will probably have been passively received, say, via a television commercial that the consumer wasn't paying particular attention to.

Alternative evaluation, if any, takes place *after* the purchase. In effect, fully formed beliefs, attitudes and intentions are the *outcomes* of purchase and not the cause. The consumer is likely to regard the cost of information search and evaluation as outweighing the benefits.

Promotions providing information, however, still do have a role to play in low involvement brand purchasing. However whilst they have a positive role, it is different from that in high involvement buying. Consumers passively receive information and process it in such a way

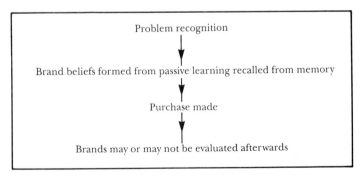

Figure 3.5   *Limited problem-solving brand purchase*

that it is stored in their memories without making much of an impact on their existing mental structure. Having stored the message, no behaviourial change occurs until the consumer comes across a purchase trigger (e.g. an in-store display of the brand) at the point at which they need to purchase the product in question.

After trying the brand, the consumer can then decide how satisfactory it is. If the brand is satisfactory, there will be a kind of belief in their particular brand, albeit a fairly 'weak' one, which will lead to the likelihood of repeat brand buying.

When *regularly* purchasing these kind of brands, consumers would establish buying strategies that reduce the effort in decision making (i.e. routine problem solving). Following a similar flow chart to that in Figure 3.3, any further purchase decisions about the brand would be based on a memory scan, which, if holding details about a satisfactory experience, would result in brand loyalty. Thus, in extended problem-solving situations, the consumer considers it important to buy the 'right brand' and it is difficult to induce brand switching. By contrast, in low involvement buying, the 'right brand' is less central to the consumer's lifestyle and brand switching may be more easily achieved through coupons, free trial incentives, etc.

In low involvement purchasing, consumers occasionally show variety-seeking behaviour. There is little involvement with the product and therefore the consumer feels little risk in switching between brands. Over time, consumers feel bored buying the same brand and occasionally seek variety by switching.

Consumers pay minimal attention to advertisements for these kinds of brands. Consequently, the message content should be kept simple and the advertisements should be shown frequently. A single (or low number) of benefits should be presented in a creative manner which associates a few features with the brand. In low involvement brand buying, consumers are seeking acceptable, rather than optimal purchases – they seek to minimize problems rather than to maximize benefits. Consequently, it may be more appropriate to position low involvement brands as functional problem solvers (e.g. a brand of washing up liquid positioned as an effective cleaner of greasy dishes) rather than as less tangible benefit deliverers (e.g. a brand of washing up liquid positioned as smelling fresh).

Trial is an important method by which consumers form favourable attitudes after consumption, so devices such as money-off coupons, in-store trial and free sachets, are particularly effective.

As consumers are not motivated to search out low involvement brands, manufacturers should ensure widespread availability. Any out-of-stock situations would probably result in consumers switching to an alternative brand, rather than visiting another store to find the brand.

Once inside a store, little evaluation will be made of competing brands so locating the brand at eye level, or very close to the check-out counter, is an important facilitator of brand selection. Packaging should be eye-catching and simple.

Tendency to limited problem solving

While the 'limited problem solving' aspect of the matrix describes low involvement purchasing with *minimal* differences between competing brands, we believe that this can also be used to describe low involvement brand purchasing when the consumer perceives *significant* brand differences. It is our view that when consumers feel minimal involvement, they are unlikely to be sufficiently motivated to undertake an extensive search for information. So even though there may be notable differences between brands (e.g. the unique dispensing nozzle on the Heinz's Tomato Ketchup), because of the consumer's low involvement, they are less likely to be concerned about any such differences. Brand trial would take place and, in an almost passive manner, the consumer would develop brand loyalty.

The brand selection process is very similar to that described in 'limited problem solving' and similar marketing issues need to be addressed.

This section has shown that, given an appreciation of the degree of involvement consumers have with the brand purchase and their perception of the degree of differentiation between brands, it is possible to identify their buying processes. With an appreciation of the appropriate buying process, the marketer is then able to identify how marketing resources can best be employed. A further benefit of appreciating consumers' buying processes is that brands can be developed and presented in such a way that consumers perceive them as having added values over and above the basic commodity represented by the brand, as the next section explains.

Consumers' perceptions of added values

Brands are able to sustain a price premium over their commodity form, since consumers perceive relevant added values. For brands with which consumers become personally involved, there may be a complex cluster of added values over and above the brand's basic functional purpose, such as, for example, the ability of a clothing brand to signify membership of a particular social group whose distinctiveness is the result of their ability always to be at the forefront of chic fashion. By contrast, for low involvement brands, the added value could be as simple as the friendly smile consistently apparent from a newsagent encouraging the busy commuter buying his daily newspaper to remain a loyal consumer.

The concept of added values is an extremely important aspect of brands, being their *raison d'être*. As there are many different ways in which added values interact with commodity forms in the branding process, we do not have just one chapter dedicated to this. Instead the topic is addressed at appropriate points in further chapters, for example, Chapters 5 and 6. Here we briefly overview the idea of added value and consider its role in relation to consumer behaviour.

Exhibit 3.3   *Promoting Bio-tex's added values of removing localized stains conveniently with the sponge tipped bottle*

The brand's added values are those that are relevant and appreciated by consumers and which are over and above the basic functional role of the product. For example, well-travelled international sales executives may recognize the prime functional benefit of Best Western Hotels as being clean, comfortable, establishments to sleep in, but they also appreciate their 'no surprises strategy' as an added value. This

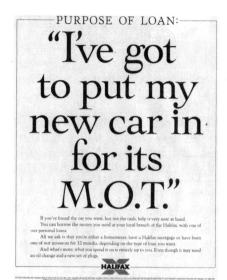

—————PURPOSE OF LOAN:—————

"I've got to put my new car in for its M.O.T."

If you've found the car you want, but not the cash, help is very near at hand.

You can borrow the money you need at your local branch of the Halifax, with one of our personal loans.

All we ask is that you're either a homeowner, have a Halifax mortgage or have been one of our investors for 12 months, depending on the type of loan you want.

And what's more, what you spend it on is entirely up to you. Even though it may need an oil change and a new set of plugs.

HALIFAX

Exhibit 3.4   *The added value consumers perceive from the Halifax loan is the unhindered ability to spend as they wish. (Reproduced with kind permission of Halifax Building Society)*

hotel group has a policy of consistency of standards throughout the world. For brands with which the consumer feels low involvement, the added values may often be other functional benefits. For example, while the prime benefit sought from a bleach may be its ability to kill germs, Domestos not only meets this requirement, but also has the added value of a directional nozzle to ensure that difficult-to-reach corners are reached. The marginal cost from the directional nozzle is an added value contributing to the overall value of the brand, enabling a price premium to be charged. Likewise, while consumers may buy a brand of salt for its taste, they may pay a premium for a particular brand, since they appreciate the added value of the small hygroscopic capsule inside the container which ensures that the salt always flows freely.

For the marketer, the challenge is to appreciate how all of the marketing resources supporting a brand interact to produce the added values which consumers perceive as being unique to a specific brand. The physical (or service) component is combined with symbols and images communicated by advertising, PR, packaging, pricing and distribution to create meanings. These meanings not only differentiate the brand, but also give it added values. Consumers interpret the meaning of the marketing activity behind a brand and project values onto the brand, endowing it with a personality. Many researchers in the 1960s and 1970s demonstrated the added value of strong brand personalities, showing that consumers tend to choose brands with the same care as they choose friends. By interpreting the personality of brands, consumers felt more comfortable buying particular brands.

This can be for a variety of reasons, such as, for example, a feeling of 'being at ease' with the brand (just as we are with an old friend) or the brand coming closest to matching the consumer's actual or aspired self-image. For example, whilst there are many credit cards, American Express has evolved such a strong brand personality that many believe 'it's the one you don't leave home without'. Likewise, whilst many firms distribute petrol, Shell is the one 'you can be sure of'.

Chapter 5 discusses the added value of brand personality in more depth, but it is worth stressing here that a strong brand personality evolves because of a consumer-focused marketing investment pro-gramme. It takes time and resources to build the brand personality and a lack of commitment to brand investment will weaken the brand's personality. For example, competitors in the lager market regard Courage's lack of brand support for Hofmeister as weakening the brand's personality, forcing the brand to concentrate on price offers.

A useful framework to help us understand the diverse types of brand added values was developed by Jones. It consists of four types:

1 *Added values from experience*   With repeated trial, consumers gain confidence in the brand and through its consistent reliability, perceive minimal risk. In grocery shopping, where a consumer is typically faced with over 20 000 lines in a grocery superstore, this added value is particularly appreciated, enabling consumers to complete their shopping rapidly by choosing known names.
2 *Added values from reference group effects*   The way that advertising uses personalities to endorse a brand is perceived by many target consumers as endorsing the brand by relating it to a certain lifestyle to which they may well aspire. An example of this is the promotion of perfume using Joan Collins.
3 *Added values from a belief that the brand is effective*   The belief that a brand is effective influences the consumer's views about the actual performance of the brand. For example, in branded pain killers, as considered in more detail in Chapter 5, it has been shown that branding accounts for approximately a quarter of the pain relief. In the suits market, one often hears of men remarking that for a certain event they 'feel' more comfortable with a certain type of suit. Further evidence of this added value is seen when consumers taste brands without their names, then with their names. In Table 3.1 it can be seen that functionally, Diet Pepsi is preferred to Diet Coke

Table 3.1   *The impact of branding on taste tests*

	Blind (%)	Branded (%)
Prefer Diet Pepsi	51	23
Prefer Diet Coke	44	65
Equal/don't know	5	12
	100	100

(blind testing), but through the strong image recalled by the name, the overall preference in the branded product test is for Diet Coke.

4 *Added values from the appearance of the brand* Consumers form impressions of brands from their packaging and develop brand preferences based on their attraction to the pack design. This is particularly so in the premium biscuit market, where designers use metal cans to enhance the premium positioning of their brand.

Thus, successful brands have consumer-relevant added values which buyers recognize and value sufficiently to pay a price premium. Accepting this, the task for the marketer is to communicate a brand's added values to consumers in such a way that the message penetrates consumers' perceptual defences and is not subject to perceptual distortion. This is not a small problem, since, as the next section shows, consumers are attentive to only a small amount of marketing information.

The extent to which consumers search for brand information

The way consumers gain information is shown in Figure 3.6 – firstly from memory, but if insufficient is held, then from external sources.

Information may be stored in memory as a result of an earlier active search process, as in the case, for example, of the assessment of a newly bought brand immediately after purchase. Alternatively, information may be stored in memory as a result of a passive acquisition process. For example, an advertisement might catch the reader's eye whilst a newspaper was being casually skimmed.

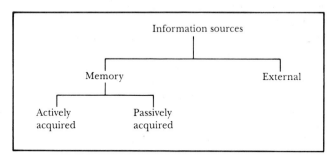

Figure 3.6 *The way consumers get brand information*

Two relevant factors which influence the degree to which consumers search their memory are the amount of stored information and its suitability for the particular problem. In a study amongst car purchasers, those repeatedly buying the same brand of car over time undertook less external search than those who had built up a similar history in terms of the number of cars bought, but who had switched between brands of cars. Repeatedly buying the same brand of car increased the quantity of *suitable* information in the memory and limited the need for external search.

If there is insufficient information already in a consumer's memory, and if the purchase is thought to warrant it, external search is undertaken. Research into consumer behaviour, however, shows that external search is a relatively limited activity, although there are variations between different groups of consumers. In one of the early studies on consumers' search for information, recent purchasers of sports shirts and major household goods (e.g. televisions, fridges, washing machines, etc.) were asked about their pre-purchase information search. Only 5 per cent of electrical appliance buyers showed evidence of a very active information search process, whilst a third claimed to seek virtually no pre-purchase information. Just under half (47 per cent) of appliance purchasers visited only one store and only 35 per cent considered another attribute in addition to brand name and price. Even less evidence of information search was found amongst purchasers of sports shirts, the conclusion being 'that many purchases were made in a state of ignorance, or at least of indifference'. As was pointed out, however, the apparent lack of deliberation does not indicate irrational decision behaviour. Some purchasers may have found it difficult to evaluate all the features of a product and instead, relied upon a limited number of attributes that they felt more comfortable with.

A further detailed study of consumers buying cars and major household appliances again showed evidence of limited external search. Less than a half of the purchasers interviewed (44 per cent) used no more than one information source, 49 per cent experienced a deliberation time of less than two weeks and 49 per cent visited only one retail outlet when making these major brand purchases. Numerous other instances have been reported of consumers under-taking limited external search for expensive brand purchases in such product fields as financial services, housing, furniture and clothing.

Not surprisingly, for low cost, low risk items (e.g. groceries), external search activity is also restricted. No doubt due to the low level of involvement that these brands engender, far more reliance is placed on memory. For example, when shopping for washing powders, consumers simplify purchasing by considering only one or two brands and by using only three to five brand attributes. Amongst consumers of breakfast cereals, only 2 per cent of the available information was used to make a decision. When using in-store observations of grocery shoppers, 25 per cent made a purchase decision without any time for deliberation and 56 per cent spent less than eight seconds examining and deciding which brand to buy.

Reasons for limited search for external information

Several reasons exist for this apparently limited external search. Consumers have limited mental capacities, which are protected from information overload by perceptual selectivity. This focuses consumers' attention on those attributes considered important. For example, one study reported that, because of perceptual selectivity, only 35 per cent of magazine readers exposed to a brand advertisement noticed the brand being advertised.

Information is continually bombarding consumers and this information acquisition is a continuous process.

The search for external information represents a cost (the time and effort) and some consumers do not consider the benefits outweigh these costs. This is particularly so for low involvement brands.

In research studies into consumer behaviour, a lot of emphasis has been placed on measuring the *number* of sources consumers use, rather than considering the *quality* of each informational source.

The prevailing circumstances of consumers also have an impact on the level of external search. Consumers may feel time pressure (e.g. newly married couples seeking a home when there is a lack of rented accommodation) or they may not find the information easy to understand (e.g. food labels). The search for information is also affected by the consumer's emotional state. For example, one study, reviewing the way funeral services are marketed, noted that due to emotional state, consumers pay little attention to information during this traumatic period.

Brand information: quality or quantity?

The preceding sections have shown the relatively superficial external search for information which is undertaken in selecting brands. The question marketers need to consider, therefore, is whether increasing levels of information help (or hinder) consumer brand decisions. In one of many studies to assess the decision-making process, consumers were presented with varying levels of information about brands of washing powders and asked to make brand selections. Prior to the experiment, they were asked to describe their preferred washing powder brand. The researchers found that accuracy (in the sense that consumers selected the brand in the survey that matched their earlier stated brand preference) was *inversely* related to the number of brands available. Initially, accuracy of brand choice improved as small amounts of brand information were made available, but a point was reached, at which further information reduced brand selection accuracy.

In another study, housewives were given varying levels of information about different brands of rice and pre-prepared dinners and were asked to choose the brand they liked best. Again, prior to the experiment, they were asked about their preferred brand. Confirming the earlier survey on washing powders, increasing information availability from low levels helped decision making, but continuing provision of information reduced purchasing accuracy and resulted in longer decision periods.

The conclusion is that marketers need to recognize that increasing the quantity of information will not necessarily increase brand decision effectiveness, even though it may make consumers more confident.

It is becoming apparent that consumers follow two broad patterns when searching for information. Some people make a choice by examining one brand at a time – for the first brand, they select information on several attributes, then for the second brand, they seek the same attribute information, and so on. This strategy is known as *'choice by processing brands'*.

An alternative strategy is seen when consumers have a particularly important attribute against which they assess all the brands, followed by the next most important attribute, and so on. This is known as *'choice by processing attributes'*.

It has been shown that consumers with limited knowledge of a product or service tend to process information by attributes, while more experienced consumers process the information by brands. Furthermore, choice by processing attributes tends to be the route followed when there are few alternatives, when differences are easy to compute and when the task is in general easier.

Clues to evaluate brands

Rather than engaging in a detailed search for information when deciding between competing brands, consumers look for a few clues that they believe will give an indication of brand performances. For example, when consumers buy a new car, they talk about them as being 'tinny' or 'solid', based on the sound when slamming the door. Clearly, then, some consumers use the sound as being indicative of the car's likely performance.

There are many examples of consumers using surrogate attributes to evaluate brands, for example, the sound of the lawn-mower engine being indicative of power; the feel of the bread pack as indicative of the freshness of bread; the clothing style of banking staff as indicative of their understanding of financial services; and high prices as being indicative of good quality. It is now widely recognized that consumers conceive brands as arrays of clues (e.g. price, colour, taste, feel, etc.). Consumers assign information values to the available clues, using only those few clues which have a high information value. A clue's information value is a function of its predictive value (i.e. how accurately it predicts the attribute being evaluated) and its confidence value (i.e. how confident the consumer is about the predictive value assigned to the clue). This concept of brands as arrays of clues also helps explain why consumers undertake only a limited search for information. If, through experience, consumers recognize a few clues offering high predictive and high confidence values, these will be selected. More often than not, the most sought-after clue, as will be later explained in this chapter, is the presence of a brand name, which rapidly enables recall from memory of previous experience. However, when the consumer has limited brand experience, the brand name will have low predictive and confidence values and thus more clues will be sought, usually price, followed by other clues. Learning, through brand usage, enables the consumer to adjust predictive and confidence values internally, which stabilize over time.

There are numerous studies showing that, when faced with a brand decision, consumers place considerable importance on the presence or absence of brand names. Not only do brand names have a high predictive value, but consumers are also very confident, particularly from experience, with this clue. Of all the marketing variables, it is the brand name which receives the most attention by consumers and is a key influencer of their perceptions of quality.

Brand names as informational chunks

The previous section has explained that brand names are perceived by consumers as important information clues, which reduce the need to engage in a detailed search for information. An explanation for this can be found by consulting the work of Miller (1956), who carried out research into the way the mind encodes information. If we compare the mind with the way computers work, it can be seen that we can evaluate the quantity of information facing a consumer in terms of the number of 'bits'. All the information on the packaging of a branded grocery item would represent in excess of a hundred bits of information. Researchers have shown that at most, the mind can simultaneously process seven bits of information. Clearly, to cope with the information deluge from everyday life, our memories have had to develop methods for processing such large quantities of information.

This is done by a process of aggregating bits of information into larger groups, or 'chunks', which contain more information. A further analogy may be useful. The novice yachtsman learning morse code, initially hears 'dit' and 'dot' as information bits. With experience, he organizes these bits of information into chunks (i.e. letters), then mentally builds these chunks into larger chunks (i.e. words). In a similar manner, when first exposed to a new brand of convenience food, the first scanning of the label would reveal an array of wholesome ingredients with few additives. These would be grouped into a chunk interpreted as 'natural ingredients'. Further scanning may show a high price printed on a highly attractive, multicolour label. This would be grouped with the earlier 'natural ingredients' chunk to form a larger chunk, interpreted as 'certainly a high quality offering'. This aggregation of increasingly large chunks would continue until final eye scanning would reveal an unknown brand name, but on seeing that it came from a well-known organization (e.g. Nestlé, Heinz, etc.), the consumer would then aggregate this with the earlier chunks to infer that this was a premium brand – quality contents, in a well-presented container, selling at a high price, through a reputable retailer, from a respected manufacturer known for advertising quality. Were the consumer not to purchase this new brand of convenience food, but later that day to see an advertisement for the brand, they would be able to recall the brand's attributes rapidly, since the brand name would enable fast accessing of a highly informative chunk in the memory.

The task facing the marketer is to facilitate the way that consumers process information about brands, such that ever larger chunks can be built in the memory, which, when fully formed, can then be rapidly accessed through associations from brand names. This relates to the category described in Chapter 2 of branding as a shorthand device. Frequent exposure to advertisements containing a few claims about the brand should help the chunking process through either passive or active information acquisition. What is really important, however, is to reinforce attributes with the brand name rather than continually repeating the brand name without at the same time associating the appropriate attributes with it.

The challenge to branding from perception

To overcome the problems of being bombarded by vast quantities of information and having limited mental capacities to process it all, consumers not only adopt efficient processing rules (e.g. they only use high information value clues when choosing between brands, and aggregate small pieces of information into larger chunks) but they also rely upon their perceptual processes. These help brand decision making by filtering information (perceptual selectivity) and help them to categorize competing brands (perceptual organization).

Amongst others, Bruner made a major contribution in helping lay the foundations for a better understanding of the way consumers' perceptual processes operate. He showed that consumers cannot be aware of all the events occurring around them and, with a limited span of attention, they acquire information selectively. With this reduced data set, they then construct a set of mental categories which allows them to sort competing brands more rapidly. By allocating competing brands to specific mental categories, they are then able to interpret and give more meaning to brands. A consequence of this perceptual process is that consumers interpret brands in a different way from that intended by the marketer. The classic example of this was the cigarette brand Strand. Advertisements portrayed a man alone on a London bridge, on a misty evening, smoking Strand. The advertising slogan was 'You're never alone with a Strand'. Sales were poor, since consumers' perceptual processes accepted only a small part of the information given and interpreted it as, 'if you are a loner and nobody wants to know you, console yourself by smoking Strand'.

It is clearly very important that brand marketers appreciate the role of perceptual processes when developing brand communication strategies and the two key aspects of perception are reviewed next.

Perceptual selectivity

Marketers invest considerable money and effort communicating with consumers, yet only a small fraction of the information is accepted and processed by consumers. First of all, their brand communication must overcome the barrier of what is known as 'selective exposure'. If a new advertisement is being shown on television, even though the consumer has been attentive to the programme during which the advertisement appears, when the commercial breaks are on, the consumer may out of preference choose to engage in some other activity rather than watching the advertisements.

The second barrier is what is known as 'selective attention'. The consumer may not feel inclined to do anything else while the television commercials are on during their favourite programme and might watch the advertisements for entertainment, taking an interest in the creative aspects of the commercial. At this stage, selective attention filters information from advertisements, so building support for existing beliefs about a brand ('Oh, its that Toyota advert. They are good reliable cars. Let's see if they drive the car over very rough ground in this advert') and avoiding contradicting claims, ('It's another advert for the Amstrad Fax machine. I had problems getting my Amstrad pc fixed last time, so I just don't want to know any more about Amstrad products').

The third challenge facing a brand is what is known as 'selective comprehension'. The consumer would start to interpret the message and would find that some of the information does not fit well with their earlier beliefs and attitudes. They would then 'twist' the message until it became more closely aligned with their views. For example, after a confusing evaluation of different companies' life assurance policies, a young man may mention to his brother that he is seriously thinking of selecting a Scottish Widows policy. When told by his brother that he knew of a different brand that had shown a better return last year, he may discount this fact, arguing to himself that his brother as a software engineer probably knew less about money matters than he did as a sales manager.

With the passage of time, memory becomes hazy about brand claims. Even at this stage, after brand advertising, a further challenge is faced by the brand. Some aspects of brand advertising are 'selectively retained' in memory, normally those claims which support existing beliefs and attitudes.

From the consumer's point of view the purpose of selective perception is to ensure that they have sufficient, relevant information to make a brand purchase decision. This is known as 'perceptual vigilance'. Its purpose is also to maintain their prior beliefs and attitudes. This is known as 'perceptual defence'. There is considerable evidence to show that information which does not concur with consumers' prior beliefs is distorted and that supportive information is more readily accepted. One of the classic examples of this is a study which recorded *different* descriptions from opposing team supporters who all saw the *same* football match. Many surveys show that selectivity is a positive process, in that consumers actively decide which information clues they will be attentive to and which ones they will reject.

Thus, as a consequence of perceptual selectivity, consumers are unlikely to be attentive to all of the information transmitted by manufacturers or distributors. Furthermore, in instances where consumers are considering two competing brands, the degree of dissimilarity may be very apparent to the marketer, but if the difference, say, in price, quality or pack size is below a critical threshold, this difference will not register with the consumer. This is an example of what is known as Weber's law – the size of the least detectable change to the consumer is a function of the initial stimulus they encountered. Thus, to have an impact upon consumers' awareness, a jewellery retailer would have to make a significantly larger reduction on a £1000 watch than on a £500 watch.

Perceptual organization

'Perceptual organization' allows consumers to decide between competing brands on the basis of their similarities within mental categories conceived earlier. Consumers group a large number of competing brands into a few categories, since this reduces the complexity of interpretation. For example, rather than evaluating each marque in the car market, consumers would have mental categories such as the Toyota MR2 as a sports car, the BMW 3.2i as a family saloon and so on. By assessing which category the new brand is most similar to, consumers can rapidly group brands and are able to draw inferences without detailed search. For example, if a consumer places a brand such as Safeway's own label washing powder into a category they had previously identified as 'own label', then the brand will achieve its meaning from the class it is assigned to by the consumer. In this case, even if the consumer has little experience of the newly categorized brand, the consumer is able to use this perceptual process to predict certain characteristics of the new brand. For example, the consumer may well reason that stores' own labels are inexpensive, thus this own label should be inexpensive and should also be quite good.

However, in order to be able to form effective mental categories in which competing brands can be placed and which lead to confidence in predicting brand performance, relevant product experience is necessary. The novice to a new product field has less well formed brand categories than his more experienced companion. When new to a product field, the trialist has a view (based upon perceptions) about some attributes indicative of brand performance. This schema of key attributes forms the initial basis for brand categorization, drives their search for information and influences brand selection. With experience, the schema is modified, the search for information is redirected and brand categorization is adjusted, eventually stabilizing over time with increasing brand experience.

An interesting study undertaken amongst beer drinkers is a useful example of how learning moulds brand categorization. Without any labels shown, the beer drinkers were generally unable to identify the brand they most often drink and expressed no significant difference between brands. In this instance, the schema of attributes to categorize brands was based solely on the physical characteristics of the brands (e.g. palate, smell and the visual evaluation). When the study was later repeated amongst the same drinkers, but this time with the brands labelled, respondents immediately identified their most often drunk brand and commented about significant taste differences between brands! With the labels shown, respondents placed more emphasis on using the brand names to recall brand images as well as their views about how the brands tasted. As a consequence of consumers using this new schema of attributes to evaluate the brands, a different categorization of the brands resulted.

Whilst it might be thought that the simplest way for consumers to form mental groups is to rely solely on one attribute and to categorize competing brands according to the extent to which they possess this attribute, evidence from various studies shows that this is not often the case. Instead, consumers use several attributes to form brand categories. Furthermore, it appears that they weight the attributes according to the degree of importance of each attribute. Thus, marketers need to find the few key attributes that are used by consumers to formulate different brand categorizations and major upon the relevant attributes to ensure that their brand is perceived in the desired manner.

Gestalt psychologists provide further support for the notion of consumers interpreting brands through 'perceptual organization'. This school of thought argues that people see objects as 'integrated wholes' rather than as a sum of individual parts. The analogy being drawn is that people recognize a tune, rather than listening to an individual collection of notes.

To form a holistic view of a brand, consumers have to fill in gaps of information not shown in the advertisement. This concept, referred to as 'closure', is used by brand advertisers to get consumers more involved with the brand. For example, Kelloggs once advertised on billboards with the last 'g' cut off and it was argued that consumers' desire to round off the advertisement generated more attention. Billboard advertising during 1991 showing a fly on a wall with the caption 'The Economist' was also developed to generate more interest through closure. Likewise, not presenting an obvious punch-line in a pun when advertising a brand can again generate involvement through closure. This was one of the reasons for the successful 'eau' Perrier advertising during 1989 (e.g. H_2 Eau, Eau la la, Eau Revoir, Eau Pair, etc.). When a brand has built up a respected relationship with consumers, the concept of closure can be successfully employed in brand advertising. For example, Schweppes is such a well-regarded brand that the name didn't have to appear in the early successful 'Schhh . . . you know who' campaign. The problem with this campaign was that closure initially worked well for the brand, but eventually the actor was being promoted more than Schweppes, a problem not dissimilar to that faced by the Bristol & West Building Society campaign using Joan Collins.

Naming brands: individual or company name?

From the previous sections, it should now be clear that consumers seek to reduce the complexity of buying situations by cutting through the vast amount of information to focus on a few key pieces of information. A brand name is, from the consumer's perspective, a very important piece of information and is often the key piece of

Exhibit 3.5   *The Amstrad brand name evolved from Alan M. Sugar Trading plc*

information. It is, therefore, essential that an appropriate brand name is chosen which will reinforce the brand's desired positioning by associating it with the relevant attributes that influence buying behaviour.

A brief consideration of some very well known brand names, shows that rather unusual reasons formed the basis for name selection. However, in today's more competitive environment, far more care is necessary in naming a brand. For example, the Ford Motor Company was named after its founder; Lloyds of London because of its location; Mercedes because of a friend's daughter; and Amstrad after conjuring various letters together (Alan M. Sugar Trading plc). Today, however, because of the increasing need to define markets on a global basis, idiosyncratic approaches to naming brands can lead to failure. For example, General Motor's Nova failed in Spain because the name means 'doesn't go', while a Beaujolais branded Pisse-Dru faced obvious problems, even though the French vigneron interprets this as a wine to his liking. Of even more intrigue is the lager 36/15 from Pecheur et Fischer marketed as La Biere Amoureuse. This brand is brewed with aphrodisiac plants and is named after the telephone number of a dating service advertised on French television!

When examining brand names, it is possible to categorize them broadly along a spectrum, with a company name at one end (e.g. British Telecom, Halifax), right the way through to individual brand names which do not have a link with the manufacturer (e.g. Ariel, Dreft, Daz, Bold and Tide emanating from Procter & Gamble). This is shown in Figure 3.7.

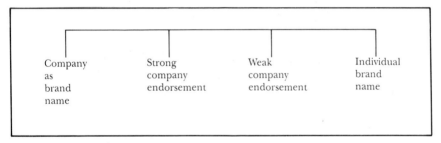

Figure 3.7   *Brand name spectrum*

There are varying degrees of company associations with the brand name. For example, there are brand names with strong company endorsement, such as Cadbury's Dairy Milk, Castrol GTX, Sainsbury's Baked Beans, and brand names with weak company endorsement, such as Kit Kat from Rowntree.

There are many advantages to be gained from tying the brand name in with the firm's name. With the goodwill that has been built up over the years from continuous advertising and a commitment to consistency, new brand additions can gain instant acceptance by being linked with the heritage. Consumers feel more confident trying a

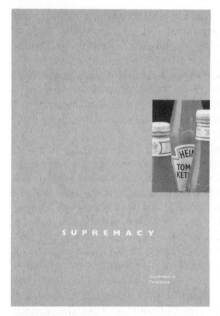

ELIDA GIBBS
CARING FOR HEALTH AND BEAUTY

SUPREMACY

THE CLEAR **No. 1**
MEN'S TOILETRIES MANUFACTURER

Exhibit 3.6   *Heinz strongly endorses its brands, whilst Elida Gibbs pursues individual brand names*

brand which draws upon the name of a well-established firm. For example, building upon high awareness and strong associations of the brand with healthy eating and children's tastes, RHM's Shreddies was rebranded Original Shreddies in 1990 and augmented by two brand extensions, Frosted Shreddies and Coco Shreddies. The heavily promoted new brands were able to benefit from similar associations built up over the years by the Shreddies name. In this example, however, the brand name was extended to a sector not dissimilar from that where the original brand's strengths were built. If this is not the case, the company's image could be diluted by following a corporate endorsement naming policy.

In the financial services sector, it is very common to see brands being strongly tied to the corporation (e.g. American Express, Guardian Royal Exchange's Choices, Leeds Liquid Gold, Abbey National 5 Star Account, etc.). With the Financial Services and Building Societies Act during the 1980s enabling more institutions to sell financial services, branding is quite a new concept in this sector. Consumers and financial advisers have traditionally evaluated policies by considering the parent corporation's historical performances, so company-linked brand names in this sector are common.

None the less, whilst a brand can gain from an umbrella of benefits by being linked with a company name, the specific values of each brand still need to be conveyed. For example, whilst organizations such as Midland Bank have been promoting the benefits associated with their corporate name, there is a danger of not adequately promoting the benefits of the individual brands (e.g. Meridian, Vector, Orchard) leading to the possibility of consumer confusion. Interestingly, when a corporation has developed a particularly novel concept, then the brand is launched without such a strong corporate name tie. For example, Midland's First Direct is a very different approach to banking and the brand was launched very much as a stand-alone brand using the black and white logo to communicate the no-nonsense approach.

There are obvious advantages in all aspects of communication to be gained from economies of scale when an organization ties a brand name in with its corporate name. This advantage is sometimes given an undue importance weighting by firms thinking of extending their brands into new markets. This whole question of brand extension is a complex issue which involves more than just the name and is dealt with in more detail in Chapter 9. However, it is worth mentioning here that in the 1990s more products and services are likely to be marketed under the same corporate-endorsed brand name. None the less, to help the brand fight through the competing noise in the market, it is still essential to know what the brand means to the consumer, how the brand's values compare with competitive brands and how marketing resources are affecting brand values.

There are also very good reasons why in certain circumstances it is advisable to follow the individual brand name route. As the earlier Procter & Gamble example showed, this allows the marketer to develop formulations and positionings to appeal to different segments in different markets. However, the economics of this need to be carefully considered, since firms may, on closer analysis, find that by trying to appeal to different small segments through different brand offerings, they are encountering higher marketing costs resulting in reduced brand profitability.

When striving to have coverage in each segment of the market as, for example, Seiko do with their watches, it is important that individual brand names sufficiently reinforce their different brand positionings. Some firms try to differentiate their brands in the same market through the use of numbers. When this route is followed, however, the numbers should be indicative of relative brand performance. For example, in the home computer market the '2000' model could have approximately double the functional capability of the '1000' model. In some markets, firms do not appear to have capitalized on naming issues. For example, in the telephone answering machine market where Panasonic has a notable presence, it brands four of its models as T1440BE, T1446, T2386DBE and T2445BE. Consumers cannot infer much about relative differences from these brand nomenclatures.

Another advantage of using individual brand names is that if the new line fails, the firm would experience less damage to its image than if the new brand had been tied to the corporation. During the 1980s many consumers became aware of the move of financial services organizations into estate agency. Some followed the route of corporate branding policies, thus changing the face of established local practices. However, the decision of The Prudential to withdraw from the estate agency market late in 1990 was a very visible signal to many consumers of the failure of this venture and may have affected some consumers' perceptions of the stability of this organization.

A strategic approach to naming brands

When looking at the way companies select brand names, many appear to follow a process of generating names and then assessing these against predetermined criteria. For example, with the opportunities presented by the opening of European markets, the following stages of questioning are usual in brand name selection:

- First, in which geographical markets does the firm intend its brand to compete? The wider the geographical coverage the more complex the decision becomes, if for no other reason than the pronounceability of the name. For example, in 1988 Whirlpool, the American white goods manufacturer, acquired 53 per cent of Philips home appliances business and are obliged by the agreement to phase out the Philips brand name by 1998. A dual brand name policy is currently being run, raising consumers' awareness of Whirlpool across Europe. However, in France Whirlpool is an extremely difficult name to pronounce.
- Secondly, even if the consumer can pronounce a name, the next question would focus on any other meanings or associations the name might have in different countries. For example, in the USA, Fairy Liquid faces the problem of sexual associations in American slang, while Big Macs (from McDonald's) is Canadian slang for big breasts.
- Thirdly, if these issues do not raise problems, the next problem is whether the brand name is available for use on an international basis and whether it can be protected. A major cosmetics house had to reschedule the launch of one of its brands, since the legal aspects of the pan-European brand name search revealed that the original name was already being used by a distant competitor in one part of Europe.

Whilst the approach described above has the strength of checking the name against a set of criteria, its weakness is that its tactical orientation doesn't relate the brand name to the wider company objectives that the brand is attempting to satisfy. A better way of developing the brand's name would be to follow the flow chart in Figure 3.8.

What little has been published about the way firms select brand names, shows that few follow a systematic process. The schema developed in Figure 3.8 builds on best current practice.

Let us now consider each of these steps in turn.

Figure 3.8   *Schema to identify most appropriate brand name*

Marketing objectives

The marketer needs to be certain about the marketing objectives that his brand must contribute towards. Clearly stated, quantified targets must be available for each segment showing the level of sales expected from each of the product groups comprising the company's portfolio. The marketing objectives will give an indication as to whether emphasis is being placed on gaining sales from existing products to existing customers, or whether new horizons are envisaged (e.g. through either product extensions or new customer groups). By having clearly defined marketing objectives, brand managers are then able to consider how each of their brands need to contribute towards satisfying the overall marketing objectives.

The brand audit

The internal and external forces that influence the brand need to be identified, such as company resources, competitive intensity, supplier power, threats from substitutes, buyer concentration, economic conditions, and so on. This audit should help identify a few of the criteria that the name must satisfy. For example, if the brand audit showed that the firm has a superior battery that consumers valued because of the battery's long life, then one issue the name would have to satisfy would be its reinforcement of the critical success factor 'battery long life'.

Brand objectives

In the brand planning document, clear statements about individual brand objectives should be made, again helping clarify the criteria that the brand name must satisfy. Statements about anticipated levels of sales, through different distributors, to specified customers, will help the marketer to identify criteria for the name to meet. For example, if the primary market for a new brand of rechargeable batteries is 10–14 year old boys who are radio control car racing enthusiasts, and if the secondary market is fathers who help their sons, the primary target's need may be for long intercharge periods, whilst the secondary market may be more concerned about purchase costs. The primary need for the brand name would be to communicate power delivery, with an undertone about cost.

Other brand objective statements about positioning and brand personality would further clarify some of the criteria that the name must satisfy.

Brand strategy alternatives

The marketer must be clear about what broad strategies are envisaged for the brand in order to satisfy the brand objectives. Issues here would include:

- Manufacturer's brand or distributor's brand?
- Specialist or niche brand?
- Value-added or low price positioning?

Again, these would clarify issues that the name must satisfy.

Brand name criteria specified

From the previous sections, the marketer should be able to list the criteria that the brand name must satisfy. They might also wish to learn from other companies' experiences what appears to work best with brand names. This issue will be addressed in the next section of this chapter.

Brand name alternatives generated

With a clear brief about the challenges that the new brand name must overcome, the marketer can now work with others to stimulate ideas for possible brand names. It is unlikely that the brand manager would work on this alone. Instead, he would be joined by others from the marketing department, by advertising agency staff, by specialist name-generating agencies where appropriate, and by other company employees. Also, at this stage a market research agency may be commissioned to undertake some qualitative research to help generate names. Some of the methods that might be used to generate names would be:

- Brainstorming
- Group discussions
- Management inspiration
- Word association
- In-company competitions amongst employees
- Computer generated names.

It is important to stress that, during the name-generation stage, any intentions to judge the names must be suppressed. If names are evaluated as they are generated, this impedes the mind's creative mode and results in a much lower number of names.

Screen and select the brand name

By scoring each name against the criteria for brand name effectiveness, an objective method to judge each option can be employed. Each name can be scored in terms of how well it matches each of the criteria and, by aggregating each name's score, a value order will result. The more sophisticated marketer can weight each of the criteria, in terms of importance, and arrive at a rank order on the basis of the highest aggregated weighted score. Whatever numerical assessment procedure is employed, it should be developed only on the basis of an agreed internal consensus and after discussions with key decision makers. Not only does this enhance commitment to the finally selected brand name, but it also draws on the relevant experience of many executives.

By following this schema, the marketer is able to select a name which should satisfy the company's ambitions for long-term profitable brand growth. This process should also result in a name which is well able not only to defend a sustainable position against competitive forces, but also to communicate added values to consumers effectively.

Issues associated with effective brand names

When considering criteria for brand name effectiveness, there is much to be gained by drawing on the experience of other marketers as enshrined in the literature on branding. Some of the guidelines include:

- *The brand name should be simple*   The aim should be to have short names that are easy to read and understand. As was noted earlier, consumers have limited mental capacities and they find it easier to encode short words in memory. Listening to consumers talk clarifies the way that long brand names are simplified (e.g. Pepsi rather than Pepsi Cola, Lewis's rather than John Lewis).
- *The brand name should be distinctive*   Brand names such as Kodak and Adidas create a presence through the distinctive sound of the letters and the novelty of the word. This creates attention and the resulting curiosity motivates potential consumers to be more attentive to brand attributes.
- *The brand name should be meaningful*   Names that communicate consumer benefits, facilitate consumers' interpretations of brands. For example, Xpelair, Tipp-Ex and Lean Cuisine leave little doubt about the benefits to be gained from these brands. Creativity should be encouraged at the expense of being too correct. A battery branded 'Reliable' would communicate its capability, but would not attract as much attention as the more interesting 'Die Hard'. The

IF MEN ARE WISE THEY SOCIALISE WITH APPLETISE.

Pure, sparkling apple juice — for a refreshingly different toast this Christmas, Appletise is your safest bet.

Exhibit 3.7   *The brand name Appletise has the virtues of being simple, distinctive, meaningful and totally compatible with its key ingredient*

brand name should also support the positioning objectives for the brand, e.g. Crown Paints.
- *The brand name should be compatible with the product* The appropriateness of the name Timex with watches is more than apparent, reinforcing the meaningfulness of the brand name.
- *Emotion helps for certain products* For those product fields where consumers seek brands primarily because they say something about

**Catch the Lufthansa Chuttle
to Germany: every 40 minutes
between 7.00 am and 8.00 pm.**

Virtually nothing gives you more freedom and flexibility than our Channel Shuttle. Because virtually nothing is as fast, frequent or convenient.

From London alone, we lift off 26 times a day, 7 days a week. Making it easier than ever getting to Germany – and back home again.

On all our jets, incidentally, you have a choice of three classes, each first-class in its class. Obviously it pays to have a look at our Chuttle Timetable, a copy of which we'll gladly send you.

Please forward me the latest Lufthansa Timetable.

Name

Street

City/Postcode

Return coupon to:
Lufthansa German Airlines
Dept. LON GH
10, Old Bond Street, London W1X 4EN.
Or just phone: London 071 3554994

 Lufthansa

Exhibit 3.8   *In the global travel market, the brand name Lufthansa, with associations of German efficiency and timeliness would appeal to the traveller seeking punctuality*

the purchaser, as, for example, in the perfume market, emotional names can succeed. Examples here include Poison and Opium.

- *The brand name should be legally protectable*   To help protect the brand against imitators, a search should be undertaken to identify whether the brand name is available and if so, whether it is capable of being legally registered.

A SAUCEPAN THAT CONDUCTS HEAT SO WELL, IT'LL COOK A CANDLE-LIT SUPPER.

Thanks to its thermocopper base, tough high grade stainless steel and a lifetime guarantee, no other saucepan can hold a candle to Prestige.

Exhibit 3.9   *The functional excellence of the firm's saucepan is reinforced through the images evoked by the name Prestige*

- *Beware of creating new words*   Marketers developing new words for their brand have to anticipate significant promotional budgets to clarify what their invented word means. For example, the successfully invented names of Kodak, Esso and Xerox succeeded because of significant communication resources.
- *Extend any stored-up equity*   When firms audit their portfolio of current and historical brands, they may find that there is still considerable good-will in the market place associated with brands

they no longer produce. There may be instances when it is worth extending a historical name to a new line (e.g. Mars to ice cream), or even relaunching several historical lines (e.g. Cadbury Classic Collection of Old Jamaica, Turkish Delight, etc.).

- *Avoid excessive use of initials*   Over time, some brand names have been shortened, either as a deliberate policy by the firm, or through consumer terminology (e.g. International Business Machines to IBM, Imperial Chemicals Industries to ICI and British Airways to BA). It takes time for the initials to become associated with brand attributes and firms generally should not launch new brands as arrays of initials. The hypothetical brand North London Tool and Die Company certainly fails the criteria of being short, but at least, unlike the initials NLT&D, it does succeed in communicating its capabilities.

- *Develop names that allow flexibility*   The hope of any marketer is for brand success and eventually a widening portfolio of supporting brands to better satisfy the target market. Over time more experienced consumers seek a widening array of benefits, so, if possible, the name should allow the brand to adapt to changing market needs. For example, with the recognition of the reliability of Caterpillar Tractors, the company wished to diversify further into the earthmoving equipment market, but the word 'Tractor' blocked diversification. By dropping this word, Caterpillar was better able to diversify.

Whilst these points should contribute to the way organizations think about the appropriateness of different brand names, we should never lose sight of the fact that it is consumers who buy brands, not the managers who manage them. For this reason, it is always wise, when short listing potential names, to undertake some consumer research and evaluate consumers' responses. For example, are the words harsh sounding?, are there any negative associations with the words?, are the names appropriate for the proposed brand?, do the words 'roll off the tongue' easily?, are the words memorable?, and so on.

Once a decision has been taken about the brand name and the brand has been launched, the firm should audit the name on a regular basis. This will show whether or not the meaning of the brand name has changed over time as a result of changes in the market place. If the environment has changed to such an extent that the firm is missing opportunities by persisting with the original name, then consideration should be given to changing the name. For example, Mars saw economies of scale with a unified pan-European brand name strategy and changed the name Marathon to Snickers in order to capitalize on this.

Brands as a risk reducer

The final issue which is of relevance to branding that will be considered in this chapter is the concept of perceived risk. Earlier parts of this chapter showed that products and services can be conceived as arrays of clues and that the most consulted clue when making a brand choice is the presence or absence of a brand name. This reliance upon brand name is also confirmed by the considerable volume of consumer behaviour research on the concept of perceived risk. It is clear that, when buying, consumers develop risk-reducing strategies. These are geared to either reducing the uncertainty in a purchase by buying, for example, only advertised brands, or to minimizing the chances of an unpleasant outcome by buying, for example, only previously tried brands. This concept also affects the way organizations buy brands and is also addressed in Chapter 4.

It must be stressed that we are talking only about consumers' *perceptions* of risk, rather than *objective* risk, since consumers react only as they perceive situations. Whilst marketers may believe they have developed a brand that is presented as a risk-free purchase, this may not necessarily be the perception consumers have. Consumers have a threshold level for perceived risk, below which they do not regard it as worthwhile undertaking any risk-reduction action. However, once this threshold level is exceeded, they will seek ways of reducing perceived risk.

We can now start to view brands as being so well formulated, distributed and promoted, that they provide consumers with the added value of increased confidence. For example, if the brand is available from a quality retailer, this should signal increased certainty regarding its performance. If there has been a lot of supporting advertising this would also be read as being indicative of a low risk product. Furthermore, should there also be favourable word of mouth, this too would allay concerns about the brand. Marketers can gain a competitive edge by promoting their brands as low risk purchases.

By viewing risk as being concerned with the *uncertainty* felt by consumers about the *outcome* of a purchase, it is possible to appreciate how marketers can reduce consumers' risk in brand buying. For example, appropriate strategies to reduce consumers worries about the *outcome* of the brand purchase, would include developing highly respected warranties, offering money-back guarantees for first-time trialists and small pack sizes during the brand's introductory period. To reduce their *uncertainty*, consumers will take a variety of actions, such as, for example, seeking out further information, staying with regularly used brands, or buying only well-known brands. Marketers can reduce concerns about uncertainty by providing consumers with relevant, high quality information, by encouraging independent parties, such as specialist magazine editors, to assess the brand and by ensuring that opinion leaders are well versed in the brand's potential. For example, by tracking purchasers of a newly launched microwave oven brand, using returned guarantee cards, home economists can call on innovative trialists and, by giving a personalized demonstration of the new brand's capabilities, ensure that they are fully conversant with the brand's advantages. This can be particularly effective, since early innovators are regarded as a credible information source.

Exhibit 3.10   *Creating interest in brands through making consumers aware of their perceptions of risk*

The favoured routes to reduce risk vary by type of product or service and it is unusual for only one risk-reducing strategy to be followed. It is, however, apparent that brand loyalty and reliance on major brand image are two of the more frequently followed actions.

When consumers evaluate competing brands, not only do they have an overall view about how risky the brand purchase is, but they also form a judgement about why the brand is a risky purchase. This is done initially by evaluating which dimensions of perceived risk cause them the most concern. There are several dimensions of risk. For example:

- Financial risk: the risk of money being lost when buying an unfamiliar brand.

- Performance risk: the risk of something being wrong with the unfamiliar brand.

- Social risk: the risk that the unfamiliar brand might not meet the approval of a respected peer group.

- Psychological risk: the risk that an unfamiliar brand might not fit in well with one's self image.

- Time risk: the risk of having to waste further time replacing the brand.

If the marketer is able to identify which dimensions of perceived risk are causing concern, they should be able to develop appropriate consumer-orientated risk-reduction strategies. The need for such strategies can be evaluated by examining consumers' perceptions of risk levels and by gauging whether this is below their threshold level. It should be realized, however, that the level of risk varies between people and also by product category. For example, cars, insurance and hi-fi are generally perceived as being high risk purchases, while toiletries and packaged groceries are low risk purchases.

Table 3.2 shows the results of a consumer study by Jacoby and Kaplan indicating how some of the dimensions of perceived risk vary by product field. From these findings, it can be seen that marketers of life insurance policies need to put more emphasis on stressing the relative cost of policies and how well they have performed compared with those of competitors. By contrast, the suit marketer should place more emphasis on reference group endorsement of their brand of suit by means, for example, of a photograph of an appropriate person in this suit.

Table 3.2 *Consumers' views about the dimensions of risk*

	Life Insurance	Suit
Financial risk	7.2	6.4
Performance risk	6.7	5.8
Psychological risk	4.9	6.9
Social risk	4.8	7.3
Overall risk	7.0	5.9

1 = very low risk, 10 = very high risk.

After Jacoby and Kaplan, 1972.

Conclusions

By adopting an information processing model of consumer behaviour, this chapter has considered how a knowledge of consumers' buying processes can help to develop successful brands. Through an appreciation of the differences consumers perceive between competing brands and their involvement in the brand buying process, we identified different consumer buying processes. According to the type of buying process, so an active or passive approach to brand information acquisition may be followed. If the consumer actively seeks information, it was shown that this would be for only a few key pieces of information regarded as highly indicative of the brand's capabilities.

When evaluating competing brands, consumers are concerned with appreciating the extent to which the brands have added values over and above the commodity form of the brand. These added values may be as simple as polite service from a bank clerk, through to a complex cluster of lifestyle associations by driving a particular car marque.

One added value often overlooked by marketers is labelling which displays only a few pieces of information, facilitating brand choice. Consumers have limited mental capabilities and seek to process a few, high quality pieces of information as quickly as possible. They often use surrogate clues, such as price, to evaluate brands and place considerable reliance on the presence or absence of brand names.

The problem facing the marketer, however, is that consumers are selective in their search for brand information and they twist some of the information to make it fit their prior beliefs. Brand promotional activity must, therefore, be regularly audited, to evaluate the extent to which consumers correctly interpreted the message.

To encourage consumer appreciation of the brand's true capabilities, the right type of brand name is needed. In certain circumstances, there are strengths in having a brand name tied to the corporation, but there are others when unique brand names are more appropriate. Brand name selection should not be based on tactical issues, but rather on a more robust, strategic basis which relates the potential name to marketing objectives and other forces influencing the brand.

Finally, marketers should appreciate that consumers perceive risk when buying brands. Through appreciating the extent of perceived risk and the factors causing consumer concern, they can develop strategies geared to reducing this perceived risk.

Marketing action checklist

To help clarify the direction of future brand marketing activity, it is recommended that the following exercises are undertaken.

1 Write down how involved you believe the consumer is when buying a brand in the product field where you have a presence. From the consumer's perspective, evaluate whether competing brands in this

product field are strongly or weakly differentiated, stating what the differentiating features are. Then, consulting Figure 3.1, identify the consumer decision process reflecting brand buying behaviour. Ask other colleagues to undertake this exercise individually. If there is a lack of consensus about the level of involvement of consumers, the degree of brand differentiation, or the basis for brand differentiation, your department may be basing its brand communication programme on erroneous assumptions about consumer behaviour. This can be resolved by undertaking qualitative research amongst target consumers to assess dimensions they use to differentiate between brands and the basis for their involvement in the purchase. This should then be followed by a survey to quantify the extent of consumers' involvement and their perceptions of brand differences. On the basis of such market research, the consumer's decision process can be evaluated and by referring to the early parts of this chapter, the appropriateness of the current brand communication strategy can be assessed.

2 When was any market research last undertaken to assess consumers' involvement and their perceptions of brand differences? If this information is more than a year old, consider whether the dynamic nature of your market necessitates a further up-date.

3 At what stages in the consumer's buying process is any brand information currently being directed? On the basis of the model of the buying process identified in the earlier exercises, when do consumers seek information? Are there any discrepancies?

4 Get your colleagues to write down what stages they believe consumers pass through in the buying process for one of your brands. Ask someone who does not work in the marketing or sales department (and ideally who is new to the firm) to narrate the stages they went through when buying this particular brand. In an open forum, resolve any differences between what managers' perceptions are and the reality of consumer buying activity.

5 Have you any information about the factors which encourage or discourage consumers to seek more information about your brand (e.g. role of family, previous experience, etc.)? How are you addressing each of these factors in your brand activity?

6 How much do you know about consumers' perceptions of your brands (and if appropriate, about perceptions of your company)? Are there any differences between the brand communications objectives agreed internally (and specified to your promotions agency) and the way consumers interpret your brands?

7 How do you help consumers evaluate your brand very shortly after it has been purchased for the first time? How well equipped are retailers to resolve consumers' doubts about the brand?

8 Has any consumer research been undertaken to evaluate the key attributes that consumers use to make a brand selection? What attributes did your last promotional campaign major on? Did these attributes match the findings from the previous research?

9 What are the added values that distinguish your brand from competitors? How relevant are these to consumers? How are *all* elements of the marketing mix being used to achieve these added values? Is there any inconsistency between the elements of the marketing mix?

10 Show several consumers a pack or brochure describing your brand, along with similar material from your competitors. Do not allow them to spend long looking at these examples. Observe how they examine the material. Remove the examples and ask what they recalled and why they recalled this. Discuss the results with your colleagues and consider which aspects of your pack/brochure are critical to the consumer and which parts clutter the central message. What informational clues were consumers using to draw inferences about the capabilities of the product or service? How much marketing attention is being focused on these informational clues?

11 List the brands against which your brand competes. Now categorize these brands into groups that show some form of similarity, starting the basis for brand groupings. Ask colleagues to do this exercise individually and collate the forms. In an open forum, discuss any differences. Commission a survey to evaluate which brands consumers see as competing in a particular product field, how they would group these brands and what was their basis for categorization. If there is not agreement between consumers' categorization of brands and yours, you may well need to reconsider your brand strategy.

12 What are the strengths and weaknesses of your brand's name? How able is the name to cope with future opportunities and yet overcome any threats? State the criteria that your experience has shown are essential for a brand name to satisfy and critically evaluate your brand name against this.

13 List the aspects of risk that consumers perceive when buying your brand and your competitors' brands. In what order of perceived risk do consumers rank these brands? What actions can you take to reduce consumers' perceptions of risk when buying your brand?

References and further reading

Allison R. I., Uhl K. P. (1964). Influence of beer brand identification on taste perception. *Journal of Marketing Research*, **1** (3), 36–9

Assael H. (1987). *Consumer Behavior and Marketing Action*. Boston: Kent Publishing.

Bauer R. A. (1960). Consumer behavior as risk taking. In *Dynamic Marketing for a Changing World. 43rd Conference of the American Marketing Association* (Hancock R. S., ed.). Chicago: American Marketing Association, pp. 389–98.

Beales H., Maziz M., Salop S., Staelin R. (1981). Consumer search and public policy. *Journal of Consumer Research*, **8**, (June), 11–22.

Bennett P., Mandell R. (1969). Prepurchase information seeking behaviour of new car purchasers: the learning hypothesis. *Journal of Marketing Research*, **6** (4), 430–3.

Bettman J. R. (1979). *An Information Processing Theory of Consumer Choice*. Reading, Massachusetts: Addison Wesley.

Bettman J. R., Kakkar P. (1977). Effects of information presentation format on consumer information acquisition strategies. *Journal of Consumer Research*, **3**, (Mar.), 233–40.

Bettman J. R., Park C. W. (1980). Effects of prior knowledge and experience and phase of the choice process on consumer decision processes: a protocol analysis. *Journal of Consumer Research*, **7**, (Dec.), 234–48.

Biehal G., Chakravarti D. (1982). Information-presentation format and learning goals as determinants of consumers' memory retrieval and choice processes. *Journal of Consumer Research*, **8**, (Mar.), 431–41.

Britt S. H. (1975). How Weber's law can be applied to marketing. *Business Horizons*, **13**, (Feb.), 21–9.

Britt S. H., Adams S. C., Miller A. S. (1972). How many advertising exposures per day? *Journal of Advertising Research*, **12**, (Dec.), 3–10.

Bruner J. S. (1957). On perceptual readiness. *Psychological Review*, **64**, (2), 123–52.

Bruner J. S. (1958). Social psychology and perception. In 1970 edition of: *Research in Consumer Behavior* (Kollat D. T., Blackwell R. D., Engel J. F., eds) 1970 edn. New York: Holt, Rinehart and Winston.

Bucklin L. P. (1969). Consumer search, role enactment and market efficiency. *Journal of Business*, **42**, 416–38

Buschke H. (1976). Learning is organized by chunking. *Journal of Verbal Learning and Verbal Behaviour*, **15**, 313–24.

Capon N., Burke M. (1980). Individual, product class and task-related factors in consumer information processing. *Journal of Consumer Research*, **7**, (Dec.), 314–26.

Chisnall P. M. (1985). *Marketing: A Behavioural Analysis*. London: McGraw Hill.

Claxton J. D., Fry J. N., Portis B. (1974). A taxonomy of prepurchase information gathering patterns. *Journal of Consumer Research*, **1**, (Dec.), 35–42.

Cox D. F. (1967). The sorting rule model of the consumer product evaluation process. In *Risk Taking and Information Handling in Consumer Behavior* (Cox D. F., ed.). Boston: Harvard University.

Derbaix C. (1983). Perceived risk and risk relievers: an empirical investigation. *Journal of Economic Psychology*, **3**, (Mar.), 19–38.

Engel J. F., Blackwell R. D. (1982). *Consumer Behaviour*. Chicago: The Dryden Press.

Gardner D. M. (1971). Is there a generalised price-quality relationship? *Journal of Marketing Research*, **8**, (2), 241–3.

Gemunden H. G. (1985). Perceived risk and information search. A systematic meta-analysis of the empirical evidence. *International Journal of Research in Marketing*, **2**, (2), 79–100.

Haines G. H. (1974). Process models of consumer decision making. In: *Buyer/Consumer Information Processing* (Hughes G. D., Ray M. L., eds.). Chapel Hill: University of North Carolina Press.

Hansen F. (1972). *Consumer Choice Behavior. A cognitive theory*. New York: The Free Press.

Hastorf A. H., Cantril H. (1954). They saw a game: a case history. *Journal of Abnormal and Social Psychology*, **49**, 129–34.

Jacoby J., Kaplan L. (1972). The components of perceived risk. In *Third Annual Conference, Association for Consumer Research. Proceedings*. Venkatesan M. (ed.). Chicago: Association for Consumer Research.

Jacoby J., Speller D. E., Kohn C. A. (1974). Brand choice behavior as a function of information load. *Journal of Marketing Research*, **11**, (1), 63–9.

Jacoby J., Szybillo G. J., Busato-Schach J. (1977). Information acquisition behavior in brand choice situations. *Journal of Consumer Research*, **3**, (Mar.), 209–16.

Jacoby J., Chestnut R. W., Fisher W. A. (1978). A behavioural process approach to information acquisition in nondurable purchasing. *Journal of Marketing Research*, **15**, (3), 532–44.

Jones J. (1986). *Whats in a Name?* Lexington: Lexington Books.

Kapfer J-N., Laurent G. (1986). Consumer involvement profiles: a new practical approach to consumer involvement. *Journal of Advertising Research*, **25**, (6), 48–56.

Katona G., Mueller E. (1955). A study of purchasing decisions. In *Consumer Behavior. The dynamics of consumer reaction* (Clark L. H., ed). New York: New York University Press.

Kendall K. W., Fenwick I. (1979). What do you learn standing in a supermarket aisle? In *Advances in Consumer Research* vol 6 (Wilkie W. L., ed.). Ann Arbor: Association for Consumer Research, pp. 153–60.

Kiel G. C., Layton R. A. (1981). Dimensions of consumer information seeking behavior. *Journal of Marketing Research*, **18**, (2), 233–9.

Krugman H. E. (1975). What makes advertising effective? *Harvard Business Review*, **53**, (Mar.–Apr.), 96–103.

Krugman H. E. (1977). Memory without recall, exposure without perception. *Journal of Advertising Research*, **17**, (4), 7–12.

Lannon J., Cooper P. (1983). Humanistic advertising: a holistic cultural perspective. *International Journal of Advertising*, **2**, 195–213.

McNeal J., Zeren L. (1981). Brand name selection for consumer products. *Michigan State University Business Topics*, **29**, (2), 35–9.

Midgley D. F. (1983). Patterns of interpersonal information seeking for the purchase of a symbolic product. *Journal of Marketing Research*, **20**, (1), 74–83.

Miller G. A. (1956). The magical number seven, plus or minus two: some limits on our capacity for processing information. *Psychological Review*, **63**, (2), 81–97.

Neisser V. (1976). *Cognition and Reality* San Francisco: W. H. Freeman.

Newman J. W. (1977). Consumer external search: amounts and determinants. In: *Consumer and Industrial Buying Behavior* (Woodside A. G., Sheth J. N., Bennett P. D., eds). Amsterdam: North Holland Publishing Company.

Newman J. W., Staelin R. (1973). Information sources of durable goods. *Journal of Advertising Research*, **13**, (2), 19–29.

Olshavsky R. W., Granbois D. H. (1979). Consumer decision making – fact or fiction? *Journal of Consumer Research*, **6**, (Sept.), 93–100.

Ray M. L. (1973). Marketing communication and the hierarchy of effects. In *New Models for Communication Research* (Clarke P., ed.). Beverley Hills: Sage.

Reed S. K. (1972). Pattern recognition and categorization. *Cognitive Psychology*, **3**, (3), 382–407.

Render B., O'Connor T. S. (1976). The influence of price, store name and brand name on perception of product quality. *Journal of the Academy of Marketing Science*, **4**, (4), 722–30.

Rigaux-Bricmont B. (1981). Influences of brand name and packaging on perceived quality. In *Advances in Consumer Research* vol 9 (Mitchell A, ed.). Chicago: Association for Consumer Research

Robertson K. (1989). Strategically desirable brand name characteristics. *Journal of Consumer Marketing*, **6**, (4), 61–71.

Rock I. (1975). *An Introduction to Perception*. New York: Macmillan.

Roselius T. (1971). Consumer rankings of risk reduction methods. *Journal of Marketing*, **35**, (1), 56–61.

Russo J. E., Staelin R., Nolan C. A. et al. (1986). Nutrition information in the supermarket. *Journal of Consumer Research*, **13**, (June), 48–70.

Schwartz M. L., Jolson M. A., Lee R. H. (1986). The marketing of funeral services: past, present and future. *Business Horizons*, Mar.–Apr., 40–45.

Shipley D., Hooley G., Wallace S. (1988). The brand name development process. *International Journal of Advertising*, **7**, (3), 253–66.

Venkatesan M. (1973). Cognitive consistency and novelty seeking. In *Consumer Behavior: theoretical sources* (Ward S., Robertson T. S., eds). Englewood Cliffs, NJ: Prentice Hall.

Zajonc R. B. (1968). Cognitive theories in social psychology. In *The Handbook of Social Psychology* vol. 1 (Lindzey G., Aronson E., eds). Reading, Massachusetts: Addison Wesley.

4 Business to business branding

Summary

The aim of this chapter is to consider the issues associated with the way organizations buy brands. We open by making the point that brands play as important a role in this sector as they do in consumer marketing. The unique characteristics of organizational marketing are considered, along with brand implications. We identify the people likely to be involved in organizational brand purchasing and discuss their roles. The stages involved in brand purchasing are presented, with a consideration of the effort put in by the buyers. Buyers' stable relationships with sellers are examined. The rational and emotional factors affecting brand choice are reviewed. The traditional way that marketers present brand information is compared with buyers' views of the most useful sources. Finally, we address the important role played by corporate identity programmes and the corporate images perceived by buyers.

Brands and organizational marketing

A distinction is frequently drawn between consumer and organizational (or business to business) marketing. Consumer marketing is principally concerned with matching the resources of the selling organization with the needs of consumers. It focuses heavily on those people at the end of the value chain who purchase brands to satisfy either their own personal needs, or those of their families or friends. By contrast, organizational marketing is concerned with the provision of products and services to *organizations*. They are not the final consumers of the products and services. For example, Eastern Electricity is actively involved in organizational marketing by buying electricity from suppliers (e.g. Power Gen, National Power, etc.). They add value by distributing this in the most effective and efficient manner to other organizations (e.g. farmers, car producers, etc.), who use the energy to produce products and services which are ultimately bought by consumers.

While there are differences between consumer and organizational marketing, brands are just as important in both areas. The phrase,

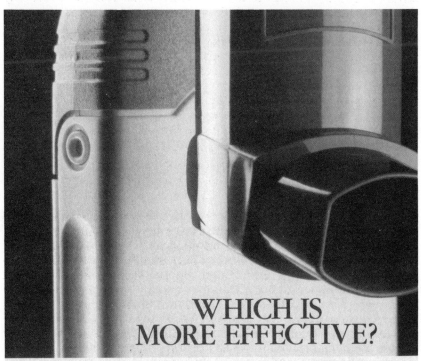

WHICH IS MORE EFFECTIVE?

'It is concluded that the Diskhaler device confers extra benefits in terms of efficacy and tolerability compared with the metered dose inhaler. This may be due to a higher proportion of the patients using the Diskhaler device correctly.'
Conclusion of a 365 patient, double-blind, double-dummy, parallel-group, multicentre general practice study comparing Becodisks 400 micrograms b.d. with Becotide 100 inhaler 2 puffs b.d.

FOR EFFECTIVE DELIVERY OF BECOTIDE

Becodisks (Beclomethasone Dipropionate BP)
Abridged Prescribing Information
(Please refer to full data sheet before prescribing.)
Uses Topically active corticosteroid for inhalation in a wide range of asthmatics including those inadequately controlled by bronchodilators and those with severe asthma who would otherwise be dependent on systemic corticosteroids.
Dosage and administration Use regularly every day. *Adults only:* Usually 400 micrograms twice a day.
Contra-indications Hypersensitivity. Special care in active or quiescent pulmonary tuberculosis.
Precautions If inadequate response after one week add short, high-dose course of systemic

steroids. When transferring steroid-dependent patients to Becodisks withdraw systemic steroids slowly. In adrenal insufficiency provide oral steroids for periods of stress. Replacement of systemic steroids may unmask other allergies. *Pregnancy:* Inadequate evidence of safety in human pregnancy. Avoid unnecessary use. Balance risks against benefits.
Side effects Oropharyngeal candidiasis. Hoarseness or throat irritation. Paradoxical bronchospasm could occur – substitute alternative therapy.
Presentation and Basic NHS cost Pack of 7 Becodisks each containing 8 x 400 micrograms Beclomethasone Dipropionate BP, dark brown, together with a Becotide Diskhaler. For inhalation. £20·90.

Refill pack of 7 x 8 Becodisks 400 micrograms, £20·33.
Product licence number Becodisks 400 micrograms 0045/0142.
Reference: L Drepaul BA, Payler DK, Qualtrough JE, Perry LJ, Reeve FBA, Charlton SC. Clinical Trials Journal 1989, 26(5): 335-344.

ALLEN & HANBURYS
Further information is available on request from:
Allen & Hanburys Limited
Greenford, Middlesex UB6 0HE
Becodisks should only be used with a Becotide Diskhaler.
Becodisks, Becotide and Diskhaler are trade marks

Exhibit 4.1 *Allen & Hanburys advertising the added value of greater efficacy from the Diskhaler device with Becodisks 400 micrograms*

'Nobody ever got fired for buying an IBM' is testimony to the role of brands in organizational marketing. Many argue that organizational buying is far more rational than consumer buying, yet emotional factors still play an important role. Some computers offer more functional benefits at a lower price than IBM, but IBM is the brand leader, not only because of functional excellence, but also because buyers feel safe and reassured by the IBM name. They value the way that the name stands for reliability and customer support.

Brands permeate all areas of organizational marketing (e.g. Prozac in pharmaceuticals, Hewlett-Packard Laserjet in printers, Novex in polyethylene). They succeed because purchasers and users value the commitment of suppliers behind their brands. Purchasers are proud to be associated with successful brands. For example, in the computer industry IBM is proud to promote the fact that their PS/2 system is based on the Intel 486 microprocessor.

In Chapter 2 we defined a successful brand as:

An identifiable product, service, person or place, augmented in such a way that the buyer or user perceives relevant unique added values which match their needs most closely. Furthermore its success results from being able to sustain these added values in the face of competition.

This definition is appropriate for both consumer and organizational marketing, since in both sectors marketers are striving to make buyers aware of their added values. In consumer marketing there is a greater emphasis on emotional aspects as added value. Non-rational considerations do influence organizational buyers, albeit to a lesser extent, and we discuss this later in this chapter.

It is more common to see organizational brand names bearing the name of the company. This enables a wide range of products from the same company to benefit from its corporate identity. As a consequence of this naming policy, many buyers see brands' added values resulting from two factors. First the added values from dealing with a particular firm and, second, the benefits from the specific product or service. As such, it is not uncommon in organizational marketing for buyers to talk about suppliers as brands (e.g. SKF, IBM, ICI). In such situations the supplier has succeeded in augmenting his product with the added value of his firm's corporate identity. Consequently, the brand selection process for these buyers will be one of company selection first and then, at a later stage in the evaluation process, consideration of each company's brands. By contrast, where other firms have concentrated less on corporate brand endorsement and more on individual product branding, buyers will be less interested in the firm as a brand. For example in the anti-ulcer drug market Zantac, from Glaxo, and Tagamet, from Smith Klein & French, compete against each other without excessively relying on the added values of their corporate origins.

Organizational marketers who think that brands have no role to play are ignoring a powerful tool. More often than not, they perceive, in a rather blinkered sense, brands to be little more than 'commodity items

The Leading Edge.

The Case International Axial-Flow is at the forefront of combine technology. No matter how many acres you have to harvest, the Axial-Flow will get the job done in record time.

But it's not only the speed of harvesting that makes our combines special. The unique Axial-Flow single rotor system eliminates the need for straw walkers, produces a cleaner grain sample and minimises crop losses.

Each of the three models in the Axial-Flow 1600 Series (1640-160hp, 1660-190hp and 1680-235hp) is powered by a fuel efficient 6 cylinder turbo-charged diesel engine offering proven reliability, and comes with a choice of cutter bar widths from 14ft to 20ft.

Whichever model you choose, you'll find the unrivalled Axial-Flow cab offers the same combination of operational ease,

comfort, excellent visibility and advanced instrumentation.

To help you reap the benefits of our world beating combine technology, Case IH are offering a superb 0% finance package with the added bonus that if you purchase today you don't have to pay a penny before 3rd January 1992.

With 55,000 already sold across 37 countries the Axial-Flow combine has the leading edge in more ways than one.

*Finance is for business purposes only in the UK and is subject to status. Written quotations are available on request.

AXIAL-FLOW

0% FINANCE

J I Case
A Tenneco Company
Wheatley Hall Road, Doncaster, South Yorkshire. DN2 4PG

case IH

Exhibit 4.2   *Case International major on their corporate name across their range of tractors*

with a name stuck on'. As several case histories show, this is naive and is an ineffective use of resources. An American study, published late in the 1980s, reported that established producers of wood and plywood panels were facing increasing competition from new entrants. Producers felt that the best way to counter this challenge was to brand their products. In this case, all they did was to develop names for their lines, with the prime objective of *differentiating* themselves from competitors. Several months after the adoption of this so-called branding strategy, interviews were conducted with timber merchants. They were asked what criteria they used when deciding between wood suppliers. In the majority of cases, the first consideration was price. The buyers clearly regarded the competing products as *commodities*, and not brands. If they had perceived any changes, they would have recognized the competing items as being *differentiated because of their added values*, for which price premiums could be charged. A further irony of this study was that the timber merchants were highly critical of the consumer confusion caused by these 'branding strategies'. The producers had used names that were only appropriate for distributors. They had ignored the fact that consumers could not relate the brand names to the performance capabilities of the different types of wood panels.

To succeed, brands in organizational markets must take into account the needs of everyone in the value chain. In the man-made fibres market, suppliers thought that it was more important to stress brand names, without carefully relating the name to the uses of the fibres. As a consequence, in a market rich with competing brands (e.g. Dacron, Terylene, Acrilan, Celon), but poor in brand explanation, users were confused about the capabilities of different fabrics. A more effective strategy would have been to identify the different customers and influencers in the value chain (e.g. the weavers, knitters, designers, manufacturers, distributors). Promotional strategies suitable for each group should have then been developed, unified by a corporate theme, to clarify the capabilities of the different fibre brands.

Our concern in this chapter is to show how an appreciation of the differences between organizational and consumer marketing can help in developing successful brands. Some of the key differences are addressed in the next section.

The unique characteristics of organizational marketing

In consumer marketing, brands tend to be bought by individuals, while many people are involved in organizational purchasing. The brand marketer is faced with the challenge of not only identifying which managers are involved in the purchasing decision, but also what brand attributes are of particular concern to each of them. The various benefits of the brand, therefore, need to be communicated to all involved, stressing the relevant attributes to particular individuals. For example, the brand's reliable delivery may need to be stressed to the production manager, its low level of impurities to the quality control manager, its low life-cycle costs to the accountant, and so on.

Consumers are generally faced with relatively inexpensive brands which, therefore, they do not evaluate thoroughly. By contrast, organizational purchasing involves large financial commitments. To reduce the risk of an inappropriate purchase decision, organizations involve several managers from different departments to help in the evaluation process. For example, when IBM was looking for a firm to manufacture transistor-transistor logic chips, it had a team consisting of engineers, accountants and a purchasing manager. After an assessment of all potential suppliers, only five were able to match IBM's requirements. Engineers then visited each firm and eliminated one of the potential suppliers because of worries about quality capabilities. Price and delivery quotations subsequently ruled out two other firms. Commissioned prototypes were then asked for so that they could choose between the final two firms. This detailed evaluation took several weeks to complete. During this time, a considerable amount of technical and financial information was sought and assessed.

It is not unusual to observe consumers making a brand choice with only a short deliberation time. By contrast, organizational buying generally involves much longer deliberation periods. Salespeople in organizational marketing are more frequently regarded as technical advisers compared with salespeople in consumer marketing. They often expect to have several meetings with potential purchasers before the firm feels sufficiently confident to make a purchase decision. The implication of this is that the effectiveness of brand support needs to be assessed over a much longer period of time than in consumer marketing.

Whilst consumers are generally loyal to particular brands, from time to time they like to experiment with new brands. In organizational marketing, however, it is much more common for purchasers to seek long-term buying relationships with particular suppliers. They have invested a considerable amount of work in the selection process and have learnt the idiosyncrasies of working with their suppliers. To experiment, by trying out new supplier's brands, has implications throughout the whole organization (e.g. delivery, quality control, production, invoice processing, etc.) and is not lightly entertained.

Just as certain groups are prone to buy certain types of brands in consumer markets, so clearly identifiable segments are also apparent in organizational purchasing. The characteristics of these segments, however, differ from those seen in consumer markets. For example, marketers of computer software brands (e.g. SPSS, BMDP, SAS) find it beneficial to segment potential purchasers according to their computing experience. Compared with more experienced users, novices appreciate a service that includes on-site programme loading facilities and training workshops to learn how to use the software.

Organizational buying is generally more rational than consumer buying, even though, emotional considerations still influence the final decision. They may not be a particularly dominant force, but they can still be part of the brand selection criteria. For example, some buyers like to be treated as very important people by sales representatives and others question whether they can 'get on with the people in that firm'. If these 'less rational' issues are not satisfied, the competitor may succeed.

Chapter 3 showed that perceived risk helps us to understand better why consumers select certain brands. Likewise, an understanding of perceived risk is useful in organizational buying. Buyers perceive risk when buying a new brand for the first time and look for ways of reducing it. For example, they may involve more people in the evaluation process. One pharmaceutical company takes heed of

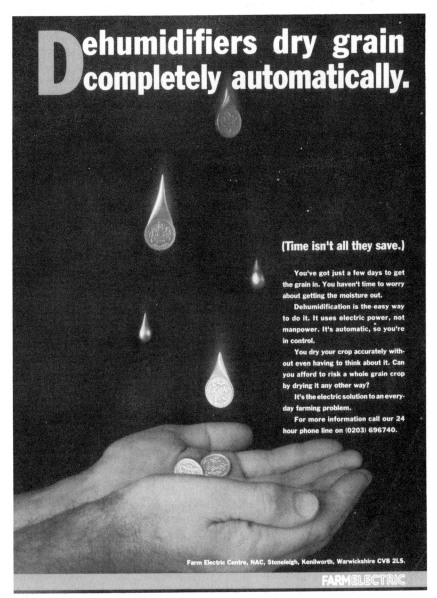

Exhibit 4.3   *Positioning electric dehumidification as a process with only a low risk of performing poorly*

perceived risk in its marketing strategy. Its sales representatives have an estimate of the extent to which each GP is risk averse. When launching a new drug, they direct their calls initially towards those GPs with a high threshold for risk. Once these GPs have prescribed it and are satisfied with the results from the new drug, they are then encouraged to talk about the new drug with their colleagues. This is facilitated by the company hosting meetings at which, for example, there may be a lecture by a hospital consultant on a novel surgical technique.

Exhibit 4.4   *KLM recognize that there is an emotional side to the highly rational businessman when presenting their brand*

It is important that marketers do not overlook the risk dimension in career advancement. Some buyers may be particularly ambitious to gain rapid promotion and are keen to show what improvements they have achieved for the firm. If approached by a new supplier, with a particularly attractive brand proposition, they are likely to be receptive to change. By contrast, the Purchasing Manager who has gradually achieved promotion may be more cautious and therefore less receptive to a new brand proposition.

In conclusion, there are differences between consumer and organizational markets. These differences, however, are subtle. Consequently, marketers do not need to get to grips with a whole new series of branding tools. Rather they have to appreciate how to fine tune the techniques widely practised in consumer marketing. One topic that warrants particular attention is the number of people involved in the organizational brand buying process.

Who buys brands?

Brand buying in organizations typically involves several people. A buying centre, sometimes also called a decision-making unit, is a group of people, from different departments, who are involved in the evaluation and selection of a particular brand. For example, when buying a particular brand of capital equipment, it is likely that representatives from engineering, purchasing, finance, manufacturing, marketing and site services will be involved. It is not unusual, particularly when larger firms buy expensive and complex brands, to see as many as twenty people involved in the buying centre. This typically occurs when the organization has little experience of a new brand, or when they perceive a high degree of risk in purchasing a complex and expensive item. One of the reasons for such a wide range of skills and functional backgrounds, is the greater sense of confidence amongst the decision makers.

Where the user has a continual need for specific items, such as, rubber seals for car doors, the buying will typically be left to the purchasing manager. Even here, however, the user is likely to produce and update the specification for the purchasing manager.

In situations where the user has expert knowledge of a particular area and is not involved in major financial expenditures, they alone will make the brand decision. An example of this is the market research manager deciding which consultant to employ for a specific project.

The matrix in Figure 4.1 is a useful guide when anticipating who is likely to be involved in the organizational brand purchase decision. This can be predicted from the commercial risk facing the organization and its perception of the degree of product/service complexity. When, for example, the firm feels there is a considerable financial commitment, both in the initial purchase cost and in running and maintenance costs, in buying a brand that is difficult to assess functionally, because it involves unfamiliar features, the organization

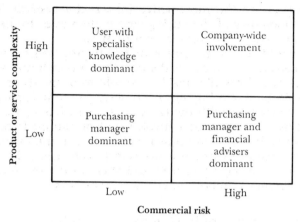

Figure 4.1   *Predicting who will be involved in brand planning*

will feel at its most vulnerable. In such a situation, there is likely to be at least one person from each of the interested departments. After they have evaluated alternative brands, it is probable that recommendations will then be channelled to more senior levels for final consideration.

As the matrix indicates, the Purchasing Manager rarely makes brand purchase decisions alone. In general, buying centres, rather than individuals, become involved in brand selection when:

- The size of the purchasing firm becomes larger.
- The firm has little experience of buying or using the brand.
- There is weak loyalty towards a supplier.
- The brand is regarded as being an important part of the production process.
- The financial size of the order increases.
- Individuals perceive risk of any kind in buying the brand.

Membership of the buying centre changes as more information becomes available. For example, if in the early stages of the evaluation process it was learnt that one of the competing brands could be either bought or leased, then the team would be supplemented by a financial adviser able to evaluate these options.

Brand marketers need to put themselves in the organization's position and consider which departments will be most affected by their brand. If the brand offers a significant opportunity for the organization to cut production costs, but after-sales service will deteriorate for a few months, it is likely that production, marketing , customer service and finance will be involved in the buying decision. The relative importance of any member in the buying centre varies according to the type of product being bought. For example, plant managers and engineers are more influential than purchasing managers when buying technically sophisticated capital equipment.

Plant managers are the most active information seekers in buying centres and members of the buying centre often refer to them rather than going to external sources for information.

Having identified the members of the buying centre, the brand marketer needs to monitor it to identify any shifts in terms of who the key deciders are. X-ray film used to be sold to hospitals on the basis that the deciders in the buying centre were the radiologists and the technicians. However, with the Government's review and changes to the NHS, this led to a greater involvement of administrators in the buying process. It has been argued that brands in the medical X-ray film market succeeded because marketers recognized the changing composition of the buying centres and altered their presentations to reflect the increasing importance of administrators.

Anticipating the role of buying centre members

Often, recommendations about brand purchases are referred to senior management or directors, because the evaluating team have a limit on how much they can spend. Yet even after this highly rational process, the decision may be overruled for an emotional reason. We learnt about one organization who employed an IT consultant to work with its managers in evaluating and recommending which computer to buy. A recommendation was made to the board about two possible brands. The decision was overruled in favour of the more expensive and less technically sophisticated option. The chairman thanked the team for its work, but felt that it was safer to stay with a well-known brand, even though he had very little knowledge of IT. If the brand marketers had had more insight into the roles played by the purchasing team, this outcome may have favoured their brand.

One of the most widely employed ways of understanding the different roles of members of the buying centre is based on the five categories: users; influencers; deciders; buyers; and gatekeepers.

Users are those people in the firm who will be using the brand. These people usually start the buying process and write the requirement specifications. Problems are sometimes created for the marketer when there are two or more groups of users, with conflicting objectives. For example, a chemist in a laboratory may want a particular brand of spectrometer because of its high resolution capabilities, but the R&D manager, who would make less frequent use of the spectrometer, is concerned about the lack of space to house the equipment. The shrewd marketer needs to identify who the primary and secondary users are and find the right balance in appealing to each group.

Influencers are sometimes difficult to identify, as they can either exert a direct influence, by defining brand criteria requirements, or indirectly, through informally providing information. For example, a manager evaluating particular brands of oscilloscopes would seek information from potential suppliers, but in a chance corridor meeting may learn from a colleague in a different department about his views. Influencers are not just those people inside the organization, but can include external consultants. Often consultants are employed to write brand specifications or to help evaluate the competing brands. They may also include individuals working in competing firms, who, because of their perceived expertise, are approached through the informal networking system.

Deciders have the power to make the final decision about which brand should be bought. Ironically, it is sometimes difficult to identify these people. For example, the user may have written the specification requirement in such a way that only one brand can be bought. Or, in the final debate, conducted in a closed session, the managing director may make the decision, but leave the purchasing manager to place the order. Thus, the purchasing manager may appear to be the decider, when in fact it is the managing director.

Buyers are those with the formal authority for arranging the purchase. While the purchasing manager may appear very forceful in negotiations, often his objectives are specified by others in the organization. For relatively routine, low cost purchases, the purchasing manager will proceed without recourse to company-wide discussion. It should be appreciated that purchasing managers are keen on maintaining and improving their status within the firm. To do this, they employ several tactics. For example some are deliberately rule-oriented. Regardless of who approaches them, they insist on working by the book and take no actions until in receipt of formal notification, even though verbal decisions were earlier reached. Such an approach causes frustration amongst all those who need to work with purchasing. Another tactic seen is that of favouring a few collegues. Just for these few individuals, purchasing managers project an aura of friendship and willingness to help, expecting in return favours to be done for them.

Gatekeepers are individuals who control the flow of information into the buying centre. This may be the managing director's secretary, opening the daily post and deciding which circulars he should see. Or it may be the purchasing manager, insisting to the receptionist that any salespeople seeking new business with the firm should always be directed to him. Gatekeepers tend to exert their influence at the early stage of the buying process when the full range of competing brands needs to be identified.

It must be appreciated that the same person can perform several of these roles. The challenge facing the brand marketer is to identify who is playing which role and when does any one member of the buying centre become more influential. Evidence suggests that the purchasing department becomes more influential when:

- Commercial considerations, e.g. delivery, terms of payment, are seen to be more important than technical considerations.
- The item is routinely bought.
- The purchasing department is highly regarded within the firm because of their specialized knowledge of suppliers.
- The technology underpinning the brand has not changed for some time, neither have the evaluation criteria.

If members of the buying centre meet, individuals from different departments with different motivations are brought together. Group dynamics may cause tension and covert attempts are made by some members to gain a more influential position. In a large buying centre, people sense that those who have expert knowledge are more powerful influencers. Surveys have shown that these individuals are also powerful when the firm does not feel it is under pressure to arrive at a rapid brand decision.

Armed with a better understanding of who is likely to be involved in the buying centre and of the roles these individuals are likely to play, the brand marketer should be better able to decide how to position his brand to appeal to the different participants. He should also be able to anticipate where the influencing power lays and thus, where more effort should be directed. By also appreciating the stages of the buying process, he should be able to assess when more effort needs to be put behind his brand, an issue which is considered next.

The organizational buying process

In common with the way we model consumer buying behaviour as a process, starting with problem recognition and progressing through to post-purchase evaluation, so the same logic satisfactorily describes organizational buying. Robinson and his team of researchers developed a model that charts the organizational buying process as an eight-stage process, shown in Figure 4.2. This model, developed in the 1960s, has stood the test of time.

```
1   Anticipation/recognition of a problem
2   Determine what item is necessary
3   Describe characteristics and quantity of item needed
4   Search and qualification of potential suppliers
5   Acquisition of proposals
6   Proposals evaluation and supplier selection
7   Selection of order routine
8   Performance feedback and evaluation
```

Figure 4.2   *The organizational buying process. (After Robinson et al., 1967)*

The process starts when the firm becomes aware of a problem. For example, their product is out-dated, an opportunity for a new line has been identified, a piece of capital equipment has broken, and so on. Someone within the organization recognizes this problem and starts to involve others. They would consider how their particular problem should be solved. A detailed specification would be drawn up at the third stage and, following internal discussions, this would be redrafted until it reflected a consensus view. If the marketer knows who will draw up the specification, he can target his brand's commercial and technical promotion. At the fourth stage, the organization searches for potential suppliers and qualifies these. The criteria for qualification are considered later in this chapter. Some of the possible suppliers will be eliminated at this stage.

The screened suppliers would then be invited to submit their brand proposals. This normally entails a series of meetings to ensure that the supplier fully understands the company's needs. Each of the proposals are analysed against the agreed evaluation criteria and a brand purchase decision made. The purchasing manager is then given the authority to place the order and undertake any negotiations about terms and deliveries. Finally, once the brand has been used, an internal review takes place and assesses how well the brand and the supplier are performing against the evaluation criteria. This would usually only be done formally if the brand proved unsatisfactory. However, it is likely that there would be an informal review, where individuals would talk amongst themselves about the brand's capabilities.

While this eight-phase model describes the buying stages passed through, the amount of time and effort devoted to any one phase depends on the type of purchase. Robinson and his team identified three types of purchases: *new task*; *modified rebuy*; and *straight rebuy*. These three types of purchases give some indication about the amount of effort undertaken by the buying centre.

In the *new task* purchase, the organization has no previous experience of buying the brand. In this situation, the purchasing firm will put in a lot of work and will seek a considerable amount of information about different brands. The marketer has to work hard explaining how his brand can solve the purchaser's problem. The buying centre feels that there is a lot of risk in this purchase and the marketer should present his brand as a low risk option, describing how other firms have successfully benefited from using the brand.

In the *modified rebuy* situation, the firm has experience of buying brands in the product field, but feels it is time to consider whether significantly better brands are available. An example of this would be the office services manager becoming aware of the benefits of fax machines with laser printers, rather than with thermal printers. The organization knows that there will be a lot of work involved in finding a new brand, as well as in adapting its internal processes to absorb the change. It feels, however, that the benefits from change warrant the review.

For the firm currently supplying the organization, news of a re-evaluation of alternative suppliers should alert them to the dangers of complacency. A thorough and rapid review should be instigated to assess:

- How the supplier is currently working with the purchaser (e.g. has there been a change in personnel causing friction? have deliveries been on time? are there any problems with quality?).
- What market changes are occurring?

- What competitive brands are available and how do these compare against their brand?

A meeting should be convened with the purchasing firm to identify their revised needs fully and a programme of change instigated. One lesson that can be learnt from this is that organizations often seek relationships with suppliers based on an expectation that they will always be trying to improve their brands, in order to give their customers an even better deal. We have worked with an industrial advertising agency which holds regular seminars for its clients about new issues in marketing. These seminars are valued by its clients, who feel that not only do they have a good advertising agency but they are also being kept up to date and are able to become more effective.

The *straight rebuy* situation involves repeat purchasing of previously bought brands. In such cases, the purchasing process is relatively fast and simple. It is handled on a routine basis, increasingly using electronic reordering as more organizations invest in computerised stock control and Electronic Data Interchange. The purchasing organization has a lot of relevant experience about the brand and, apart from the re-ordering mechanics, little other effort is expended. In some industries (e.g. packaging), it is not unusual for the purchaser to split the order between two suppliers. If problems occur with one supplier, the purchaser immediately increases the order with the second supplier. It is clearly in the interest of the 'in' supplier not only to ensure customer satisfaction with his brand, but also to make the reordering procedure as easy as possible.

Once the customer starts to order the brand routinely, it may well prove profitable for the marketer to develop and pay for his customer to have a computerized reordering system. Otherwise, the 'in' supplier may face the problem of technological developments in purchasing making it easier for buyers to change brands. For example, AT&T Istel have developed a computer system, Formtrac, facilitating the purchasing of business stationery. Business customers enter their requirements in a computer network and promptly receive a list of potential suppliers. Should the user wish, he can then send an electronic invitation for quotations to specified suppliers through the system and subsequently place an electronic order.

The importance of the different departments in the firm varies according to the type of purchase. One study looked at the top two influential departments in firms buying small components. In Table 4.1 we see how the source of influence varied through the buying process according to the firm's buying experience.

In the *new buy* situation, engineering emerged as the most influential department throughout most stages of the buying process, surpassed only in the final brand selection stage by purchasing. In the *modified rebuy* situation, purchasing took the initiative in suggesting the need to reconsider alternative suppliers, with engineering being the dominant party when preparing the revised specification. From this stage onwards, purchasing played the leading role, supported by

Table 4.1   *Most influential departments*

Purchase stage	Purchase situation		
	New buy	Modified rebuy	Straight rebuy
Need identification	Engineering Purchasing	Purchasing Production	Production Purchasing
Prepare specification	Engineering Purchasing	Engineering Purchasing	Purchasing Engineering
Evaluate proposals	Engineering Purchasing	Purchasing Engineering	Purchasing Engineering
Brand selection	Purchasing Engineering	Purchasing Engineering	Purchasing Engineering

After Naumann *et al.*, 1984.

engineering. In the *straight rebuy* situation, production alerted the firm about the need to buy component parts, from which point onwards, purchasing was the dominant department.

Brand buying as a means of establishing relationships

A weakness of the Robinson model is that it does not address sufficiently well the relationships between buyers and sellers. In the 1980s, our understanding of organizational brand buying was increased by an international project undertaken by the IMP group. They found that both buyers and sellers were seeking close, long-term relationships. Many of their interviews with different industrialists showed a desire for stability. The broad implications for brand marketers are that they should look at brand marketing, not just in terms of marketing resource management, but also in terms of employing the right interpersonal skills and managing relationships through the most appropriate negotiation style.

Buyers were reticent about switching between competing brands because:

- They did not want to keep on spending more time in finding and evaluating alternative brands.
- They were worried about technical problems in adapting their production processes for the new brand.
- They might have had internal production problems which could be easier to resolve by involving a loyal supplier.

Many purchasers were of the opinion that they had a very good working relationship with their suppliers. As such, any brand alternative had to be extremely good to warrant any thought about change.

The IMP group showed that the relationship between the brand marketer and the purchasing organization was influenced by four factors: the interaction process; the organizations involved; the atmosphere affecting and affected by the interaction; and the environment within which the interaction took place.

In the *interaction process*, a series of 'episodes' take place between an order being placed and delivered. For example, the brand exchange, information exchange, financial exchange and social exchange. Over a period of time, these exchange episodes lead to institutionalized expectations about the respective roles of buyer and seller. For example, there are unwritten rules about which party will hold stock. Many case histories showed that stable relationships were characterized by frequent social and information exchange.

Growth through partnership.

Safeway has a big and growing commitment to British farming. Just one example is our partnership with the Malton Bacon Factory.

Working together with Safeway, Malton proved able to ensure animal welfare standards, product quality, supply for over 300 stores, and value to consumers.

The result: mutual satisfaction. All bacon sold in the Safeway delicatessen is now British, and supplied by the Malton Bacon Factory.

We look for partners who can grow with us. You?

Please contact Barry Martyn, Commercial Director, Safeway plc, 6 Millington Road, Hayes, Middlesex. UB3 4AY.   **SAFEWAY**

Exhibit 4.5   *Safeway seeking long-term relationship with suppliers*

By looking at the characteristics of the two *organizations*, there is some indication of the likely relationship. Technical issues are often important indicators of the likely buyer–seller relationship. Ultimately the interaction process is concerned with matching the production technology of the seller to the application technology of the buyer. Where the two organizations are at different stages of technological development, then their working relationship will be different to that where two firms have a similar level of technical expertise. Likewise, where the two firms are of a different size, or have little experience of working together, or have individuals with differing backgrounds, then the relationship between buyer and seller will take a lot of work to ensure harmony.

The relationship between the two firms is affected by the overall *atmosphere*. The atmosphere between two firms can be characterized by several factors. For example, the firms' mutual expectations, the overall closeness or distance of the relationship, whether there is a sense of conflict or cooperation and whether the dominant firm is trying to use its power over the weaker partner. Where there is an atmosphere of overall closeness, cost advantages can be gained through a variety of sources, for example, more efficient negotiations and administration, joint work on redesigning existing brands and more effective distribution. Some atmospheres may be characterized by a power-dependence relationship. For example, to ensure brand deliveries are scheduled primarily for the convenience of the powerful purchaser, the negotiation's agenda will take advantage of the supplier's dependence on the purchaser.

The wider *environmental issues* such as social systems, channel structure and market dynamism have an effect on the interaction relationship. The buyer and seller have to appreciate the type of social system they are working in. For example, the brand supplier has to be aware of any nationalistic buying preferences that they are facing. The relationship will also be affected by the type of channel used. For example, an electronic components' producer may sell to an actuator producer who in turn sells a range of actuators to another firm working on aircraft systems. The relationship between any two firms in this extended channel will be influenced by the relationships between other members of the channel. Highly dynamic markets, characterized by frequent new brand launches, make suppliers and purchasers aware of the need for a large number of relationships, which are not as intense as may be the case with much more stable markets.

By taking account of these four influencing factors, brand marketers can better appreciate the basis for their relationships with purchasing organizations. They should make all of the brand team aware of the institutionalized activities that each purchaser takes for granted and protect these from being cut in recessionary periods. Making changes to institutionalized activities, without thorough negotiation, is likely to sour the working relations.

The IMP research shows that the same brand support teams cannot work as effectively with every customer. The relationship of trust and mutual respect will be nurtured when people are selected because their backgrounds and personalities are ideal for sustaining a long-term working relationship with certain customers. This research makes the point that both rational and emotional factors influence brand selection, an issue that is now considered in more detail.

Factors influencing brand selection

When choosing between competing brands, a thorough evaluation, particularly for brands new to the firm, takes place, often with an agreed list of attributes. This reflects the views of all members of the buying centre. But a more covert assessment also takes place. This is based on social ('can I get on with this rep?') and psychological ('will I be respected if I'm seen to be buying from that firm?') considerations. Let us now examine some of these rational and emotional issues.

Rational brand evaluation criteria

In business to business marketing, considerably more emphasis is placed on the use of resources which appeal to buyers' rational, rather than emotional considerations. For instance, a survey amongst firms marketing high technology brands showed that considerable import-ance was placed on having state-of-the-art technology, employing effective salesmen, backing the brand with a strong service capability, being price competitive and offering a complete product range. Much less importance was placed on engendering a favourable attitude between the buyer and the sales representative.

It is not possible to generalize about the kinds of functional components of a brand that might appeal to buyers, since this depends on several factors, some of which include:

- The different requirements of members of the buying centre.
- The type of industry buying the brand.
- The type of product being bought.

It is unlikely that all *members of the buying centre* will be equally interested in the same attributes. People work in different depart-ments, with different backgrounds and different expectations of the brand. In fact, the brand marketer may well face a situation where different members have opposing views about relevant brand criteria. A chief chemist may be particularly concerned about the purity of the brand of solvent, while the purchasing manager's sole concern is keeping costs down. In a study considering the marketing of solar air conditioning systems, it was shown just how diverse the evaluation criteria were amongst members of the buying centre. Plant managers were more attentive to operating costs, whilst general managers were more concerned about the modernity of the brand and its potential for energy saving.

If the same brand is being sold to *different industries*, it is unlikely that they will be using the same evaluation criteria. In a study comparing the evaluation criteria used by manufacturing companies and hospitals, it was found that while there were some similarities, there were also major differences. For example, both manufacturers and hospitals regarded reliability and efficiency as being very

The new SII Combines

ANOTHER POWERFUL REASON TO CHOOSE A JOHN DEERE COMBINE

210 *horsepower*

If it's power you're looking for, look no further than a new John Deere SII Combine. Up to 210 DIN hp on the 1188 SII Hydro/4 Combine and 190 DIN hp on the 1177 SII Hydro/4. Plus a new 150 DIN hp 1166 SII Hydro/4 Combine rounds out the SII line.

But extra engine performance is just the start. Check out the fuel tank on both top models ... 33 percent larger for longer hours in the field. New larger tyre sizes are offered for less compaction and better riding comfort.

A new fine-cut chopper with hardened, serrated knifes cuts any straw more efficiently and evenly distributes it into the stubble. Simplifies your autumn tillage.

Grain quality? Just check the grain tank. You'll find cleaner grain and more of it in all crops thanks to a high-capacity cleaning shoe with redisigned cleaning fan.

See your John Deere dealer for more powerful reasons to buy an SII Combine.

RELIABILITY IS OUR STRENGTH   JOHN DEERE Ltd., Harby Road, Langar, Nottingham NG13 9HT Telephone (0949) 60491

Exhibit 4.6   *In common with many business to business brands, John Deere appeal predominantly to buyers' rational considerations*

important issues. Hospitals, however, saw after-sales service as a key factor, whilst the manufacturers rated the technical capabilities of the brand as very important.

The greater the similarity between purchasing industries, the greater the likelihood of similar evaluation criteria being used. When comparing the use of twenty brand evaluation criteria between electric power generating industries and electronic manufacturers, there were only four criteria not considered to be of the same importance (i.e. repair service, production facilities, bidding compliance and training aids).

The *type of product* also influences brand evaluation criteria. One particularly informative study was able to classify industrial products into four categories and showed that similar attributes were considered according to the category. Specifically, the four most important considerations for each category were:

1 For frequently ordered products that pose no problems in use: reliable delivery; price; flexibility; and reputation.
2 For products requiring training for use: technical service; ease of use; training offered; and reliability of delivery.
3 For products where there is uncertainty about whether the product will perform satisfactorily in a new application: reliability of delivery; flexibility; technical service; and information about product reliability.
4 For products where there is considerable debate amongst the buying centre: price; reputation; information on product reliability; and reliability of delivery.

There is an erroneous belief amongst some business to business marketers that brands succeed if they offer an attractively low price to purchasers. This is not so. A team of researchers examined the buying records of large manufacturing companies. They focused on 112 purchases of capital equipment. From this database they found that, on average, three competing brands were evaluated before a purchase decision was made and, in 41 per cent of the purchases, the successful brand was *not* the lowest priced bidder. The buyers paid a price premium for:

- Interchangeability of parts.
- Short delivery time.
- Working with prestigious suppliers.
- Full range of spare parts rapidly available.
- Lower operating costs.
- Lower installation costs.
- Higher quality materials.

Only when competing brands are perceived as being very similar does price becomes an important criteria. A study investigated buyers' perceptions of different brands of electrical devices (oscilloscopes, switches, resistors, etc.). When buyers perceived *little* brand differentiation, the three main choice criteria were price, specifications and delivery. By contrast, when buyers perceived *significant* differences between competing brands, price was not one of the ten criteria considered. A similar finding resulted in another study amongst buyers purchasing undifferentiated brands of industrial cleaners, lubricants and abrasives. Price was viewed as being one of the key choice criteria when choosing between mainly undifferentiated brands.

Even when price is a dominant choice criterion, different aspects of price are considered by the buyers. The purchase price of the brand may appear to be high, but when taking into account longer term economies resulting from the brand, such as lower defect rates in production, the buyer may well look at the purchase in terms of the long-term savings and quality improvements. Buyers also consider the brand's life cycle costs, i.e. the total costs likely over the lifetime of the brand. Mercedes-Benz trucks were once advertised using the slogan 'Are you buying a truck or an iceberg?' underneath which was an iceberg depicting the fact that over the vehicle's life, the buying price represented 15 per cent of the cost and the running costs 85 per cent.

Going with too low a price makes the buyer wonder what has been cut. We are aware of one consultant who lost a project because his price was too low compared with the other bidder. The client could not understand how the consultant could do a sufficiently thorough piece of work at such a low price. It transpired that as he worked alone he had much smaller overheads and was content to operate at lower margins than the more expensive firms, yet his low price lost him the contract. Thus, in common with consumer brand marketing, there exists a feeling of 'you get what you pay for'.

There are other reasons why pitching the brand at a low price may not be wise. Some buyers are evaluated on their ability to negotiate discounts and pricing low allows little leeway for negotiations. There are also some buyers who seek the satisfaction of always being able to negotiate a better price.

In conclusion, functional issues are important components of organizational brands which appeal to the rational side of the buyer. It should not, however, be thought that the decision processes of the members of the buying centre are totally logical. They are not solely concerned with quantitative measures to assess technical and commercial performance. The next section explores some of these non-rational criteria.

Emotional brand evaluation criteria

The individuals involved in the brand selection process enjoy the challenge of finding the best solution to the firm's problems. They are also motivated by more personal issues such as job security, a desire to be well regarded by colleagues inside and outside the firm, the need for friendship, ego enhancement, aspirations of career advancement, loyalties based on their beliefs and attitudes and a whole host of other social and psychological considerations. In a study we undertook for a tin packaging manufacturer, we became very aware of these emotional brand selection issues. Our brief was to find out why purchasers only awarded small contracts to this firm. In a depth interview, one purchaser told us that he used to place large orders with this firm, but felt that the quality standards were too variable and only used this supplier for small runs. When asked why he still bothered to use them, he spoke about the good social relations he had built with the firm's managing director. He viewed our client

'As an old friend, whose company you value because of the years you've been together. But as you get older, you develop particular idiosyncrasies, which as a good friend you just accept and try to still enjoy their company'.

He clearly valued his friendship with the managing director, and, at a lower level of commitment, was still prepared to buy tin packaging, albeit for jobs where tin quality was not a critical issue.

Buyers, as emotional individuals, take account of how the brand will affect them socially and psychologically. Having a brand delivered late not only affects production schedules, but also causes personal anguish. Late delivery is interpreted by some buyers as 'you're not that important to us'. It is a broken agreement, which is read as an attitude of complacency, and hurts their pride. They feel that the supplier is not serious about their business and start to wonder whether they can trust someone who shows such disinterest.

Buyers like to deal with prestigious suppliers as they feel this increases their status within the firm. They are proud to tell their colleagues that they are using particular suppliers, as they believe they gain more credibility and authority, particularly when the supplier's corporate identity has clearly communicated associations of excellence.

The size of a supplier is not just considered in terms of production capabilities, but also as indicative of the type of relationship. Larger suppliers are sometimes viewed as impersonal, unapproachable, self-centred, bureaucratic firms, who are unlikely to be flexible. By contrast, smaller firms are perceived as warmer, friendlier, more attentive and more flexible in responding to the supplier's problems.

One purchasing manager was part of a team deciding whether to buy glass or tin packaging for a new grocery brand. In spite of the fact that technical data was obtained and evaluated, he recommended tin because he personally found glass aesthetically unappealing. To get around this personal dislike, the glass packaging manufacturer appealed to his emotional instincts by leaving a small glass statue on his desk. He hoped that the sight of this expensive statue on his desk would change his attitude. In this case, functional issues were less important to the buyer than emotional considerations.

This is but one of many examples showing the importance of positioning organizational brands to satisfy the emotional needs of buyers. For example, a surgical instrument manufacturer succeeded when they spoke about their brands not in cold, medical terms, but using instead the terms of surgeons – 'smooth and elegant'. In this case the manufacturer won through by blending a technical approach to the communication with a more personal tone.

Understanding the psychological concerns of organizational buyers can give the brand an edge if other competitors are focusing solely on

Exhibit 4.7 *Allen & Hanburys presenting Beconase b.d. to GPs in a manner which not only satisfies their rational considerations but which also emotionally communicates the satisfaction of their patients*

functional issues. As was pointed out earlier in this chapter, managers perceive risk when buying brands. By understanding managers' concerns about brand buying, marketers should then be able to devise ways of presenting their brand as a risk reducer. One study investigated purchasers' perceptions of personal risk when choosing between competing brands in a modified rebuy situation. Their concern, after feeling personal remorse due to purchasing incompetence, was that relations with the internal user would be strained, the

Exhibit 4.8   *The Philips Pocket Memo appealing to managers' emotional desire to succeed in their careers*

Table 4.2   *Rankings of perceived personal risk in a modified rebuy*

Perceived personal risk	Ranking of buyers' concerns
You will feel personally incompetent	1
Your relations with the company user will be strained	2
The status of the purchasing department will fall	3
Your performance review will be less favourable	4
You will have less chance of promotion	5
Your annual rise will be smaller	6
You will lose status among your peers	7
You will lose your job	8
Your popularity will fall	9

After Hawes and Barnhouse, 1987.

status of the purchasing department would decrease and there would be a less favourable annual career performance review, with less chance of promotion. Further details are shown in Table 4.2.

In order of importance, the buyers in Table 4.2 felt that the most effective way of reducing personal risk was to visit the supplier's plant and then to ask some of the supplier's customers about their opinion of the supplier. The rankings of the preferred ways of reducing personal risk are shown in Table 4.3. Armed with results like these, brand marketers can develop strategies that position their brand as an effective risk reducer.

The Caterpillar Corporation is but one of many firms who benefited from understanding buyers' perceived risk. They were faced with the problem of firms producing inferior quality spare parts for after-sales service. These looked similar to the genuine Caterpillar part, but sold at a considerably lower price. Their lifetime was less than the genuine part and premature failing, while in use, could cause considerable engine damage. To counter this threat, Caterpillar developed a series of leaflets for its customers showing dice next to Caterpillar

Table 4.3   *Rankings of preferred ways to reduce personal risk*

Personal risk reduction	Buyers' preference ranking
Visit the supplier's plant	1
Talk with the supplier's customers	2
Multi-source the product	3
Insert penalty clauses in the contract	4
Ask colleagues' opinions	5
Only buy from firms used before	6
Seek senior managers' opinions	7
Only use well-known suppliers	8

After Hawes and Barnhouse, 1987.

equipment. The headlines were 'Don't gamble with it', 'Don't play games with it', 'Don't risk it'. Each brochure showed photographs of the damage caused by using pirate parts. These successfully communicated the functional excellence of the brand, as well as resolving the buyer's personal risk about using only genuine parts.

Providing organizational buyers with brand information

In business to business brand marketing, buyers undertake a thorough evaluation of competing brands. Due to the more complex and expensive nature of brands, they rely much more on personalized messages. As such, more emphasis is placed on using sales representatives to present brand information. Their task, particularly when approaching new firms, is that much easier when the brand is recognized as emanating from a well-respected organization. Corporate advertising, reinforcing a clear corporate identity, can pave the way for a more effective sales presentation. The sales representatives don't have to spend long reassuring the buyer about the company, and can devote more time to explaining the brand's benefits.

This promotional push, using advertising to give reassurance to customers and to enable salespeople to focus on brand capabilities, is seen in many industrial sectors. A survey amongst high technology firms, detailed in Table 4.4, showed that suppliers felt that it was most important to promote their brands using the salesforce, advertising in trade magazines and displaying at trade shows. In fact, the average high technology firm spent 9 per cent of its annual revenue on the salesforce, 3 per cent on advertising and 2 per cent on trade shows.

Table 4.4   *Sellers' importance ranking of promotional methods*

Promotional methods	Sellers' importance ranking
Sales representatives	1
Advertising in trade magazines	2
Trade shows	3
Technical seminars	4
Sales promotion materials	5
Direct mail advertising	6
Packaging	7
Newspapers/television/radio advertising	8

After Traynor and Traynor, 1989.

Promoting brands through the trade press is the most popular advertising media used by business to business advertisers. In a 1986 survey it was found that 35 per cent of business to business advertising budgets were directed at buyers via trade magazines. This was followed by brochures and exhibitions, each accounting for 14 per cent of advertising budgets, and then direct mail at 8 per cent.

We need to be careful, however, not to place too much emphasis on figures that talk about the importance that brand manufacturers place on different types of promotions. It emphasizes branding as an *input*, rather than an *output* process. It is more relevant to appreciate, from the buyer's perspective, how useful they believe different sources to be.

A study amongst purchasers of capital equipment and component materials found that buyers rated their purchasing records as the most useful source of information. This was followed by visits from salesmen and then discussions with their colleagues in other departments. The marketer who has a *range* of brands may find it easier to widen his business with his existing customers, since they can reassure themselves about his track record from their purchasing records. These results also indicate that the brand marketer should build a favourable relationship with other departments in the firm, to give the purchaser a greater sense of confidence when he talks with other colleagues. The fourth most useful way of finding out about the brand was by visiting the supplier's factory and glancing through the relevant brochures. The results, in Table 4.5, show that trade advertisements are not seen as being that useful, mainly because the buyers consider these as being too general.

Table 4.5   *Buyers' ranking of information sources*

Information sources	Buyers' importance ranking
Consult purchasing records	1
Visit from salesman	2
Talk with other colleagues	3
Visit vendor's factory	4
Brochures	5
Look through purchasing directories	6
Credit and financial reports	7
Telephone calls from salesmen	8
Talk to external purchasing manager	9
Articles in trade press	10
Trade advertisements	11
Trade shows	12

After Dempsey, 1978.

The key points that the organizational brand marketer should not lose sight of are that the buyer and his colleague in the buying circle may well:

- Perceive the contents of the brand message differently from the marketer, and
- May perceive the content of the brand message differently between themselves.

As Chapter 3 showed, people have limited mental capabilities and, to protect themselves from excessive amounts of information, their

Exhibit 4.9 *Due to perceptual processes, the target audience's skim reading of this advertisement may not have registered that it is promoting Valentine Wood Business Park*

FRAME 2
THE ZANTIC AD TESTED IN THE *ÄRZTE ZEITUNG*

Exhibit 4.10   *Due to legal requirements medical advertisers have to give considerable information about prescriptions when advertising their brands. Providing such a large quantity of information to busy GPs results in many skimming the points*

perceptual process filters much out. An example of this is shown in the advertisement, in Exhibit 4.10, for Zantac in Germany (where it is known as Zantic). Glaxo wanted to communicate the anti-ulcer capabilities of this drug to GPs in Germany and took a one-page advertisement in a respected medical journal. At the bottom of the advertisement there is a detailed explanation of the brand's pharmacology. Subsequent research showed that none of the doctors read the detailed explanation about the drug. Most read the caption, skimmed over the brand name, but took little further notice of the advertisement.

Loctite is a good example of an organization that took steps to avoid the problem of different perceptions amongst members of the buying circle. It was concerned about the way different types of engineer in the buying firm interpreted their trade advertisements for its range of industrial adhesives. They conducted some market research and found that design engineers felt strong pressure on themselves to be 'right' and not make a bad decision. They were risk avoiders who liked to see diagrams, charts and graphs in brand advertisements, with explanations of how the brand works. By contrast, plant engineers saw themselves as fixers, who kept things running by being creative in solving problems. They felt more comfortable with advertisements showing photographs of products rather than graphs. With this understanding of the different needs of members of the buying circle, Loctite then developed trade advertisements to appeal to specific types of engineers. A consequence of this was that there was a greater similarity of perceptions amongst engineers about Loctite's industrial adhesives and this in turn led to greater sales success.

The company as a brand

To present themselves in the most favourable way, firms develop a *corporate identity* programme, ensuring that all forms of external communication are coordinated and presented in the same way. The problem is that corporate identity is akin to 'branding as an input process', as dicussed in Chapter 2. Due to the problems created by the buyer's perceptual process, the resulting perception buyers have of the firm – its *corporate image*, may well be different from those intended.

Corporate identity is a valuable asset, which, if efficiently managed, can contribute to brand success. As such, any firm needs to manage its corporate identity programme in such a way that all members of a particular buying unit perceive a similar corporate image, encouraging a feeling of trust and confidence in the supplier.

Each member of the buying unit could have a different line of contact with a particular supplier. Without a cohesive approach to managing the corporate identity, this may result in each member of the buying unit perceiving a different corporate image – a result which bodes badly for the brand. Buyers are impressed by the consistency with which the firm presents itself. Their increased confidence places the brand in a more favourable light.

Any corporate identity programme is supported by a myriad of resources. For example, the firm's name, its structure, its employees, its offices, its letter-headed paper, its promotional activity, its core values, its culture, its logo, its promotional work and even the way the telephone is answered. It is wrong to think that corporate identity equates to the logo – this is but the tip of the iceberg. Many people were amazed late in the 1980s to see ICI spending large sums of money on what amounted to only a slight change to their logo. In reality, the logo change was but a small part of the corporate identity. ICI had undergone a major review to question why their performance was not better. They had carefully evaluated their strategy and were signalling a move to more added value products. Internally and externally they were communicating that the good things about ICI were remaining and that the 'World Class ICI' had changed to take advantage of the new environment.

To maximize the assets of the company as a brand, more enlightened firms expect their employees to act as 'ambassadors' for the firm. Most employees come in contact with other firms and they must be able to present a personality of knowledgeable helpfulness. The personnel director should no longer be concerned just with an *internal* focus on strategic human resource management, but should also take an *external* orientation, by looking, for example, at recruitment in terms of the individual's abilities to 'sell' for the firm. Training programmes need to be devised that give employees the skills to talk knowledgeably with all external contacts. They need to take 'ownership' of problems and structure their department around customers' needs. Partly because it recognized that it was structured more to suit itself, rather than its customers, British Telecom instigated a major corporate identity review in 1990.

There are many advantages from adopting a well thought through corporate identity programme. The first advantage is coping with shorter brand life cycles. The dynamic nature of markets and the continual pressure on performance improvement is resulting in shorter brand life cycles. To succeed, the brands must be adaptable. Uncompromising, staid brands blur the firm's image. Courtaulds recent corporate identity change reflected the corporation's desire to communicate modernity and the logical interlinkage between its divisions. Buyers associated Courtaulds as being in the textile market, and mentally pictured them as trading in a hostile, declining sector. Yet the reality is that Courtaulds has evolved six strong businesses, all of which have very clear strategic intents. To help communicate this externally, as well as making employees aware of their relations with other divisions, Courtaulds developed a new corporate identity in 1989.

A second advantage of corporate identity is that it sustains a real point of differentiation. It is more often the case that functional advantages are soon surpassed by technology leapfrogs. This is particularly so in financial services, where it is only a matter of days before new 'look-alikes' follow the innovator. Where, however, the point of difference is based on an emotional rather than a functional discriminator, buyers normally perceive extra value and competitors take longer to copy this. For example, the buyer may constantly receive fast responses from a technical representative who takes an active interest in their business and, on the odd occasion when the rep is unobtainable, receives a similar level of service. The emotional benefits from customer service are valued by buyers, who are unaware of the fact that this is one of the core values that the supplier has worked hard to instill internally (e.g. communication systems and training). This aspect of corporate identity is not just apparent from the promotional campaign, but from the way that *all* points of contact with the customer are geared to delivering customer service.

A third advantage is that in the current environment, where media inflation exceeds retail price increases, it can be a cost-effective means of communicating the broad values to which the company subscribes. The presence of the letters ICI before the individual company brands instantly enables the buyer to form an image about what the brand might be like.

We do not believe, however, that the promotions budget should just be directed towards corporate communication. Instead, a process has to be developed whereby the corporate advertising helps communicate the corporate identity, allowing each brand to benefit from the corporate goodwill, yet not stifling the individual brands' personalities.

Corporate identity can be a powerful tool helping business to business marketers to promote their brands. However, its power is limited by the extent to which all of the component parts are coordinated and whether they reinforce each other. The supplier needs to identify the different ways in which it comes into contact with all members of the buying centre, for example, brochures, staff, delivery vehicles, stationery, etc. For each of these elements, it then needs to assess whether a unifying device (e.g. logo) should be displayed and whether each of the elements supports the corporate identity objectives. The corporate identity objective of communicating concern for quality may be well supported by impressive brochures, smartly presented and knowledgeable sales staff, but will fail when dirty lorries deliver the products, with impatient lorry drivers thrusting badly typed invoices at the goods inward clerk.

It should now be very apparent that the logo is not the sole basis for such programmes, although it is a useful device to communicate corporate objectives. Particularly when the firm is responding to a changed environment, it can be a very visible way of communicating change to all interested publics. An example of this is Allied Irish Banks. Over the years its growth had taken it into international markets, with a widening range of financial services. Yet, it was still perceived as being Irish, it did not have a cohesive identity in the capital markets and its logo, a roundel with three spokes, was confused with Mercedes Benz. As part of a strategic push to become more customer orientated, the mission statement changed from being:

'The premier Irish financial Services Organisation, capable of competing worldwide by consistently delivering high quality service on a competitive basis to our customers in Ireland and throughout the world'

to:

'Value and service are at the heart of our business. We aim to provide real value to every one of our customers and to deliver the highest standards of service in banking and financial services.'

Consistent with this new mission, all aspects of the bank's activities were audited and changed where necessary. An ark was chosen as the new logo, since it was thought this communicated the bank's heritage, security and the many groups that it serves.

Conclusions

This chapter has shown that branding plays as important a role in business to business marketing as it does in consumer marketing. The organizational buyer has the encouragement to assess rationally competing brands, yet emotional considerations also influence brand buying. Not only do buyers seek performance reassurance, but they are also influenced by emotional aspects such as the prestige associated with specific brands.

Aspects of organizational marketing are different from consumer marketing and these issues need considering when developing organizational brands. For example, several people, from different departments, are likely to be involved in the brand selection decision, each having different brand expectations. By appreciating the needs of the different individuals, presentations can be tailored to different groups.

Non-routine purchasing in organizations typically involves about five people, but increases for more complex purchases. One way of anticipating which departments are likely to be involved in the brand purchase is through a consideration of the organization's view about the commercial risk and technical complexity of the brand. High technology brands from a well-respected supplier will attract considerable interest from technical specialists, but only a small amount of interest from company accountants.

Further insight to the challenges facing the brand can be gained by identifying which members of the buying centre will be the users, influencers, deciders, buyers and gatekeepers. Brand marketers must work to ensure that brand information is not blocked by gatekeepers. Brand presentations then should not just be directed at the needs of the decider, but also to the needs of key influencers, such as architects influencing the choice of office heating systems.

An eight-stage model of the buying process enables marketers to anticipate the way organizations go about deciding which brand to select. The amount of work undertaken by members of the buying centre will vary according to how much previous experience they have of buying the particular product. With little experience, they seek a considerable amount of information and undertake a detailed review of alternative brands. As they gain more experience, so they demand less data from suppliers and eventually they place considerable value on the ease of rapid reordering. The IMP Group have shown that many buyers seek a long-term relationship with their suppliers, due in no small part to the joint benefits to be gained from the supplier continually improving his portfolio of brands.

To facilitate the buying centre's evaluation of both rational and emotional aspects of the brand, personal visits by sales representatives are of considerable value. However, buyers also place a lot of importance on the supplier's track record with the firm, as well as discussing matters with colleagues and visiting the supplier's factories. The brand purchase decision is more confidently made when the buyer favourably associates the supplier's brand with a well-respected corporate image.

Marketing action checklist

To help clarify the direction of future brand marketing activity, it is recommended that the following exercises are undertaken:

1 Write down the criteria that you believe your customers use to evaluate your brands. If you only have rational reasons shown, discuss this with your colleagues and identify the emotional issues that your customers take into account. Does your marketing programme take account of your customers' rational and emotional needs?
2 For one of the contracts that your firm is trying to win, work out with the rest of the team the composition of the buying centre. Do you know who is playing the roles of user, influencer, decider, buyer and gatekeeper? How are you tailoring your brand presentation to appeal to the different members of the buying centre? Have you made sure that *all* members of the buying centre have relevant brand information?
3 For a contract that you recently lost, work with your colleagues to identify who was in the buying unit and the roles they played. With hindsight, were you correctly targeting and tailoring your brand presentation?
4 For a new contract that you are bidding for, assess whether the buying centre's experience makes the purchase a new task, modified rebuy or straight rebuy. With this assumption made explicit, use Figure 4.2 to map out the stages that the buying centre is likely to pass through, and estimate where it will devote most effort. For each of these stages identify the action you need to take to help the buyers.
5 What actions are you taking to ensure that your customers can place repeat orders? Have you investigated developing a computer-ized reordering process for each of your customers?

6 When did you last audit the way that all members of your organization interact with your major customers? For each major account, do you know whether:
- There have been any organizational changes?
- There is any personal friction between your staff and the buying centre?
- Deliveries are always on time, with the correct product mix?
- The buyers are satisfied with the consistency of quality?
- There are market changes occurring that will result in the buyer changing his brand purchasing?

7 What are you doing with your major customers to make them feel that you are always trying to improve your brands and help their business grow?

8 For a contract that you are currently bidding for, prepare a table comparing your brand against the other competing brands showing
- Purchase price
- Installation costs
- Operating costs
- Regular maintenance costs
- Depreciation costs

If any of this information puts your brand in a favourable perspective, how could you incorporate this into your brand presentation?

9 When was a market research study last undertaken to assess buyers' views of your brands and those of your competitors? If this was longer ago than two years, it may be worth while commissioning a new study. This should identify buyers' evaluation criteria and their assessment of competing brands. It should also investigate those aspects of risk that buyers perceive when buying your brand and their preferred ways of reducing risk.

10 Do you know which sources buyers most value when seeking information about competing brands? If not, interviews should be undertaken with key buyers and your promotional strategy adjusted accordingly.

11 What are your corporate identity objectives? How well do these match the corporate image buyers have of your firm? What actions are you taking to reduce any differences between your objectives and buyers' perceptions?

12 When did you last evaluate the appropriateness of your corporate identity? How much has the market changed since this was last done? Is your corporate identity programme able to adapt to market changes or is it now necessary to undertake a major review?

References and further reading

Berkowitz M. (1986). New product adoption by the buying organization: who are the real influencers? *Industrial Marketing Management*, **15**, 33–43.

Chisnall P. (1985). *Strategic Industrial Marketing*. Englewood Cliffs: Prentice Hall.

Choffray J., Lilien G. (1978). Assessing response to industrial marketing strategy. *Journal of Marketing*, **42**, (Apr.), 20–31.

Dempsey W. (1978). Vendor selection and the buying process. *Industrial Marketing Management*, **7**, 257–67.

Dichter E. (1973). Industrial buying is based on same 'only human' emotional factors that motivate consumer market's housewife. *Industrial Marketing*, (Feb.), 14–18.

Diefenbach J. (1987). The corporate identity as the brand. In *Branding: A Key Marketing Tool* (Murphy J., ed.). Basingstoke: Macmillan.

Hakannson H. (ed). (1982). *International Marketing and Purchasing of Industrial Goods*. Chichester: J. Wiley.

Hawes J., Barnhouse S. (1987). How purchasing agents handle personal risk. *Industrial Marketing Management*, **16**, 287–93.

Hill R., Hillier T. (1986). *Organizational Buying Behaviour*. Basingstoke: Macmillan.

Hutt M., Speh T. (1985). *Industrial Marketing Management*. Chicago: The Dryden Press.

Ind N. (1990). *The Corporate Image*. London: Kogan Page.

Kelly J., Coaker J. (1976). The importance of price as a choice criterion for industrial purchasing decision. *Industrial Marketing Management*, **5**, 281–93.

King S. (1991). Brand building in the 1990's. *Journal of Marketing Management*, **7**, (1), 3–13.

Kiser G., Rao C. (1977). Important vendor factors in industrial and hospital organizations: a comparison. *Industrial Marketing Management*, **6**, 289–96

Kohli A. (1989). Determinants of influence in organizational buying: a contingency approach. *Journal of Marketing*, **53**, (July), 50–65.

Lehmann D., O'Shaughnessy J. (1974). Difference in attribute importance for different industrial products. *Journal of Marketing*, **38**, (Apr.), 36–42.

Mattson M. (1988). How to determine the composition and influence of a buying centre. *Industrial Marketing Management*, **17**, 205–14.

McQuinston D. (1989). Novelty, complexity and importance as causal determinants of industrial buyer behavior. *Journal of Marketing*, **53**, (Apr.), 66–79

Naumann E., Lincoln D., McWilliam R. (1984). The purchase of components: functional areas of influence. *Industrial Marketing Management*, **13**, 113–22.

Parket I. (1972). The effects of product perception on industrial buying behavior. *Industrial Marketing Management*, **3**, 339–45.

Patton W., Puto C., King R. (1986). Which buying decisions are made by individuals and not by groups? *Industrial Marketing Management*, **15**, 129–38.

Robinson P., Faris C., Wind, Y. (1967). *Industrial Buying and Creative Marketing*. Boston: Allyn and Bacon.

Saunders J., Watt F. (1979). Do brand names differentiate identical industrial products? *Industrial Marketing Management*, **8**, 114–23.

Sheth J. (1973). A model of industrial buyer behavior. *Journal of Marketing*, **37**, (Oct.), 50–6.

Shoaf F. (1959). Here's proof – the industrial buyer is human. *Industrial Marketing*, **43**, (May), 126–28.

Sinclair S., Seward K. (1988). Effectiveness of branding a commodity product. *Industrial Marketing Management*, **17**, 23–33.

Stewart K. (1990). Corporate identity: strategic or cosmetic? In *Marketing Educators Conference Proceedings* (Pendlebury A., Watkins T., eds). Oxford: MEG.

Traynor K., Traynor S. (1989). Marketing approaches used by high tech firms. *Industrial Marketing Management*, **18**, 281–87.

Webster F., Wind Y. (1972). *Organizational Buying Behavior*. Englewood Cliffs: Prentice Hall.

Woolfson K. (1990). British Telecom plans a name with a new ring. *The European*, 5–7 October.

5 How consumer brands satisfy social needs

Summary

The purpose of this chapter is to consider the social roles played by brands. When consumers buy brands, they are not just concerned with their functional capabilities. They are also interested in the brand's personality which they may consider appropriate for certain situations. They look to brands to enable them to communicate something about themselves and also to better understand the people around them.

The chapter focuses on consumer rather than organizational brands, reflecting the greater emphasis placed on brand personality and symbolism in consumer marketing. This does not necessarily mean they are inappropriate, rather that they do not have the impact seen in consumer marketing.

We open this chapter by considering the added values from the images surrounding brands. We then address the symbolic role played by brands, where less emphasis is placed on what brands *do* for consumers and more on what they *mean* about consumers. Different symbolic roles for brands are identified, along with a consideration of the criteria necessary for brands to be effective communication devices. We draw on self-concept theory to explain how consumers seek brands with images that match their own self-image. A model of the way consumers select brands is presented, which shows how consumers choose brands to project images appropriate for different situations. Finally, we review the way that semiotics, the scientific study of signs, can contribute to brand effectiveness.

Added values beyond functionalism

Brands succeed because they represent more than just utilitarian benefits. The physical constituents of the product are augmented through creative marketing to give added values that satisfy social and psychological needs. The surrounding of the intrinsic physical product with an aura, or personality, gives consumers far greater confidence in using well-known brands. Evidence of this is shown by one study which investigated the role that branding played in drugs sold in retail stores. Women suffering from headaches were given an analgesic. Some were given the drug in its well-known branded form, the rest had the same drug in its generic form, lacking any branding. The branded analgesic was more effective than the generic analgesic and it was calculated that just over a quarter of the pain relief was attributed to branding. What had happened was that branding had added an image of serenity around the pharmacological ingredients and, in the consumers' minds, had made the medication more effective than the unbranded tablets.

The images surrounding brands enable consumers to form a mental vision of what and who brands stand for. Specific brands are selected when the images they convey match the needs, values and lifestyles of consumers. For example, at a physical level, drinkers recognize Guinness as a rich, creamy, dark, bitter drink. The advertising has surrounded the stout with a personality which is symbolic of nourishing value and myths of power and energy. The brand represents manliness, mature experience and wit. Consequently, when drinkers are choosing between a glass of draught Guinness or Murphys, they are subconsciously making an assessment of the appropriateness of the personality of these two brands for the situation in which they will consume it, be it amongst colleagues at lunch or amongst friends in the evening.

Particularly for conspicuously consumed brands, such as those in the beer and car market, firms can succeed by positioning their brands to satisfy consumers' emotional needs. Consumers assess the meanings of different brands and make a purchase decision according to whether the brand will say the right sort of things about them. They do not just base their choice on rational grounds, such as perceptions of functional capabilities, beliefs about value for money or availability. Instead, they recognize that to make sense of the social circles they move in, and to add meaning to their own existence, they look at what different brands symbolize. For example, they question how well a particular brand might fit in with their lifestyle, whether it helps them express their personality and whether they like the brand and would feel right using it.

Brands are part of the culture of a society and as the culture changes, so they need to be updated. For example, the Oxo brand has been portrayed in television advertisements over the past 30 years by the personality Katie. In the 1960s she epitomized the home-centred housewife devoted solely to the well-being of her family. With the changing role of women in society, the brand has had to move with the times. In the 1990s Katie stands for the busy women with a full-time job as well as a growing family to take care of. In both of these roles she is shown as a successful person who conveys a no-nonsense, warm, modern personality. Oxo's brand image has been updated to match the lifestyle of the modern consumer and its continuing success is partly due to this.

Exhibit 5.1   *In this 1980s advertisement, Heinz was playing on the way consumers choose brands to say the right sort of thing about them*

Brands and symbolism

A criticism often voiced is that many models of consumer behaviour do not pay sufficient attention to the social meanings people perceive in different products. A lot of emphasis has historically been placed on the functional utility of products, at the expense of ignoring the way that some people buy products for good feelings, fun and in the case of art and entertainment, even for fantasies. Today, however, consumer research and marketing activity is changing to reflect the way that increasingly consumers are evaluating products not just in terms of what they can *do*, but also what they *mean*.

Some brands have the added value of symbolism – meanings and values over and above the functional element of the product or service. Symbolism helps people to interpret things like images, feelings and stereotypes. Symbolism is sought by people in all walks of life, to help them better understand their environment. Different marques of cars succeed because they enable drivers to say something about who they are. We buy different brands of ties, for example, Yves St Laurent, as opposed to Burton, not just for their aesthetic design, but in anticipation of enhancing self-esteem.

To cope with the numerous social roles we play in life, brands are invaluable in helping set the scene for the people we are with. As such, they help individuals join new groups more easily. The new member at a golf club interprets the social information inherent in the brands owned by others and then selects the right brand to communicate symbolically the right sort of message about himself. When playing golf, the smart chequered trousers may be seen to be necessary to communicate the social role, but to play with a particular group of people, it's important to have the right *brand* as well.

Brands as symbols can act as efficient communication devices, enabling people to convey messages about themselves and to facilitate expressive gestures. Using Barclaycard Gold, rather than the standard Barclaycard, enables owners to say something about themselves to their friends when paying for a meal in a restaurant. Giving Black Magic chocolates for instance, says something about a sophisticated relationship between two people, while After Eight Mints imply an aspiration for a grand and gracious living style.

Advertising and packaging are crucial in reinforcing the covert message that is signified by the brand. Charles Revlon of Revlon Inc succeeded because he realized that women were not only seeking the functional aspects of cosmetics, but also the seductive charm promised by the alluring symbols with which his brands have been surrounded. The rich and exotic packaging, and the lifestyle advertising supporting perfume brands are crucial in communicating their inherent messages. On a similar basis, Marlboro have used the symbol of the rugged cowboy to communicate the idea of the independent, self-confident, masculine image. Consumers of this brand are not only buying it for its physical characteristics, but also as a means of saying something about themselves.

Brands are also used by people as ritual devices to help celebrate a particular occasion. For example, Moet & Chandon champagne is often served to celebrate a wedding, a birthday, or some other special event.

They are also effective devices for understanding other people better. The classic example of this was the slow market acceptance of Nescafe instant coffee in the USA. In interviews, American housewives said they disliked the brand because of its taste. Yet, blind product testing against the then widely accepted drip ground coffee showed no

Exhibit 5.2 *Jameson Irish Whiskey as a ritual device associated with making friends*

problems. To get to the heart of the matter, housewives were asked to describe the sort of person they thought would be using a particular shopping list. Two lists were given to the samples. Half saw the same list of groceries, but including Nescafe instant coffee, and the other half saw the list, but this time with Maxwell House drip grind coffee rather than Nescafe. The results of these interviews showed that switching coffee brands led respondents to infer two different personalities. The person who had the Nescafe grocery list was perceived as being lazy while the drip grind person was often described as a 'good, thrifty housewife'. As a consequence of this research, the advertising for Nescafe was changed. The campaign featured a busy housewife who was able to devote more attention to her family because Nescafe had freed up time for her. This change in advertising helped Nescafe successfully establish their brand of instant coffee.

Brands are also effective devices for symbolically expressing something to ourselves. For example, amongst final year undergraduates there is a ritual mystique associated with choosing the right clothes for job interviews and spending longer on shaving and hair grooming than normal. These activities are undertaken not only to conform to the interview situation, but also to give the person a boost to their self-confidence. In these situations, the consumer is looking for brands that will make them 'feel right'. A further example of this is in the specialist tea market, where Twinings advertised their teas using the theme 'Teas to match your mood'. The emphasis of brands here is to help consumers communicate something to themselves.

Exhibit 5.3   *PG Tips is positioned in this advertisement in terms of its functional capabilities, while Twinings add an emotional dimension to its functional capabilities*

So, consumers look to brands in highly conspicuous product fields, as symbolic devices to communicate something about themselves or to better understand their peer groups. Consumer behaviour in these situations becomes more akin to consumers encoding messages through buying certain types of brands. For example, a consultant

"You can't put too high a price on love. This summer, you don't have to."

Brighten someone's summer by sending them a Summer Pageant Bouquet of roses and carnations. Costing only £14.95, including VAT and local delivery, from any Interflora florist displaying the Summer Pageant banner. Standard relay orders cost just £2.85 extra; although in some cases extra charges may apply. Prices apply almost anywhere in the UK, Channel Islands and Republic of Ireland. Content and colour may also vary, depending on best available locally. Offer ends 30th September 1990. To order, visit or telephone your Interflora florist or, after shop hours, ring the Interflora Flowerline on 0529 304545.   GUARANTEED TO GET TO HER

Interflora

Exhibit 5.4   *Interflora's use of Eros to reinforce the symbolic association between their flowers and love. (Reproduced with the kind permission of Interflora (FTDA) British Unit Ltd)*

having his first meeting with a particular client may wish to convey a message of being successful and would be more likely to choose Dunhill aftershave, rather than Aramis. His hope is that the brand will be decoded by his client in the manner that he intended. The symbolic interpretations of some brands are well accepted. For example, Interflora makes use of Eros in their television and press advertisements to symbolize the giving of flowers as a sign of love. Not only are they building on the mythological associations of Eros, but they are further reinforcing this by bringing the character to life in their commercials to reinforce associations with Interflora.

Consumers also strive to understand their environment better through decoding the symbolic messages surrounding them. A client working with an architect sees things like certificates on the architect's wall, his tastefully designed office, the quality of the paper on which his report is word processed, the binding of his report and the list of clients he's worked for. All of these are decoded as messages implying a successful practice.

Symbols acquire their meaning in a cultural context. As such, the culture of the society consuming the brands needs to be appreciated to understand the encoding and decoding process. For instance, in Britain, Mr Kipling Cakes play on the association of the traditional master baker, yet, in the Arabic countries, this symbolism would not be decoded this way. Symbols acquire their meaning through everyday socialization that starts in childhood. People learn the inherent meaning of different symbols and through regular contact with each other, there is a consistent interpretation of them. To take a brand into a new culture may require subtle changes to ensure that the symbol acquires the right meaning in its new cultural context. For example, Red Cross becomes Red Crescent in the Middle East.

If a brand is to be used as a communication device, it must meet certain criteria. It must be highly visible when being bought or being used. It must be bought by a group of people who have a clearly distinguishable characteristic, which in turn facilitates recognition of a particular stereotype. For example, *The Times* newspaper is bought most often by the upper social classes and the reader is often stereotyped as a middle-aged 'City Gent'. In the newspaper market, readers select different brands as value-expressive devices. They provide a statement about who they are, where they are in life and what sort of person they are. Since brands can act as self-expressive devices, users prefer brands which come closest to meeting their own self-image. The concept of self-image is important in consumer branding and is reviewed in the next section.

Self-concept and branding

In consumer research, it is argued that consumers' personalities can be inferred from the brands they use, from their attitudes towards different brands and from the meanings brands have for them. Consumers have a perception of themselves and they make brand decisions on the basis of whether owning or using a particular brand, which has a particular image, is consistent with their own self-image. They consider whether the ownership of certain brands communicates the right sort of image about themselves. Brands are only bought if they enhance the conception that consumers have of themselves, or if they believe the brand's image to be similar to that which they have of themselves. Just as people take care choosing friends who have a similar personality to themselves, so brands, which are symbolic of particular images, are chosen with the same concern. As brands serve as expressive devices, people therefore prefer brands whose image is closest to their own self-image.

This way of looking at personality in terms of a person's self-image can be traced back to Rogers' self-theory. Motivation researchers advanced the idea of the self-concept, which is the way that people form perceptions of their own character. By being with different people, a person experiences different reactions to himself and through these clues starts to form a view about what sort of person he is. A person's self-concept is formed in childhood. From many social interactions, the person becomes aware of their *actual self-concept* – an idea of who they think they are. However, when they look inward and assess themselves, they may wish to change their actual self-concept to what is referred to as the *ideal self-concept* – who they think they would like to be. To aspire to the ideal self-concept, the person buys and owns brands which he believes supports the desired self-image.

The purpose of buying and using particular brands is either to maintain or to enhance the individual's self-image. By using brands as symbolic devices, the person is communicating certain things about himself. Most importantly, when he buys a particular brand and receives a positive response from his peer group, he feels that his self-image is enhanced and, will be likely to buy the brand again. In effect, he is communicating that he wishes to be associated with the kinds of people he perceives as consuming that particular brand.

There is a considerable amount of research supporting this idea of the self-concept, based on research in product fields such as cars, cleaning products, leisure activities, clothing, retail store loyalty, electrical appliances and home furnishing. Several studies have looked at car buying and have shown that the image that a car owner has of himself is congruent with the image of the marque of car he owns. Owners of a particular car hold similar self-concepts to those they attributed to other consumers of the same car. Also, if the car purchaser's self-image is dissimilar to the image he perceives of different brands of cars, he will be unlikely to buy one of these brands.

To check whether an appreciation of self-image as an indicator of buying behaviour is as useful for conspicuously consumed brands as it is for privately consumed brands, a study was specially designed to look at car brands (conspicuous consumption) and magazine brands (private consumption). In both of these product fields, people chose brands whose images came closest to matching their own self-concepts. What this study also showed was that for less conspicuously consumed product fields, actual, rather than ideal, self-image appeared to be more strongly related to brand choice.

There has been a lot of debate about which type of self-concept (actual or ideal) is more indicative of purchase behaviour. To understand this better, a study was designed which looked at nineteen different product fields ranging from headache remedies, as privately consumed products, through to clothes, as highly conspicuously consumed products. There was a significant correlation between the purchase intention for the actual and ideal self-concept results. This indicated that both are equally good indicators of brand selection.

However, the behaviour of individuals varies according to the situation they are in. The brand of lager bought for drinking alone at home in front of the television is not necessarily the same as that bought when out on a Saturday night with friends in a pub. Situational self-image – the image the person wants others to have of them in a particular situation – is an important indicator of brand choice. According to the situation that the individual is in, so they match their situational self-image to the social expectations of that particular group and select their brands appropriately. The impact of situation on brand choice can be modelled, as shown in Figure 5.1.

Consumers anticipate and then evaluate the people that they are likely to meet at a particular event, for example those going to an important dinner party. They then draw on their repertoire of

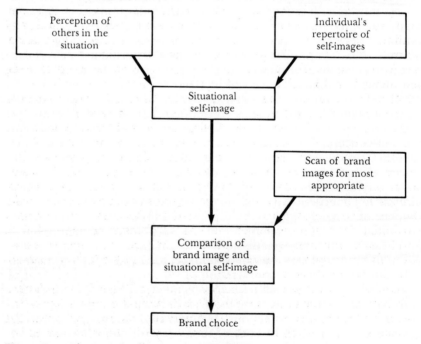

Figure 5.1   *The impact of situation and self-image on brand choice. (After Schenk and Holman, 1980)*

self-images to select the most appropriate self-image for the situation ('I can't let my hair down on Saturday night, as there are too many of my husband's colleagues there. Better be a lot more reserved, especially as his boss is hosting this party.'). If the situation requires products to express the situational self-image, for example a certain type of clothing, the consumer may decide to buy new clothes. When shopping they will consider the images of different clothes and select the brand which comes closest to meeting the situational self-image they wish to project at the dinner party.

Finally, it needs to be realized that there is an interaction between the symbolism of the brand being used and the individual's self-concept. Not only does the consumer's self-image influence the brands that they select, but the brands have a symbolic value and this in turn influences the consumer's self-image.

The contribution of semiotics to branding

People also make inferences about others from the brands they own, since some brands act as cultural signs. Semiotics, the scientific study of signs, is a qualitative market research technique that is widely used in France and is beginning to gain popularity in the UK. It helps clarify how consumers learn meanings associated with products and brands. If marketers are able to identify the rules of meaning that consumers have devised to encode and decode symbolic communication, they can make better use of advertising, design and packaging. For example, gold has been enshrined in our culture as a symbol of wealth and authority and can convey meanings of luxury, love, importance, warmth and eternity. But to use this as the prime colour on a box for a cheap, mass-produced plastic moulded toy car runs the risk of it being interpreted as vulgar.

Some have argued that brands act as communicative sign devices at four levels. At the most basic level, the brand acts as a utilitarian sign. For example, a particular brand of washing machine may convey the meaning of reliablity, effectiveness and economic performance. At the second level, a brand acts as a commercial sign conveying its value. For example, Porsche and Skoda signify the extremes in value perceptions. At the third level, the brand acts as a sociocultural sign, associating consumers with particular groups of people. For example, having certain brands 'to keep up with the Joneses', or wearing a particular tie to signify membership of an exclusive club. At the fourth level, the brand can be decoded as a mythical sign. For example, Napoleon Brandy, Cutty Sark Whisky and the Prudential Corporation, all build on mythical associations.

Semiotics provides a better understanding of the cultural relationship between brands and consumers. Checking the communications' briefs for brand advertising against the way consumers interpret the messages, can result in the more effective use of brand resources. For example, British Airways wished to increase the number of female executives using its airline. They developed an advertising campaign, targeted at women business travellers, which spoke about the ergonomics of seats. Semiotic Solutions undertook research to evaluate the proposed new campaign. They found that the campaign was not sufficiently sensitive to the fact that women are not as tall as men, and the copy was rejected by women business travellers who felt that 'talking about 6½ foot women was an insult'.

Semiotics can help in the design of brands, as was the case with a hypermarket in the Mammouth chain, opened in Lyon in 1986. Using group discussions, the different values consumers ascribed to hypermarkets were identified and designs developed to match these. Patterns of similarity were sought in terms of the way consumers associated different values with hypermarkets and four segments were tentatively identified from the qualitative research:

- *Convenience values*, characterized by 'Find the product quickly, always enough in stock, always on the same shelf'.
- *Critical values*, characterized by 'My husband isn't interested in frills and friendliness. He's only bothered about his wallet. He looks at the quality of the products, and at the prices'.
- *Utopian values*, expressed by comments such as 'I like being somewhere on a human scale, and not somewhere vast and overwhelming'.
- *Diversionary values*, such as 'I get the basic stuff out of the way first, and then I give myself a little treat, such as browsing in the book department'.

In the group discussions, consumers spoke about spatial issues, and it was inferred that:

- Convenience values were associated with interchanges and avenues.
- Critical values were associated with roundabouts and orientation maps.
- Utopian values related to markets and public gardens.
- Diversionary values encompassed covered arcades and flea markets.

Further analysis revealed that consumers expressing convenience and critical values wanted simple, continuous space. By contrast, consumers with utopian and diversionary values preferred complex, discontinuous space. Then, by considering customers in these two broad categories, the semiotic analysis led to the suggested design shown in Figure 5.2. It was anticipated that as they gained more experience shopping in the hypermarket, the two consumer groups would use separate entrances. As such, a different store design was conceived for each entrance. Most consumers would seek all four values of the hypermarket, but would be particularly drawn to the section that reflected their values. Decisions about where to locate the produce were aided by the group discussions. After the store accepted these designs, they had to be adjusted to cope with operational issues, such as ease of rapidly replenishing shelves, lighting, safety regulations, etc. However, overall, Mammouth found this approach helpful in conceiving a new design for their hypermarket.

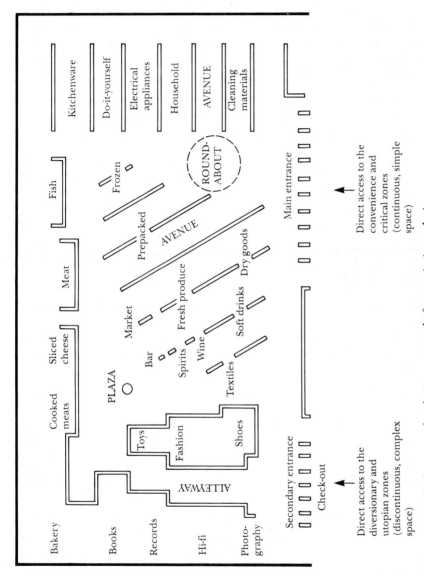

Figure 5.2   *The hypermarket design proposed after semiotic analysis*

Conclusions

This chapter has shown how brands perform a social role beyond that provided by their physical features. Consumers rely on brands to help them understand and communicate with different groups of people. The fact that consumers report greater pain relief after using a branded, rather than a generic version of the same analgesic, provides evidence of added values from brand images. Creative marketing has successfully positioned brands as effective problem solvers, with personalities that contribute to greater effectiveness.

Brands have the added values of symbolism – meanings and values over and above their physical constituents. Consumers look to brands not only for what can they do, but also to help say something about themselves to their peer groups. Rolex watches are not worn just for their functional excellence, but also to say something about who the owner is. To ensure that brands are effective symbolic devices, it is crucial for marketers to communicate their capabilities to users, and their peer groups, through advertising, public relations, packaging, merchandizing, etc.

The symbolic aspect of brands makes them all the more attractive to consumers since they:

- Help set social scenes and enable people to mix with each other more easily.
- Enable consumers to convey messages about themselves.
- Act as ritual devices to celebrate specific occasions.
- Provide a basis for better understanding of the way people act.
- Help consumers say something to themselves.

In effect, consumers are encoding messages to others by buying and using particular brands and are hoping that their target audience decodes the message the right way. Unfortunately, this is not always the case. For example, two friends meeting after several years may decide to go for a drink. One may order a Britvic Orange Juice, encoded to communicate his concern about not drinking when having to drive. The second person may decode this as: 'time has dulled his sociability'.

When consumers buy brands, they are making decisions about how well specific brands maintain or enhance an image that they have of themselves. Just as consumers have distinct personalities, so do brands. Consumers take as much care choosing highly conspicuous brands as they do choosing their friends, since they like to be surrounded by like-minded personalities. Brands whose images match consumers' actual or ideal self-images are likely to be bought. When friends or colleagues admire someone's newly bought brand, that person feels pleased that the brand reinforces his self-image and will continue to use the brand. The situation in which consumers find themselves will dictate, to some extent, the type of image that they wish to project. Through anticipating, and subsequently evaluating, the people that they will meet at a particular event, consumers then seek brands to reflect the situational self-image that they wish to display.

Semiotics, the scientific study of signs, can help brand development by assessing the cultural signs portrayed by different brands. For example, our culture brands the 07.00 train running ten minutes late as the late 07.00, carrying critical associations of inefficiency. However, in lesser developed economies, the train would be branded as the 07.10, portraying the triumph of mass transportation running against many odds in an under-resourced environment. Semiotics analyses brands' communication capabilities at four different levels: utilitarian, commercial, sociocultural and mythical. Successful brands blend well with their cultural environment, since consumers' decoding of brand values does not break any cultural mores. Brand advertising and design can benefit from checking communication briefs against the ways that consumers have interpreted the marketing activity as part of the social system.

Marketing action checklist

To help clarify the direction of future marketing activity, it is recommended that the following exercises are undertaken:

1 When did you last evaluate the added value of image surrounding your key brands? If this has not been done within the past 12 months, it may well be advisable to assess this.

One way of doing this is to identify the main competitor to one of your brands. Recruit a representative sample of consumers to try your brand and also that of your nearest competitor, seeking their comments about which brand they most preferred and why. This is a 'branded product test'. With another matched sample of consumers, repeat the product test but, this time, remove any branding and use identifying codes when presenting the brands. This is referred to as a 'blind product test'. Again, ask consumers which one of the two brands they most preferred, with their reasons. Calculate the proportions who prefer each of the two brands on the branded and the blind product test. Comparing the preference scores when the brands are assessed blind and then branded gives an indication of the value consumers ascribe to functional and emotional aspects of the brand.

2 Do you know what image surrounds your brand? If little is known about this, it would be wise to conduct some qualitative depth interviews with consumers. Ideally, this should be done by a skilled qualitative market researcher, preferably with a background in psychology. Some of the ways of gauging the image associated with a brand are to ask consumers the following types of questions:

'If ——(**brand**)—— came to life, what sort of person would it be?'
'If ——(**brand**)—— were a person, and they died what would be written on their epitaph?'
'If ——(**brand**)—— were to be a car, what sort of car would they be?'

'Tell me the first thing that comes to mind when I say ——(**brand**)——'
'What would a friend of yours most like about ——(**brand**)——, and what would they most dislike about ——(**brand**)——?'.

They could also be asked to role play the way your brand solves a problem and then repeat this for a competitor's brand.

Once you have identified the image dimensions of your brand, it would then be useful to see how strongly your brand is associated with each of these statements, comparing this against competitors' brands. This could be done using a questionnaire which asked respondents to use a five-point agreement–disagreement scale to state how well they felt each of the statements described each of the brands. By administering this to a representative sample of consumers, the image profiles of your brand, and those of your competitors, can be assessed.

3 When did you last evaluate whether the characters portraying your brands are appropriate for today's consumers? If you feel your brands compete in a fashion-driven market, it would be advisable to undertake qualitative market research to assess the suitability of the people in your brand advertising.

4 To what extent do your key brands satisfy the following symbolic roles. Do they:

- Enable people to join new groups more easily?
- Enable people to convey messages about themselves?
- Help celebrate special events?
- Aid people in understanding the actions of their peer group?
- Allow consumers to say something about themselves to themselves?

Having undertaken this symbolic brand audit, evaluate how well your marketing activity helps support these symbolic roles.

5 If, on exporting your brands, you found a hostile consumer response, did you subsequently conduct qualitative market research to assess why your brands failed? Was any work undertaken to assess whether the symbols surrounding your brands meant something different overseas, from that in the UK? For example, putting your hand to your ear in the UK indicates that the person is talking too quietly, but in Italy is taken as an insulting gesture.

6 How well matched is your brand's image with the self-image of your target consumers? One way of assessing this is by comparing the image profile of your brand against the self-image profile of your target market. If you have no data on this, point 2 in this section explains how to measure the image of your brand quantitatively. The same battery of attributes should also be administered to a representative sample of your consumers, asking them to use a five-point scale to assess how much they agree or disagree with each of the statements describing themselves. Compare the average brand image scores against the average self-image scores to assess how well your consumers' self-image matches that of your brand.

Highlight the attributes showing the largest differences – these indicate areas where your brand does not meet consumers' expectations and should be investigated further.

7 How much is your brand the subject of situational influences? Do you know what supporting roles your brand plays when consumers use it in different situations? Does your marketing activity promote the appropriateness of your brand for particular situations?

8 Take one of your recent brand advertisements and evaluate, with your colleagues, what the brand is communicating as a utilitarian sign, as a commercial sign, as a socio-cultural sign and as a mythical sign. Are these messages consistent at all four levels? Were the interpretations consistent across your team?

Repeat the exercise with consumers and compare the findings between yourselves and the consumers. Any dissonant findings should be considered in more detail and corrective action taken.

References and further reading

Belk R., Bahn K., Mayer R. (1982). Developmental recognition of consumption symbolism. *Journal of Consumer Research*, **9**, (June), 4–17.

Birdwell A. (1968). A study of the influence of image congruence on consumer choice. *Journal of Business*, **41**, (Jan.), 76–88.

Branthwaite A., Cooper P. (1981). Analgesic effects of branding in treatment of headaches. *British Medical Journal*, **16**, (May), 282, 1576–8.

Broadbent K., Cooper P. (1987). Research is good for you. *Marketing Intelligence and Planning*, **5**, (1), 3–9.

Chisnall P. (1985). *Marketing: a behaviourial analysis*. London: McGraw Hill.

Combs A., Snygg D. (1959). *Individual Behavior: a perceptual approach to behavior*. New York: Harper & Bros.

Dolich I. (1969). Congruence relationships between self images and product brands. *Journal of Marketing Research*, **6**, (Feb.), 80–4.

Floch J. (1988). The contribution of structural semiotics for the design of a hypermarket. *International Journal of Research in Marketing*, **4**, (3), 233–52.

Gordon W., Langmaid R. (1988). *Qualitative Market Research. A practitioners and buyers guide*. Aldershot: Gower.

Grubb E., Hupp G. (1968). Perception of self-generalized stereotypes and brand selection. *Journal of Marketing Research*, **5**, (Feb.), 58–63.

Hirschman E., Holbrook M. (1982). Hedonic consumption: emerging concepts, methods and propositions. *Journal of Marketing*, **46**, (Summer), 92–101.

Landon E. (1974). Self concept, ideal self concept and consumer purchase intentions. *Journal of Consumer Research*, **1**, (Sept.), 44–51.

Lannon J., Cooper P. (1987). Humanistic advertising. *International Journal of Advertising*, **2**, 195–213.

Levitt T. (1970). The morality (?) of advertising. *Harvard Business Review* (July–Aug.), 84–92.

Munson J., Spivey W. (1981). Product and brand user stereotypes among social classes. In *Advances in Consumer Research* (Munroe K., ed.) vol. 8. Ann Arbor: Association for Consumer Research, 696–701.

North W. (1988). The language of commodities: groundwork for a semiotics of consumer goods. *International Journal of Research in Marketing*, **4**, (3), 173–86.

Ross I. (1971). Self-concept and brand preference. *Journal of Business*, **44**, (Jan.), 38–50.

Schenk C., Holman R. (1980). A sociological approach to brand choice: the concept of situational self image. In *Advances in Consumer Research* (Olson J.,ed.) vol. 7. Ann Arbor: Association for Consumer Research, pp. 610–15.

Sirgy M. (1982). Self-concept in consumer behavior: a critical review. *Journal of Consumer Research*, **9**, (Dec.), 287–300.

Solomon M. (1983). The role of products as social stimuli: a symbolic interactionism perspective. *Journal of Consumer Research*, **10**, (Dec.), 319–29.

Wilkie W. (1986). *Consumer Behavior*. New York: Wiley.

6 Developing and sustaining added values

Summary

The aim of this chapter is to consider the issues involved in developing and sustaining brand added values. The chapter begins by making the point that it is only worth developing added values if they are relevant to the target market and noticeably different from those of competitors. Any marketing activity then needs to integrate these added values and present brands as *holistic* offerings. In other words all, rather than one single aspect, of the brand's assets should be developed, enabling customers to appreciate their points of difference, the way they satisfy both functional and emotional needs, reduce perceived risk, and make purchasing easy.

One way of identifying possible added values for brands is to consider a four-level model of a brand as a *generic* product with an *expected*, *augmented* and *potential* branding surround. We describe the development of brands using this conceptual model and employ it to identify appropriate ways of adding value. We also consider the problem of sustaining brands' added values against imitators through trademark registration. Counterfeiting, however, is but one of the challenges facing brands. We conclude the chapter by considering some of the other challenges.

Positioning brands as added value offerings

Brands succeed because customers perceive them as having added values, that is, values over and above their commodity constituents. But success comes from developing added values which make brands *noticeably different* from competitive brands and which result in *relevant* and *welcomed* attributes.

17% OF TRAVELLERS WILL FORGET SOMETHING ANYWAY.

No matter how you pack, there's often that small but essential item that gets left behind. Like a toothbrush, a comb or a razor. That's why at Holiday Inns we provide those items we know our guests most often forget.

We call it our "Forget Something?" programme. It's just a small example of our big commitment to service. So next time you travel, why not give us a call? And take a load off your mind.

STAY WITH SOMEONE WHO REALLY KNOWS YOU.   ✳ *Holiday Inn*®

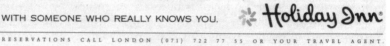

FOR RESERVATIONS CALL LONDON (071) 722 77 55 OR YOUR TRAVEL AGENT.

Exhibit 6.1   *The forgetful traveller may no doubt perceive Holiday Inn's 'Forget Something?' programme as being a welcome added value*

The conveyancing solicitor who publicizes the fact that his clerk drives papers round to clients' homes is more likely to win in the commodity conveyancing market than the undifferentiated firm of solicitors who try to negotiate lower priced conveyancing. The winner in the commodity car hire market is the firm who delivers the car the night before it is needed for a very long journey. The hire cars from competing firms may well be replaced every 6 months, but ultimately, it is the smile, civility and genuine personal concern that often prove to be the real discriminators that make some firms more successful than others.

To be successful, it is crucial for firms to have a very clear view about precisely what added values their brands offer as well as understanding the relevance of these added values to consumers. A kitchen kits sales director perceived his brands as having the added value of 'quality'. The problem was that many of the competitors also saw quality as *their* added value. When forced to define more precisely what he meant by 'quality', he spoke about the kits not breaking when the flat packs were dropped from a height of five metres! But, as consumers are hardly likely to test the durability of their kitchens in this manner, and are more concerned about designs, types of facias, dimensions and delivery times, this is hardly likely to be relevant. In other words, little thought had been given to identifying *relevant* added values and his brands were not being marketed with a point of differentiation that was relevant to the consumer. Consequently, their long-term future was at risk.

Once there is a clear internal appreciation about the brand's added values, a holistic strategy then needs to be developed, integrating the added values into all parts of the supply chain. For example, the added value of reliability in a new brand of testing equipment starts by having good quality components and stringent testing procedures at every stage of production. This is followed through by having everyone who works on the brand committed to satisfying this goal. This means that if the testing equipment does fail in the customer's factory, there is a facility to provide a rapid temporary replacement while the instrument is being repaired. This enables the firm's brands to be differentiated from those of their competitors by positioning them in such a way that their added values are clearly appreciated.

To succeed, a holistic approach is needed when developing a brand, which would need to be recognized as:

- Being *differentiated* from competition, in such a way that the name is instantly associated with specific added values.
- Having added values which satisfy both *functional* and *emotional* needs.
- Being perceived as a low *risk* purchase. ✳
- Making purchasing easy through being presented as an effective *shorthand* device.
- Being backed by a registered trademark, *legally* guaranteeing a specific standard of consistency.

In other words, successful brands do not stress just one part of the brand asset. They blend all of these components together. Further-more, they ensure that a coherent approach is adopted, with each component reinforcing the others.

In the 1990 consumer survey undertaken by Landor & Associates, Coca-Cola emerged as the most well known brand. Furthermore, it is held in very high esteem by consumers, being ranked sixth on this measure, as seen in Table 6.1. The success of this brand resulted from a coherent strategy that draws on *all* of the brand's assets. It does not stress just the brand name in its strategy, but also draws on other assets such as its ability to satisfy both functional and emotional needs. After the debacle in the 1980s with diet Coca-Cola, it recognized the need to establish clear brand personalities for each of its individual brands and in spring 1991 launched different advertising approaches, separating the core Coca-Cola brand from diet Coke.

Exhibit 6.2   *Bells Old Scotch Whisky is a good example of a coherent, holistic approach to branding*

Table 6.1   *Consumers' assessment of global brands*

| | Rankings of: | |
	Familiarity	Esteem
Coca-Cola	1	6
McDonald's	2	85
Pepsi-Cola	3	92
Sony	4	1
Kodak	5	9
Toyota	6	23
Nestle	7	14
Disney	8	5

After Landor & Associates, 1990.

In a similar manner, another successful brand, Levi, continues to be a leader by developing propositions in tune with changing market needs. During the 1980s, young peoples' attitudes changed and, while the core values of Levi jeans were retained – American-ness, rebelliousness, toughness and masculinity – a new campaign was developed to build on these values as well as communicating the new theme of independence.

Brands succeed because they have clearly defined added values which match consumer needs. In East Europe, where manufacturers' brands can take advantage of significant market opportunities, success will probably be linked to the way that West European brands will be repositioned to reflect consumer needs in the East. For example, brands of washing powder positioned as being environmentally friendly, with biodegradable packs, may not be as well received as brands that go back to the 1960s claims of washing 'whiter than white'.

While these points show the need to use *all* the elements of a brand's assets, a consideration of some branding approaches in our sophisticated society shows an excessive reliance on only a few, or worse still, just one component of the brand. The most frequent branding error appears to be an undue emphasis on using the brand name purely as a differentiating device. For example, John Cleese, in an Australian advertisement for Planters Pretzels, does little more than introduce a group of dancers to chant the brand's name. The advertisement is shot against a white set and no clues are presented about what, or who, the brand represents. Tacking a name on a pack, and saying it as many times as possible in advertisements, does little more than create initial interest. It is often subsequently quickly forgotten. Consumers look to brands as problem solvers and in so doing need to be able to associate instantly a brand name and a specific added value. Incantations, such as those referred to in the Planters case, which do not facilitate associations of added values with specific brands, can actually hinder marketing programmes.

Identifying added values

When faced with the need to find a removal company, the home-owner may initially notice very little difference between removers. However, when a few firms are asked to give quotations, very clear differences become apparent. There are those estimators who can call at a time convenient to the home-owner, while others cannot be definite. Some will appear with a brochure describing their firms' capabilities, provide advice on how to minimize packing effort and will provide lightweight, collapsible cardboard cartons. Others will wander round the house, making comments about the difficulty of having spiral staircases and the irritation of having to wait for the key to the new home to be released. In other words, while the basic service is akin to an undifferentiated commodity, the way that it is offered can be differentiated.

By recognizing that buyers in consumer, service and industrial markets regard products and services as clusters of value satisfactions, marketers can start to differentiate their brands by developing relevant added values. For example, removal firms can differentiate themselves by providing values such as responsiveness to unusual handling requests, politeness, the confidence they give home-owners through the care they take when packing, reliability and the guarantees they offer, and so on. All of these features present opportunities for differentiation.

As a further example, many would argue that the salt market comes close to being a commodity market, yet Reichenhaller is marketing its brands of salt to satisfy consumers' needs for health and flavour. For example, for health-conscious consumers, there is the choice of Alpine Light Salt (sodium reduced) or No Salt (salt-free flavouring). For consumers looking for new flavours, there is Alpine Salt With Herbs, Alpine Salt for Meat & Poultry and Alpine Salt for Fish & Vegetables.

The model in Figure 6.1 is a helpful conceptualization of the way that brands can be constructed to satisfy consumers' needs.

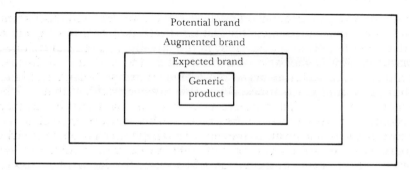

Figure 6.1 *The four levels of a brand. (After Levitt, 1980)*

The generic level

At its most basic, there is the *generic* product or service functionality, that enables firms to be in the market. For example, the cars produced by Ford, Vauxhall and Toyota; the home loans advanced by the Abbey National and Halifax; the computers from IBM, Hewlett Packard and Fujitsu. At this level, it is relatively easy to develop 'me-too' versions. For example, a small, hatchback, town car is offered by Ford, Renault and Peugot, amongst others. In developed countries, this is rarely the basis for differentiation.

The expected level

Buyers and users have a perception about the minimum character-istics that differentiate competing brands in the same product field. At the *expected* level, products and services are made to satisfy purchasers' minimum requirements for attributes such as name, packaging, design, availability, price, quantity and so on.

One of the most helpful ways of identifying what these characteris-tics should be is through depth interviews with buyers and users.

The expected level of brand competition is typically seen when buyers do not have much experience of competing brands. In such cases, they look at product attributes to assess how well different brands will satisfy their motivational needs. For example, some of the motivating reasons for having a hot drink are relaxation (Ovaltine), energy (Cadbury's Chocolate Break), stimulation (Nescafé coffee) and warmth (Bovril). Buyers consult the brand names, the packaging details, price and promotional details to form an overall assessment of the extent to which competing brands may satisfy different moti-vational needs. At an early stage in any market's development, it is unlikely that several brands will be perceived as being equally able to satisfy the same motivational need. The added values here tend to be functional characteristics, reinforcing the positioning of what the brand *does*.

The augmented level

With more experience, buyers become more confident and experiment with other brands, seeking the best value and they begin to pay more attention to price. To maintain customer loyalty, and price premiums, marketers *augment* their brands, through the addition of further benefits, such as, for example, the inclusion of a self-diagnostic fault chip in washing machines. The chip was something that a less experienced user might perceive as having minimal value, but as they become more dependent on the brand, so they learn to appreciate the way it reduces delays due to the service engineer arriving with the right spare part. To assess what types of added values would enhance their brands at this stage, marketers should arrange for depth interviews to be undertaken amongst experienced users. They should be asked to talk about the problems they have with different brands and the sorts of ways in which they could be improved.

At the augmented stage, several brands may well come to be perceived as satisfying the same motivational needs. For example, Heineken, Skol and Carling Black Label all offer refreshment. So

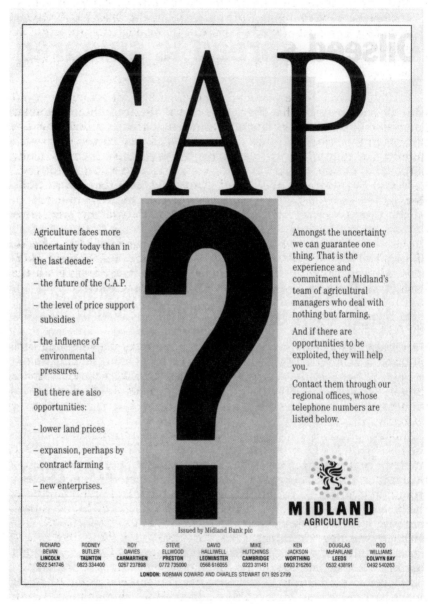

Exhibit 6.3 *Midland Bank present their agricultural division as a brand augmented by the experience gained from focusing solely on farming*

consumers focus on the *discriminating* factors. These may be functional features such as size, shape, colour, availability. Several different ways of positioning brands using functional discriminators are:

- With respect to use: 'once a day' for a pharmaceutical brand.
- With respect to the end user: Calpol for children, Anadin for adults.
- With respect to the competitor: the number two brand, Avis, trying to take share from Hertz, the brand leader through its campaign 'we try harder'.
- With respect to a specific attribute: the long life of Duracell Batteries.

Possibly an even more powerful *discriminator* is endowing the brand with a personality. The Ford Fiesta and Renault 5 are similar hatchbacks, which satisfy the motivational need for cost-effective town transport, but they also have unique brand personalities that differentiate them. For example, some might perceive the personality of the Ford Fiesta as a male, not very ambitious, but conscientious and hard working and who plays football on Saturdays. By contrast, the Renault 5 is a trendy young girl who enjoys being surrounded by people, likes to make decisions on the spur of the moment and reads *Cosmopolitan*.

In effect, at the *augmented* stage, buyers have narrowed down the list of suitable brands by considering those which match their *motivational* needs, then they differentiate between these brands on the basis of *discriminators* relevant to their particular lifestyles.

The potential level

Eventually, however, buyers and users come to regard such augmentation as a standard requirement for brands. To stop the augmented brand slipping back to the expected level, where buyers would be more interested in prices, the brand marketer needs to become more innovative and develop new added values to push the brand into the *potential* phase.

This is a much more challenging task, inhibited predominantly by the creativity of the brand's team and their financial resources. One way of identifying new added values for these highly experienced buyers is to map out the channels through which the brand passes, from manufacturer to end user. At each stage in this chain of events, the brand marketer needs to appreciate exactly how the brand is used and who is using it. A sample of these individuals coming in contact with the brand should be interviewed to assess their likes, dislikes and views about improvements. The opinions of factory floor workers are just as important as those of senior managers in the chain of events.

An example of a brand that was managed from the *augmented* to the *potential* level is American Airlines (AA). With deregulation in the American air travel market, the barriers to entry for new airlines were lowered. This resulted in new airlines increasing travellers' choice, along with more price competitive routes. As a brand, AA could have slipped to the expected level, competing against the others on price. Instead, it evaluated how people used its services and identified every point where it came into contact with customers. Based on this, it identified a few areas where it believed customers and consumers

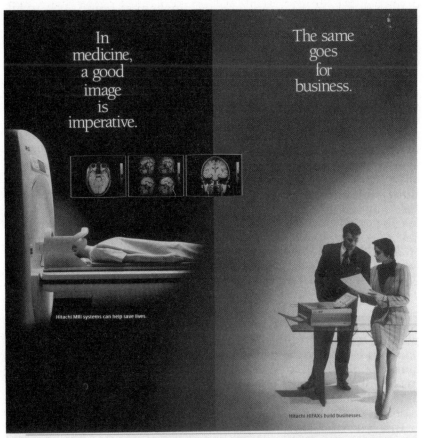

In medicine, a good image is imperative.

The same goes for business.

Hitachi MRI systems can help save lives.

Hitachi HIFAXs build businesses.

Many people think of Hitachi as a consumer electronics company. Which is true – to a point. We're also a technological leader in medicine. Business equipment. Science. Industry. Computers. Our 20,000 products include everything from TVs to image processing equipment. Such as facsimile machines and magnetic resonance imaging (MRI) systems.

Take MRI. It's the most significant advancement in diagnostic imaging since the X-ray. MRI enables doctors to detect problems early

on and to make more accurate diagnoses.

Hitachi is a world leader in high-resolution, compact MRI equipment. What's remarkable, however, is that MRI equipment only begins to tell the story of our commitment to medicine. Our involvement encompasses clinical analysers. Electron microscopes. X-ray CT scanners. And ultrasound equipment.

Chances are you already use Hitachi facsimile machines. You'd be in good company. Our unique technological advancements enable

business people to quickly and efficiently transmit super clear images. Even very small characters come out with a remarkable high degree of precision.

Taken together, Hitachi is a people company. Responding to the wants and needs of individuals everywhere.

And that's not an advertising image. That's a fact.

◉ HITACHI

Exhibit 6.4 *Hitachi promotes itself at the potential level as the firm that has extremely broad experience of displaying high quality images*

would welcome new added values. It undertook a review of its in-flight service and improved its quality. It recognized the need for being on time, both when departing and arriving, and, by assessing all of the events that influence flight operations, developed systems, resulting in it becoming the most punctual airline. The problem of overbooked seats was lessened through better information technology. They also developed far stronger relationships with travel agents, who were previously regarded as an evil necessity. A computerized booking system, Sabre, was specially developed for them. This automated the booking of tickets. Finally, it communicated all of these added values to its customers and consumers.

In the mature tea market, Tetley managed to push its brand to the potential level when in 1989 it launched round tea-bags. Both Tetley and the brand leader, PG Tips, are of an equally high quality, both being based on approximately 25 blends of tea. Previous marketing activity had been directed at satisfying consumers' motivational needs by differentiating brands along dimensions such as their ability to restore, revive and refresh. But, in addition to these functional characteristics, consumers also see teas as satisfying emotional needs through being comforting and soothing. It was the emotional needs that Tetley concentrated on. They discovered that consumers actually felt that round tea-bags were more appropriate emotional satisfiers, besides which they overcome the problem of square bags – dripping from the edges! Cynics were critical, arguing that large tea-bags facilitate infusion by allowing the tea to circulate. However, the change, supported by a £4.9m press and television campaign during 1990, helped the brand increase its market share by 25 per cent.

Eventually, competitors will follow with similar ideas and buyers will gain more confidence, switching between brands that they perceive as being similar. Yet again, the brand may slip back to the expected level unless the brand marketer recognizes that he must continually track buyers' views and be prepared to keep on improving his brand.

The problems with continually enhancing the brand is that the extra costs may not be recovered by increased sales, resulting in falling brand profitability, and there is the additional problem that competitors may soon find a way of copying the change. In such cases, an audit needs to be undertaken to evaluate whether the brand has a viable future. The audit needs to look at consumers' views, competitors' activities and the firm's long-term goals. If it is not thought viable to further enhance the brand, a different strategy for its future needs to be identified. This could entail selling the brand off, freezing further investment and reaping profits until a critical sales level had been reached, withdrawing the brand or becoming an own label supplier if there is sufficient trade interest.

The problem of competitors copying a brand can be better analysed if we consider the 'coding' or the building blocks that constitute the brand. For example, a restaurant owner may find that his restaurant is so successful that he wishes to open a second one and let one of his managers run it. To ensure that the new manager is effective, the owner needs to reveal all the codes that constitute the successful formula. On the other hand, he may wish to hold something back, for fear of the manager leaving with the formula, or of competitors copying it. Researchers have argued that successful brands are difficult to copy even if the nature of all the component parts is well understood, as long as secrecy is maintained about the manner in which these components are integrated. As a result of this, the owner should explain to the manager all the systems that support the restaurant, such as, types of menu, the pricing policy, staff recruitment, and so on. He need not insist on always being consulted when decisions are needed on operational issues, but the development of the restaurant's image or brand personality should be the sole responsibility of the owner. The brand personality is the unifying device that integrates the component parts and it is this that competitors find difficult to copy.

Protecting brands through trademark registration

By blending all of the assets constituting brands, marketers are able to develop brands which build goodwill between the brand producer and the consumer. As one advertising executive at Saatchi and Saatchi commented, 'Powerful brands are just like families. They persist through thick and thin'. The goodwill that Coca-Cola has built up over the years is such a valuable asset that if all its production facilities were destroyed, it could get adequate funds to rebuild these using the goodwill from the brand name as security. Likewise, even though Mars confectionery does not own property, hires its distribution vehicles and leases its machinery, to buy this firm would cost any potential acquirer hundreds of millions of pounds, since what is being bought is not the tangible assets, but also the goodwill and reputation from the Mars name. Consumers recognize the value of brands because, over the years, their unique pack designs have represented a commitment to maintaining key added values. In fact, it was once estimated that the distinctive design of all Campbell Soups was worth around £13m.

Unfortunately, though, the success of some brands has driven certain competitors to respond by developing counterfeits, that is to say, illegally produced look-alikes, which take advantage of the inherent goodwill in brand names. It has been estimated that the value of counterfeit goods in Europe was £30bn in 1989 and, with less stringent customs controls, is forecast to rise to £52bn in 1992. Some markets are particularly prone to illegal imitators. For example, 25 per cent of tapes worldwide are unauthorized copies.

Some counterfeiters have invested heavily in production facilities. For example, when Yves St Laurent unearthed one illegal copier and destroyed £11m of fake perfumes, they found production machinery valued at £33m. Unfortunately, with such large sums to be made from counterfeiting, more sophisticated production facilities are being built. Glaxo, for example, seized a consignment of 6000 counterfeit packets of Zantac in 1990 and were dismayed to discover that the packaging was so professionally copied that only under microscopes could any differences be noticed. Some examples of counterfeit brands are shown in Exhibit 6.5.

To reduce the scope for counterfeiters, marketers can register their trademarks, employ firms to track down copiers and devise more sophisticated packaging and batch-numbering processes. All of these enable brand owners to halt counterfeiters legally – until they find another way of circumventing the obstacles!

Marketers in the UK are normally advised to register their brands under the appropriate acts, for example, Trademarks Act (1938) and Copyright Designs and Patents Act (1989). If the registration process is followed, this provides legal protection against the copying of trademarks, such as words, logos, symbols and labels used to distinguish brands. Other legal routes have to be followed to gain protection in different parts of the world.

The legal environment is becoming more hostile to counterfeiters. For example, the European Customs Code enables customs officials to hold brands that infringe registered trademarks. Different countries, however, process legal complaints in different ways, and at different speeds. Italy is notorious for not bringing cases to court rapidly and some cases have taken around five years to be heard. In one Italian case, a judge refused to shut down a counterfeiter of silk scarves, since it was the largest local employer in a small town. The only way that the brand owner could maintain his brand quality was to grant the firm a licence to manufacture in return for a royalty!

Trademark registration can be professionally expedited using trademark agents. They would first check if anyone else has registered a particular trademark, avoiding expensive and embarrassing litigation. For example, the Kuwait Petroleum Company encountered stiff legal opposition from Duckmans over the use of the brand Q8, which was shown to infringe the QX8 trademark on fuels and oils.

There are a variety of reasons why some brand names cannot be registered. For example, brand names that are descriptive of the character or quality of the good, or that are deceptive, disparaging, confusing, or being a generic term, cannot be registered. When evaluating new brand names, legal advice has to be balanced against marketing needs. For example, lawyers argue that firms' existing trademarks are the most protectable legal option. When IBM first entered the personal computer market, it did not develop a new brand name. Instead, it launched the 'IBM PC'. Not only did it have sound legal protection, but also it deliberately wanted to take advantage of its image of being the most dependable computer manufacturer. In IBM's case, there was little danger of the brand's equity being diluted. However, as we discuss later in this chapter, there are cases where it is not appropriate to extend an existing brand name.

A balance also needs to be struck between the distinctiveness of the name and the extent to which it describes the goods that the brand

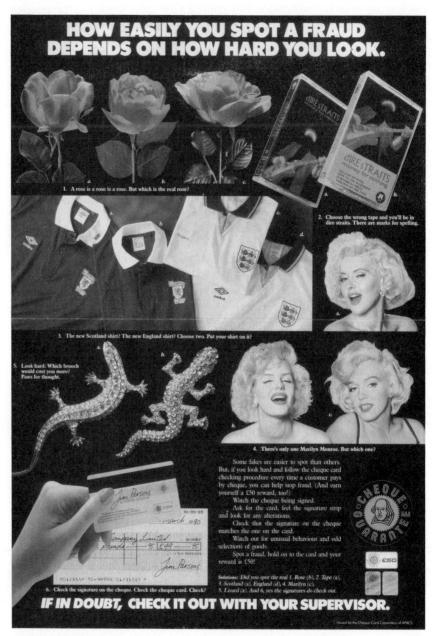

Exhibit 6.5   *Examples showing concern about counterfeit copies*

Exhibit 6.5 *(continued)*

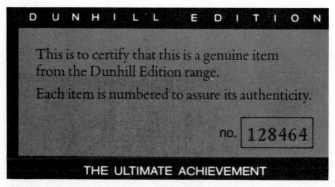

Exhibit 6.6   *Inside the box containing Dunhill After Shave, a certificate of authenticity is enclosed in an attempt to fight counterfeiters*

name stands for. The more it describes the goods, the more difficult it is to register it. PaperMate is a good example of a company getting the balance right between the brand name's communicability and its registrability. Late in the 1970's, it launched an erasable ballpoint pen in Europe, branded Replay. This was felt not to be so descriptive of the product, but it was protectable, yet the name was not so abstract that it did not need a large promotional budget to explain its benefit.

Once the trademark has been successfully registered, it should be used as soon as possible and implemented with care. If sufficient attention is not paid to promotional details, there is a danger of the brand name lapsing into a non-protectable generic term. In its advertising copy, the Otis Elevator Company did not insert a line, 'Escalator is a registered trademark of the Otis Elevator Company', and in a subsequent court case, the registration of its 'Escalator' trademark was cancelled.

To ensure that the brand name is not being infringed, some firms employ their staff to monitor retail activities. For example, Coca-Cola employees visit outlets that do not stock Coca-Cola and, without identifying themselves, they ask for a Coca-Cola. If they are served a drink which is clearly not Coca-Cola without any comment, a sample is sent for chemical analysis, and if it is not the actual brand, the outlet is asked to refrain from this action. Failure to comply results in legal action.

An alternative way of policing the brand is to use private investigators, such as Carratu International. Particularly when there is evidence of a very sophisticated channel being used by counterfeiters, as was the case in 1991 with Caterpillar parts, this is a very effective way of blocking imitators. Some firms are now so concerned about brand infringements, that detectives and legal costs are a significant expenditure. For example, 0.5 per cent of Givenchy's turnover is spent on this.

Some firms are trying to make the copying of their brands much harder. Glaxo started printing holograms on its packets of Zantac drugs to deter copiers, but it is only a matter of time before counterfeiters become more sophisticated. In some markets, such as car parts, it is much more difficult to apply an inexpensive security device.

Whilst counterfeiting is likely to pose a continuing threat to manufacturers, it is only one of the many challenges that face marketers, who must continuously devise added value strategies to succeed. Some of the other challenges are reviewed in the following section.

The challenges to brands

In order to develop the right sort of brand added values, brand marketers need to be aware of the environmental factors which cause problems. Some of these are:

The shift from strategy to tactics

With the increasing pressure to generate ever improving profitability, it is often considered to be a luxury for managers to develop long-term strategic plans. This is further exacerbated by short-term goal setting, which is frequently designed primarily for the convenience of The City.

A consequence of this is that organizations adopt a 'crisis management' attitude. This short-sightedness is dangerous, since successful brands have evolved through long-term commitments to brand support. Furthermore, it illustrates a rather naive managerial style, which is incapable of responding appropriately to crises. This can best be explained by asking: 'what is meant by a crisis?'. We argue that a crisis is a three-dimensional issue, consisting of the size of threat, awareness of the threat and the time to respond to the threat, as shown in Figure 6.2.

Through the use of this conceptualization, marketers can prioritize the crisis that their brands face. For example, there is a grave crisis when a brand faces a large threat, such as delisting by a major customer, had little warning that this was going to occur, since one of

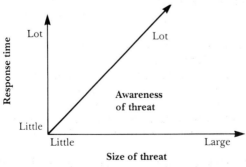

Figure 6.2 *The basis for understanding a crisis*

its competitors has just adopted a promotional drive to 'buy business', and has little time to respond – typically a few days before the account will close. By analysing each crisis using this conceptualization, marketers should be able to prioritize brand activities.

In addition, some marketers prefer to focus on just two of the crisis dimensions, since they feel these are more helpful when assessing how actions should be prioritized. Typically the two more useful dimensions are size of threat and time to respond to the threat. The value of these two dimensions can be appreciated from the matrix in Figure 6.3.

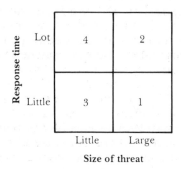

Figure 6.3   *Two of the crisis dimensions*

In quadrants 3 and 4 the size of threat is small and as such there is little urgency to act, regardless of response time. By contrast, quadrants 1 and 2 represent large threats and require a swift response. In particular, when faced with two different threats, the brand marketer should first deal with the one where there is less time to respond. The numbers in the quadrants represent the order in which actions should be taken.

The shift from advertising to promotions

Between 1982 and 1989, retail prices rose by 42 per cent, while media inflation (press and television) rose by 69 per cent. It is clearly becoming increasingly more expensive to launch new brands and there is a move away from advertising support to short-term promotions for existing brands.

The reality of this is best summarized by Broadbent's analogy: If a pilot cuts his plane's engines, believing it could cruise adequately without them (as indeed it would, for a while), one would question his sanity. When the plane subsequently goes into freefall and the engines are switched on, and then off several seconds later, because they were not making that much difference, he would be regarded as a suicidal maniac. There is an accepted view that advertising works in a similar manner by building up a 'stock' of brand goodwill in consumers' minds. This takes time, however. If advertising is subsequently stopped, there may be only a small reduction in sales for several months, while the stock of goodwill is depleting, but then there will be a rapid fall in sales. Furthermore, a disproportionately large spend is needed to raise a fallen brand back to its original position.

With such high advertising costs encountered in the launch of new brands, many brand marketers are questioning whether they have fully exploited the potential of their old brands before embarking on risky new brand development. There is increasing caution about new brand development. This can be appreciated from an analysis Tesco did of their top 100 lines. Only twelve of these were launched in the past ten years: only eighteen were launched in the past twenty years. Horlicks, which was launched in 1883, is a good example of old brand development. It was originally promoted as a warming food drink to help elderly people to sleep. In the 1970s, a marked reduction in sales was noted due to demographic changes, warmer homes and later eating. Rather than withdrawing the brand and following an expensive strategy of launching a new brand, Horlicks was successfully repositioned in the late 1970s to a much broader target market as the natural way to relax. The strategy resulted in a 63 per cent volume increase between 1976 and 1981. Some of the many examples of successful old brand development are Equitable Life with their focus on personal pensions and Lucozade, repositioned from being a health tonic for the sick to a refreshing energizer.

Retailers' names as brands

An examination of advertising spend during 1990 reveals that Tesco Stores was the most advertised brand (£26.3m), followed by McDonald's (£19.5m), Woolworth Stores (£16.3m) and Asda (£14.6m). The fifth most advertised brand was a manufacturer's brand (B&H Special Kingsize) with £14.3m support. Further examination shows that Unilever was the top advertising company, but its total spend of £83.1m was shared across 24 brands. In other words, retailers spent more money developing a clear proposition for their stores and their own brands than did any single manufacturer's brand. With virtually three-quarters of packaged grocery sales going through multiple retailers, the challenge to manufacturers from powerful retailers' own brands is indeed daunting. Furthermore, retailers such as Boots, Laura Ashley, Marks & Spencer and Sainsbury have a particularly innovative policy of developing new products under their own names.

The challenges of a Single Market

Pan-European buying groups are emerging with retailers forming alliances to source brands at the lowest possible price. For example, Argyll is collaborating with Casino in France and Ahold in The Netherlands to form the European Retail Alliance, accounting for 8 per cent of the European grocery market. In grocery retailing, manufacturers' brands will face increasing price pressures. In other product fields, however, the challenges may not be as great. For example, in the car market, cars still have to be tailored to specific markets – yellow headlights in France, catalytic exhausts for Germany and extra high ground clearance for Turkish potholes.

The 'Single Market' currently consists of a community speaking nine different languages with strong nationalistic preferences. Eventually, there will be a more homogeneous community, as consumers recognize the advantages of powerful Euro-brands such as American Express, Kellogg's, Marlboro, Kodak, IBM, Sony and Nescafe. More emphasis on symbolism will help overcome linguistic differences within the Single Market. Examples are: the distinctive shape of Jiff Lemon; the Perrier bottle; the Marlboro man; the VW badge. It is more likely that brands will be developed at the outset to appeal to consumers in many different countries. For example, Chee-tos, a cheese flavoured snack from PepsiCo was developed and tested in the USA and subsequently extended to fifteen further countries with little change.

Opportunities from technology

Brand marketers are now more able to take advantage of technology to gain a competitive advantage through time. Technology is already reducing the lead time needed to respond rapidly to changing customer needs and minimizing any delays in the supply chain. General Motors in the USA, for example, implemented a computer-controlled system, 'Saturn', which significantly reduced the order-delivery time. Furthermore, as a result of the dealer inputting customers' requirements for colour, trim and other accessories, the system is able to ensure not only that cars are tailored to customers' needs, but also that they are delivered more promptly. Another example is the way home builders in Japan use rapid response to customer needs to differentiate themselves. Potential home-buyers visit estate agents and describe their ideal home. Equipped with a unique CAD-CAM program, the agent sketches a design on a computer screen in front of the prospective purchaser. The program instantly tells the cost of building the new home, and if this is too high, it enables the home dimensions to be scaled down until an acceptable price is reached. If the purchaser then wishes to buy the new home, the agent confirms this in the computer program and the builder usually offers completion 6 weeks later.

To succeed, marketers are going to have to use technology to stay ahead of competitors. For example, global brand manufacturers, such as Unilever, have well-conceived marketing intelligence systems that rapidly inform relevant divisions in different continents of any new competitive launches in any part of the world. In some markets it is now realistic to anticipate responses to new brand launches within a week – in the financial services sector it is only a matter of hours.

With new technology, brand marketers are also likely to be served by better marketing intelligence systems. The vast amounts of data in company databanks will be filtered so that decision makers will be presented with key information to help formulate and evaluate brand strategies. The emphasis will be on smaller *quantity*, but higher *quality* information. British Home Stores is a good example of an organization that is developing strategic marketing information systems. Using scanning systems at point of sale, its buyers are fed with critical sales information and by having computerized production information from all their suppliers, along with financial information, they are quickly able to respond to market changes.

New technologies such as computers, fax machines, flexible factories and rapid distribution should enable brand marketers to become more effective at micromarketing. Rather than having to dilute marketing resources by directing campaigns at broad consumer groups, information technology is enabling marketers to target their activities more accurately. With the advent of geodemographic segmentation systems, such as ACORN, consumers' buying behaviour can be analysed at the level of groups as small as 150 households. Powerful computers, linked in with good marketing research data, enable marketers to identify new brand opportunities that would have previously been dismissed on the grounds that these small groups could not be economically targeted.

In the biotechnology sphere, Genetech, a company acquired by Roche, helped its brands grow through a deliberate policy of encouraging everyone to take advantage of technology. For example, its sales representatives were all issued with laptop computers, initially to send and receive electronic mail, file reports and place orders. However, it was quickly realized how these could give the firm a competitive advantage by transforming their sales staff into marketing consultants. Doctors valued the way that the reps used their laptops to access the latest medical articles and technical reports and in so doing, could keep them up to date. When unable to answer complex medical questions, the reps also used their laptops to send questions through electronic mail to their internal specialists and rapidly respond to doctors' requests.

More sophisticated buyers

In business to business marketing, there is already an emphasis on bringing together individuals from different departments to evaluate suppliers' new brands. As interdepartmental barriers break down even more, sellers are going to face increasingly sophisticated buyers who are served by better information systems enabling them to play off brand suppliers against each other.

Consumers themselves are also becoming more confident and sophisticated. They expect higher standards from brands and appreciate brands that deliver real values. But the values being sought are not just functional ones. In fact, in an ever changing and increasingly turbulent environment, they seem to prefer consistent brand personalities which provide some stability and help them better understand their social environments.

Consumers are becoming much more marketing literate and are increasingly critical of advertising. None the less, the danger for some brands is that advertisers make assumptions about consumers' involvement with advertisements and exceedingly 'clever' approaches are developed. For example, recently there has been a move towards cross-fertilizing advertising ideas and blending different campaigns together. Polo mints used the Perrier approach in the 'Refreshing Poleau' advertisement, using the slogan, 'The mint with the heaule', while Canon adopted the slogan 'Some things in life are as reliable as a Volkswagen'. There is a danger that, without a good appreciation of consumers' perceptions, weaker brands may well lose out with these clever approaches.

The growth of the company brand

With media costs inhibiting individual brand advertising, some firms are putting more emphasis on corporate branding, stressing the company as the brand. In this way functional aspects of brands can be increasingly augmented by corporate images, enabling consumers to select brands through an assessment of the personalities of competing firms.

Conclusions

Brands succeed because they have real added values which are relevant to the target market and which the market welcomes. The longer it takes competitors to develop an equivalent, if not better, added value, the longer the brand has to capitalize on the goodwill it builds with customers and consumers. Added values are not about superficial, one-off issues such as a smile or the greeting, 'have a nice day'. Instead, they are about integrating relevant ideas into every point of contact the brand has with consumers. So, for the car hire company differentiating itself through customer concern, it means such things as checking each car before the hirer is given the keys, recruiting staff with a genuine interest in consumers, training staff, manning a twenty-four-hour breakdown recovery service and making car reservations as simple as possible. All aspects of the brand's assets are employed to communicate rapidly the point of difference from competition, so that the consumer instantly associates the brand with functional reliability, and 'no hassle' administration, reinforcing the car hire service as a low risk event that only the firm with this specific logo can provide.

One of the problems marketers face is finding added values which are relevant to the brand's stage of development. Even if the marketer erroneously thinks he has a commodity, it can still be developed as a brand through the way it is offered to consumers. The sorts of added values appropriate for both young and mature brands, can be identified by considering a brand as growing from solely being a generic product, to being a product surrounded by an expected, an augmented and a potential layer. The generic product is the commodity form which enables firms to compete.

The expected brand represents the minimum criteria needed for purchasers to perceive sufficient added value to warrant a price premium in excess of the commodity costs of producing the brand. Here the added values tend to be functional, reinforcing what the brand can do. For example, a new type of petrol could be positioned as kind to the environment, or as being able to help cars develop more power. As consumers gain more experience they expect more from competing brands. To satisfy this, brands are augmented with added values that new consumers would not necessarily appreciate. A strong brand personality can be an effective added value at this stage. Over time though, competitive activity and consumers' variety-seeking behaviour necessitates new added values to push the brand to the potential level. Once at the potential level, a time will be reached when consumers become disenchanted with the brand. At this stage, an audit is needed to evaluate whether the brand has come to the end of its useful life, or whether there is scope for the future through introducing a new added value.

If the brand augmentation is successful, competitors may try to develop similar versions, so marketers need to protect their brands against blatant imitators. Trademark registration provides a legal route to protection, but necessitates continual vigilance to discover the first signs of counterfeiting.

Brands face other challenges, however, besides those of imitators, so marketers need to anticipate these new challenges. In this respect, some of the issues that need to be addressed are:

- Resisting the temptation of short-term tactical thinking.
- Adopting a commitment to continually communicating brand benefits.
- Recognizing the support retailers are placing behind their own brands.
- Developing strategies to capitalize on the opportunities of the Single Market.
- Integrating new technologies.
- Responding to more sophisticated buyers.
- Building on the assets of the company brand.

Marketing action checklist

To help clarify the direction of future marketing activity, it is recommended that the following exercises are undertaken:

1 List the added values you believe your brands have. Evaluate the strength of these added values by undertaking interviews with your customers and consumers to assess how relevant and unique they are, and how much people appreciate these values compared with those of your competitors.

2 Scan your company brochures and check whether you use very broad terms to describe your brands' added values. For example, 'quality', 'dependable', 'caring'. If you have some of these all-encompassing added value terms, get your team together and clarify amongst yourselves what you mean. Once you have reached a consensus, evaluate the strength of these added values and incorporate the most appropriate new added values in your brochures.

3 Map out all the main groups of people who are involved with each brand as they evolve from raw material entering the factory, right through to the point of consumption. Check the extent to which each group knows about each brand's added values. Has any of these groups ever been asked for their comments about how their task could be changed to better contribute to the brand's added values? Do the tasks of all of these groups contribute to the brand's added values?

4 For each of your brands, assess the extent to which your marketing programme incorporates these added values in order to:

   a   differentiate you from competition;
   b   satisfy customers' functional and emotional needs:
   c   reduce customers' perceptions of risk;
   d   aid rapid selection;
   e   be backed by a registered trademark.

   If your assessment shows an excessive reliance on only one of these points, consider the relevance of developing a more balanced programme.

5 If there is a view in your firm that you are competing in a commodity market, evaluate the differing needs of the channels that your brand passes through and consider ways of tailoring your offerings to better satisfy the needs of each group.

6 For each of your brands, identify from the model shown in Figure 6.1 the level on which each brand is competing. Have you a clear view about the motivational needs that your brands satisfy and the discriminators people use to differentiate between you and your competitors? How have each brand's added values developed? What plans do you have to enhance your brands when customers become more demanding and competition becomes more intense?

7 What systems do you have to identify when another firm is illegally copying your brand?

8 With your colleagues, go through the 'challenges to brands' section of this chapter and for each of the challenges, consider the implications for your brands and identify what types of actions are most appropriate.

References and further reading

Anon (1990). Coke's kudos. *The Economist*, 15 Sept., p. 120.

Bidlake S. (1989). Reaching across the seas. *Marketing*, 5 Oct., pp. 31–2.

Bidlake S. (1990). Levi's changes course for 90's. *Marketing*, 7 June, p. 9.

Bidlake S. (1991). Coca-Cola changes ad strategy to bolster its spin-off brands. *Marketing*, 7 Feb., p. 4.

Blois K. (1990). Product augmentation and competitive advantage. In *Proceedings of the 19th annual conference of the European Marketing Academy* (Muhlbacher H., Jochum C., eds). Innsbruck: EMAC.

Brownlie D. (1988). Protecting marketing intelligence: the role of trademarks. *Marketing Intelligence and Planning*, **6**, (4), 21–6.

Cohen D. (1986). Trademark strategy. *Journal of Marketing*, **50**, (Jan.), 61–74.

Davidson H. (1987). *Offensive Marketing*. Harmondsworth: Penguin Books.

de Chernatony L., McWilliam G. (1989). The varying nature of brands as assets: theory and practice compared. *International Journal of Advertising*, **8**, (4), 339–49.

Doyle P. (1989). Building successful brands: the strategic options. *Journal of Marketing Management*, **5**, (1), 77–95.

Drucker P. (1990). *The new realities*. London: Mandarin Paperbacks.

Hemnes T. (1987). Perspectives of a trademark attorney on the branding of innovative products. *Journal of Product Innovation*, **4**, 217–24.

Johnson M. (1991). Brewing up an all round alternative. *Marketing*, 2 May, p. 19.

King S. (1991). Brand-building in the 1990s. *Journal of Marketing Management*, **7**, (1), 3–13.

Leadbeater C. (1991). Moles unearth spare part scam. *Financial Times*, 14 March, p. 1.

Levitt T. (1980). Marketing success through differentiation of anything. *Harvard Business Review*, Jan.–Feb., 83–91.

McKenna R. (1991). Marketing is everything. *Harvard Business Review*, Jan.–Feb., 65–79.

Midgley D. (1990). World brand leaders. *Campaign*, 21 Nov., pp. 39–40.

Mitchell A. (1990). Back to basics. *Marketing*, 26 July, pp. 26–7.

Peters T., Austin N. (1985). *A Passion for Excellence*. Glasgow: William Collins Sons & Co.

Porter M. (1985). *Competitive Advantage*. New York: Macmillan.

Sambrook C. (1991). The top 500 brands. *Marketing*, **7**, Mar., pp. 27–33.

Thomas T. (1990). A new golden gate for great pretenders. *The European*, 19 Oct., p. 24.

7 Retailer issues in branding

Summary

The purpose of this chapter is to look at the way branding is influenced by retailers. It opens by reviewing the changing nature of own labels, examines the resources retailers are using to back their quality positioning and reviews the way information technology presents further opportunities for own label profitability. It discusses the launch of generics and clarifies why this secondary own label tier failed. The shift in the balance of power from manufacturers to retailers is documented and the response of weak and strong brand manufacturers is compared. Brand manufacturer strategies appropriate for convenience and non-convenience retailer types are reviewed. The expansion of retailers and manufacturers across Europe is considered and the problems of finding pan-European positionings discussed. The issues manufacturers should consider before working on own labels are reviewed along with the criteria retailers use to assess potential own label suppliers. The brand strength–distributor attractiveness matrix is presented as a device to prioritize the effort behind different brands being sold through specific major accounts.

Brands as a sign of ownership

Retailers' interest in own labels, stemmed originally from being able to circumvent resale price maintenance (RPM) and offer a lower priced range of goods to compete against manufacturers' brands. Up until 1964, when RPM was abolished, retailers' pricing policy had to follow manufacturers' stipulations about selling prices. By commissioning manufacturers to produce and pack products to their own specification, retailers were able to sell their own labels cheaper than manufacturers' brands.

The era of own labels being positioned primarily as a cheap alternative to manufacturers' brands lasted from the turn of this century up until the mid 1970s. One of the ways retailers achieved a price advantage was to accept quality levels lower than those normally associated ·with manufacturers' brands. Consumers were content to accept this, since they were trading off quality frills against price savings.

During the 1960s, multiple retailers began to take advantage of the economies of scale that could be achieved by owning even more stores. Particularly in the grocery retailing sector, a few companies emerged, such as Sainsbury's and Tesco, who controlled an increasingly large number of stores. Multiple retailers, that is those owning ten or more outlets, became more powerful. For example, in 1961 only 27 per cent of grocery products were sold through multiple retailers. By 1975 this had risen to 49 per cent.

Ironically in their quest for growth, multiples saw that further profit opportunities could be achieved by reducing the number of stores, but each store remaining being of a much larger size. The advent of superstore retailing, where stores in excess of 25 000 square feet became increasingly common during the 1980s, enabled retailers to capitalize further on the opportunities presented through economies of scale. For example, in 1980 there were 238 grocery superstores. By 1990 this had grown to 644. Superstores strengthened the position of the multiple sector, which accounted for 75 per cent of packaged grocery sales by 1990.

As multiple retailers became more professional in managing their stores, so they began to realize the value of own labels in reinforcing their positioning. Up until the 1970s own labels were generally used to help communicate a store's low prices proposition. However, multiple retailers shifted away from competing against each other just on price, and instead began to emphasize quality and service. This became increasingly apparent as more Superstores were opened with much wider product ranges. With a change in retailer positioning came a change in own label emphasis. Retailers became more concerned with the quality of their own labels, which were no longer 'cheap and cheerful' alternatives to quality brands. Instead, higher quality standards were stipulated in own label briefs. Advertising strategies were also prepared, aimed at refreshing own labels' personalities and giving them a quality element.

With new, well-conceived identities for stores and own labels, consumers began to recognize and appreciate the distinctive qualities and personalities of own labels. This can be seen from the following quotes from a consumer research study. To assess brand personalities, respondents were asked to describe the sort of person each of the own labels would be if they came alive. As is apparent from the quotes, these own labels have very strong brand personalities

I'm classy. I'm confident, I'm smart enough to put on the dinner table. I ape no one and I broadcast a simple message: 'I'm a classic'.

Waitrose Tartar Sauce

You feel comfortable with me. I don't have to be flash because you trust me. I'm Sainsburys and this is a packet of stuffing mix. Enough said.
                                        Sainsburys Sage and Onion Stuffing Mix

In 1961, when multiple grocery retailers accounted for 27 per cent of packaged grocery sales, own labels were generally 20 per cent cheaper than manufacturers' brands, but were of a *poorer* quality level. By 1989, with multiple retailers controlling 74 per cent of packaged

Exhibit 7.1   *An example of the premium positioning for Sainsbury's own labels*

grocery sales, own labels are of an *equivalent*, if not *better* quality level than manufacturers' brands, yet offering a 10 per cent price advantage. Grocery multiple retailers are increasingly setting high standards for the quality of own labels. Some are only prepared to launch a new own label if it at least matches, and preferably exceeds, the brand leader in consumer product testing.

This change in own labels, and manufacturer brands, particularly in packaged groceries, is shown in Figure 7.1. With some manufacturers feeling the squeeze of retailer expansion, they cut back on their quality standards. For example, one study was critical of the way that some ice cream manufacturers had increased air content in their brands to cut costs in meeting the demands of retailers. Also, more manufacturers began to compete on price, while in some instances retailers increased the prices of their own labels. In fact, in some product fields, such as fresh fruit juice, many own labels are more expensive than manufacturers' brands.

Figure 7.1 *The changing nature of brands and own labels*

Own labels are becoming increasingly popular. An estimate by Euromonitor indicates that in 1980 own labels accounted for 17 per cent of all retail sales and by 1988 this had grown to 23 per cent, with a forecast of 27 per cent by 1992. Consumers have become much more confident using own labels and are now proud to display them. For example, in one study, we came across a consumer who used to fill a branded bottle of whisky with a retailer's own label whisky and poured this when his less discerning visitors asked for whisky. With his increased respect for own labels, however, he now has the retailer's own label whisky on display when entertaining friends.

The backing behind own label

Retailers in many sectors are committed to growing their own labels. They are using *promotional activity* to communicate their high quality levels and to reinforce their 'brand' personalities. In 1990, as Table 7.1 indicates, Unilever was the company with the largest advertising support behind its brands. It spent £83.1m, but this backed twenty-four different brands. By contrast, Tesco Stores was the ninth biggest advertiser, with £26.3m, all being used to promote *the* umbrella Tesco name.

Table 7.1   *Top ten advertisers in 1990*

Company	Media spend	Number of brands advertised
Unilever	£83.1m	24
Procter & Gamble	£71.4m	18
Mars	£48.0m	12
Kelloggs	£47.3m	11
Kingfisher	£44.7m	4
Philip Morris/Kraft Foods	£34.5m	10
Ford	£30.2m	7
Gallaher	£29.6m	3
Tesco Stores	£26.3m	1
British Telecom	£25.1m	4

Source: *Marketing*, 7 March, 1991 p. 27.

Table 7.2   *Top ten advertised brands in 1990*

Brand	Media spend
Tesco Stores	£26.3m
Regional Electricity Company Share Offer	£19.5m
McDonald's	£16.9m
Woolworth Stores	£16.3m
Asda	£14.6m
Benson & Hedges Special Kingsize Filter	£14.3m
B&Q	£14.0m
British Satellite Broadcasting	£13.8m
Whiskas Supermeat	£12.8m
MFI Store/Hygena	£12.7m

Source: *Marketing*, 7 March, 1991 p. 27.

Further evidence of the support retailers are putting behind their own labels is shown in an examination of the 'top ten' advertised brands. As Table 7.2 shows, six of these are in fact retailers, many of whom have a strong commitment to own labels.

The commitment behind good value own label is apparent, both in the tight *product specifications* given to manufacturers and in the considerable effort invested in identifying and evaluating potential own label producers. Some retailers have significant R&D departments which undertake preliminary product development research prior to briefing potential producers. For example, at Marks & Spencer there are over 200 people working in its food R&D laboratories.

In terms of striving for higher quality standards and communicating these to consumers, Safeway launched its 'Refund & Replace' promotion in 1991. To communicate their backing to higher quality

Exhibit 7.2   *An example of the innnovative range expansion from Sainsbury's*

levels for own labels, they erected posters in their stores stating that if their consumers are not completely satisfied with their own label, they will be offered a refund and replacement. This was not just for damaged goods, but for perfectly packaged groceries. The guarantees were aimed at encouraging consumer loyalty, stimulating more adventurous shopping and trial purchases of new products.

Retailers are responsive to changing consumer needs and have *innovative own label* programmes which rapidly take advantage of market opportunities. The fact that they are in direct contact with the consumer no doubt gives them a slight advantage over manufacturers in identifying new trends. A good example of innovative own label development was Tesco's launch of chlorine-free own label paper products. They became aware of increasing consumer interest in environmentally friendly, 'green' products. A major market research programme was undertaken which identified different consumer groups, such as:

- 'Bright Greens' who are very concerned about the damage being done to the environment and who actively campaign for green products.
- 'Light Greens' who, as mothers of young children, are aware of the damage being done to the environment and are worried about whether food is safe for their children.
- 'Hints of Green' are well-off people, probably with two cars, aware of environmental issues, but not quite sure about what role they should play in environmental protection.
- 'Turquoise' are rural people keen on preserving their way of life who like the countryside the way it is.

The study showed that 67 per cent of people were prepared to pay more for having environmentally friendly products. With all these findings, they started to work on launching their own range of green products, under the banner 'Tesco cares'. For example, to compete against Ark Washing Powder they had their own phosphate-free product.

While developing their new 'green' range, a *World in Action* television documentary was broadcast. This showed that bleaching paper with chlorine to make it white can leave small traces of the deadly dioxin chemical. Peaudouce nappies were featured showing how they had to be withdrawn and relaunched with a safer creamy coloured nappy, bleached with peroxide.

Shortly after this programme, Tesco received lots of letters from worried consumers, asking if chlorine bleaching was being used. They quickly sensed the market's awareness of the issue and cut short a market research programme, and instead launched their own brand of non-chlorine-bleached toilet paper. To find a pulp mill that didn't use chlorine bleaching, Tesco technologists visited numerous mills throughout Europe, eventually awarding the contract to a firm in Sweden.

BACKGROUND

For many years, Tesco has shown a responsibility towards the environment. More recently it has been at the forefront of environmental initiatives.

In January 1989, Tesco Cares was launched to help address issues current at that time. It involved all areas of our business and included not only products, but also giving away information in simply explained, free leaflets. These leaflets are in all our stores and are helpful for customers when deciding which products to buy.

Today, more is known about the problems that face the environment. So we can now make products which have even less of an impact on it. We can also give more detailed information to our customers.

GREEN CHOICE
The Brand

All Tesco products are always of the highest quality. For the Green Choice range this means it must also have much less of an impact on the world around us. This applies before, during and after we use these products.

In order to make sure that this is the case, we have looked at six of the main environmental issues: Global Warming, Ozone Depletion, Air Pollution, Waste Disposal, Land Pollution and Water Pollution. With these in mind, we have set out four aims that must be applied to each Green Choice product.

 Reduce: The amount of raw materials and the volume of packaging must be reduced. Only vital ingredients and packaging will be allowed.

 Recycle: Packaging should be recyclable. Where fitting, products and packaging should be made from material that has already been recycled.

 Reuse: Where it is practical, packaging will be made to be either reusable or refillable.

 Replace: Materials that could have a harmful effect on the environment are to be removed. Any from non-renewable resources should be replaced where possible.

ACTION ON THE ISSUES
Global Warming and Ozone Depletion

When most types of energy are used, for example in manufacturing or running a car or lorry, carbon dioxide is released into the atmosphere. It then adds to the 'Greenhouse Effect' and leads to global warming.

CFCs (Chlorofluorocarbons) are used in aerosols, as well as in foam packaging and fridges. They present a twofold problem because they add to the 'Greenhouse Effect' and also damage the ozone layer.

We therefore aim to reduce the total amount of energy that we use. Cutting down on the number of raw materials in a product or on the amount of packaging, both save energy in manufacturing. Concentrated products save energy in transport.

We are also dedicated to the elimination of CFCs and other harmful gases.

♥ Green Choice products contain only the ingredients that are vital to make them work properly. This reduces the use of energy and releases of gas into the environment.

♥ As far as possible, Green Choice paper products will be made entirely out of recycled material, ideally using low grade waste such as newspapers. Using recycled rather than raw materials makes a very large energy saving.

♥ We will use the least amount of packaging for Green Choice products. Where fitting, some recycled content will be added; again this reduces the amount of energy used.

♥ We will strive to use methods that need the least amount of energy to make Green Choice products.

♥ We have removed CFCs in all Tesco own brand aerosol products. Where we can, we will only use packaging that is produced without CFCs.

Air Pollution

Whenever anything burns, such as the coal or oil used to make electricity or the petrol used in motor cars, polluting gases are given off into the atmosphere. These gases can then return to earth as acid rain. They can also cause many other problems such as smog.

We therefore aim to reduce our use of energy; chiefly the use of electricity and fuel.

Since saving energy also helps reduce global warming, the five actions listed above also cut air pollution.

Waste Disposal and Land Pollution

When products are finished, the packaging is usually thrown away. Firstly, this creates problems of where to put it, as landfill sites are filling up. Then even once it is buried it causes problems of pollution as it slowly rots.

We are committed to recycling waste in order to reduce the amount going to landfill.

♥ Where it is fitting, we will use recycled materials in both Green Choice paper goods and packaging.

♥ We will produce refill packs for many products. These use less material and take up less space when they are empty, than the standard pack.

♥ We will aim to use the least amount of packaging material for Green Choice products. We will also use the thinnest material that still ensures product safety.

♥ We will make sure that Green Choice containers and lids/caps are made from compatible materials. This makes future recycling easier. We will also label this packaging with details of its recyclability.

♥ We will only allow pump action sprays for Green Choice products. This is because they do not contain the gases that are used in aerosols.

♥ We will make sure, where we can, that Green Choice products are transported in recycled board display trays or boxes. Trials are currently taking place to recycle the shrink wrap used around the products whilst in transit.

Water Pollution

Non biodegradable ingredients in products and some of the chemicals used in manufacturing can cause problems of pollution in our streams and rivers. We aim to reduce water pollution and also to dispose safely of any waste that could be harmful.

♥ Only biodegradable surfactants (washing agents) will be used in Tesco products.
♥ All Green Choice products will be phosphate-free.
♥ We will only use non-chlorine bleached pulp in Green Choice products.

OTHER PRODUCTS AND INITIATIVES

The principles behind Green Choice are not only restricted to Green Choice brand products.

Throughout our business, products and practices are under review. Hundreds of energy saving initiatives are being taken; they range from the development of a new lighting system which greatly cuts energy use, to the provision of recycling centres at almost all our stores.

We have also made changes to many of our standard products. Changes so small that you won't even notice them, like reducing the thickness of film wrapping around our toilet tissue or making lighter bottles for household products. Refill packs are starting to appear for many products and, where possible, cardboard packaging is made from recycled board.

THE FUTURE

GREEN CHOICE brand products are already on sale in our Household Department and the range is now being extended to include toiletries. Research is always taking place to develop more Green Choice products and we will look for areas where environmental improvements can be made on all Tesco products.

 For further information, please contact:
Customer Services, Tesco Stores Ltd, P.O. Box 18, Delamare Road, Cheshunt, Herts EN8 9SL

TESCO

The Tesco New Quality Initiative

GREEN CHOICE

♡ Printed on Recycled Paper

Exhibit 7.3 *As part of its innovative own label development programme, Tesco brochures promote their commitment to protecting the environment. (© Tesco Stores Ltd)*

Retailers have stringent standards about own label *pack designs*, insisting that they not only communicate the characteristics of the individual line, but also reinforce their store's image. To ensure consistency in design, the major retailers, who typically may be handling 200 pack design projects a year, prefer to have a small core group of design consultancies. In the past, it was not unusual to have numerous agencies pitching for different design projects. Now, there is an emphasis on long-term relationships with just a few designers. For example, Safeway uses four design consultancies who are virtually an integral part of the organization. As they have worked for Safeway for a long time, they are finely tuned to their own label needs. Often, the retailer will work with its designers in establishing a design manual, as Texas Homecare have done. This provides guidelines about different design procedures and ensures long-term consistency.

In the 1970s, when retailers fought on a low price proposition, their own label packaging was functional and stark. Graphics did little more than identify the name of the store and convey an impression of low cost. Today, retailers recognize the 'silent persuader' value of own label packaging. The basic bottle containing beer now has a gold label on it and a design that implies the retailer is a specialist in the beer sector. The pack satisfies the functional requirements of being easy to carry and enables the beer to be easily poured, while at the same time promoting its message of quality. Some own label designs, particularly those from Tesco, have made many manufacturers re-think their design policy. In the late 1980s, it was not uncommon for design consultancies to be asked 'Have you seen what Tesco has done? We think we should be doing something similar.'

Quite clearly, retailers are using well-tried branding techniques to develop quality propositions for their own labels. They have devised well-conceived personalities for their own label ranges that support the image of their stores. They are using innovative advertising campaigns which memorably reinforce their positioning. In view of the way that they are developing their 'brands', we believe it is misleading to call them own labels. A more appropriate term is 'retailers' brands'.

More profitable own labels through information technology

There is evidence of multiple retailers becoming more committed to the use of information technology to increase profitability. With more brands being bar coded, retailers are able to take advantage of laser scanning at point of purchase. It allows them to adjust their product mix rapidly to reflect changes in buyer behaviour and to control stock more effectively. More recently, industry committees have started to agree common standards which allow manufacturers' and retailers' computers to communicate directly with each other. Electronic Data Interchange (EDI) is becoming more common. For example, by August 1991 over 500 of Tesco's main suppliers were using the

Tradanet EDI system. Orders can be electronically transmitted, as can invoices, saving the effort of trying to match up which invoices relate to which stores. The average cost of processing an order and its invoice is halved and the typical document matching error rate is reduced from 14 per cent to 2 per cent.

Using EDI, retailers are able to share their forecasts with manufacturers to become more efficient. At Tesco, suppliers have access to the rolling thirteen-week forecast system, enabling them to receive provisional orders a week ahead of the supply date, by day and by individual Tesco depot. In the early 1980s the sharing of sales data and forecasts was unheard of, but retailers now recognize that as own label business grows, more information needs to be shared.

EDI is being used in many different sectors. For example, in grocery, clothing, DIY and pharmaceutical retailing, in the automotive industry and in the insurance sector. It is highly likely that EDI will become the preferred method of trading during the 1990s, reducing costs and increasing customer service. With a considerable amount of retailer interest in EDI, own labels can grasp a further opportunity to become even more profitable.

The arrival and demise of generics

As was briefly discussed in Chapter 2, some retailers in the 1970s and 1980s experimented with a second tier in own labels – generics. Thinking that consumers were sceptical of the frills associated with some brands and that they would be more receptive to an even lower price proposition, particularly in a worsening economic climate, generic ranges were launched in grocery and DIY sectors. Generics are products distinguishable by their basic and plain packaging. Primary emphasis is given to the contents, rather than to any distinguishing retail chain name.

Carrefour in France pioneered this route in 1976 with its Produits Libres, and was quickly followed by Promede's Produits Blancs, Paridoc's Produits Familiaux and Euromarche's Produits Orange. In Germany, Carrefour, Deutsche Supermarkt and the Co-op encountered problems of poor quality perceptions, due to the low prices. In Switzerland, where there is a significant own label presence and consumers are primarily concerned about quality, generics had little success.

In the UK, as Table 2.1 showed, several retailers experimented with generics. Some were very committed to the concept, such as Fine Fare. Others, notably Tesco, were less certain, particularly as this conflicted with their move to shift their store's positioning up-market.

The problem was that a cheaper range was being introduced, with a quality level inferior to that of own labels. Consumers had previously been experiencing improvements in quality and service and were confused by the return of the 'pile it high, sell it cheap' era.

Furthermore, what had happened was that retailers had not launched a unique, stand-alone range. Instead, they had created a secondary own label range, perceived by consumers as an alternative to the current own label range.

The true generic concept had not been implemented. By definition, generics have no promotional backing nor any distinctive labelling. Yet, their launch was heralded by a considerable promotional spend. For example, during 1977, Carrefour spent 10m French Francs promoting generics, compared with Euromarche's 6m French Francs. A not insignificant effort was devoted to pack designs, which, while less sophisticated than conventional own labels, still clearly linked each range with a specific store. In particular, Fine Fare's bright yellow packs with black print resulted in a range which was very prominent on the shelves and which was quickly recognized as 'Fine Fare's house colours'.

As consumers began to think of generics as an extension of own labels, so they switched from the higher margin own labels to the lower margin generics. This was contrary to retailers' hopes that generics would take sales from manufacturers' brands. Retailers saw generics weakening their overall profitability and tarnishing the quality image that they were striving for. They had misjudged consumers' needs. Low prices are no longer the prime reason driving choice. Instead, consumers, as experienced buyers, are seeking value for money – rather than low prices – along with a cluster of added values.

The increasingly powerful retailer

The past thirty years have seen a swing in the balance of power from manufacturer to retailer. The early 1960s saw a boom in retailing, due to such issues as relaxation of building controls, the success of self-service and more professional management, who identified smaller retailers ripe for acquisition. The abolition of resale price maintenance in 1964 gave a further boost to retailers, who were freed from the pricing stipulations of brand suppliers. As evidence of retailer power, one study estimated that in 1960, 80 per cent of the grocery market was controlled by 1621 buying points, yet by 1970 only 647 buying points controlled 80 per cent of the grocery market.

Retailers became more efficient through centralized buying and centralized warehousing. They shut their smaller stores and opened a smaller number of stores, all of much larger selling areas. For example, between 1971 and 1979, the number of multiple grocers' stores fell by approximately 5000 outlets, yet this sector's selling area increased from 21.9 to 27.6 million square feet. Part of their increased profitability was passed on to consumers in the form of cheaper prices, further enhancing their attractiveness to consumers. By 1986, multiple chains across all sectors of retailing accounted for 59 per cent of sales. The grocery sector is characterized by particularly powerful multiple retailers. For example, Nielsen estimates showed that in 1987, 60 per cent of packaged grocery sales were accounted for by five retailers.

The reasons for the increasing concentration of multiple retailers

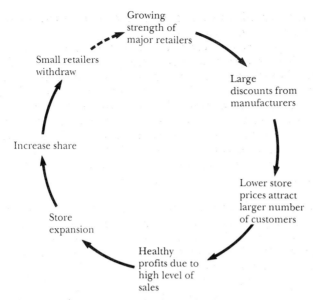

Figure 7.2   *The wheel of increasing multiple retailer dominance*

can be appreciated from Figure 7.2. As certain groups became larger, many manufacturers found it difficult not to pass on more favourable volume discounts. They rationalized these above average discounts on the basis that they justified very large orders. Retailers used some of these discounts to fund their own label programmes and to present their range as being better value than those of independent or cooperative retailers. More consumers were attracted by this proposition, contributing to the profitability of multiples. Ever aware of the future, they invested in better stores and further increased their share, forcing out less profitable smaller retailers.

Manufacturers were aware of this shift in power to the retailers, but surprisingly, took little action. Their response lacked any long-term strategic thinking. They failed to appreciate how retailers were becoming more innovative, more consumer driven, more concerned about developing strong images for their stores and increasingly committed to growing their own labels. Instead of communicating their brands' added values to consumers, they cut back on brand advertising, in favour of buying shelf space. For example, between 1970 and 1979, the top fifty grocery leaders allowed their advertising budgets to fall, in real terms, by 64 per cent. Yet, the top four grocery retailers showed a 40 per cent real increase in their advertising activity.

This shift in the balance of power resulted in retailers no longer being passive pipelines for branded goods. Instead, they became highly involved coordinators of marketing activity. As one retailer said: 'We now see ourselves as the customer's manufacturing agent, rather than the manufacturer's selling agent'.

The response of weak and strong manufacturers

Weaker brand manufacturers, particularly those lacking a long-term planning horizon, were unable to find a convincing argument to counter retailers' demands for extra discounts. They were worried about being delisted and saw no other alternative but to agree to disproportionately large discounts. Many erroneously viewed this as part of their promotional budget and failed to appreciate the implication of biasing their promotions budget to the trade, at the expense of consumers. Retailers' investment in own labels brought them up to the standard of manufacturers' brands. For example, a Lockwood's subsidiary supplying own labels invested in new equipment, which cut down the soaking and blanching of baked beans from the traditional twenty hours to less than an hour, before most of its major competitors. With increasing investment in own labels and less support behind manufacturers' brands, consumers began to perceive less differences between brands and own labels, and choice began to be influenced more by availability, price and point-of-sale displays. As retailers had more control over these influencing factors, weaker brands lost market share and their profitability fell.

Weak manufacturers' brands were not generating sufficient returns to fund either maintenance programmes or investments in new products. At the next negotiating round with retailers, it was made clear that their sales were deteriorating and again they were forced to buy shelf space through even larger discounts. In the vicious circle shown in Figure 7.3, they were soon on the spiral of rapid decline.

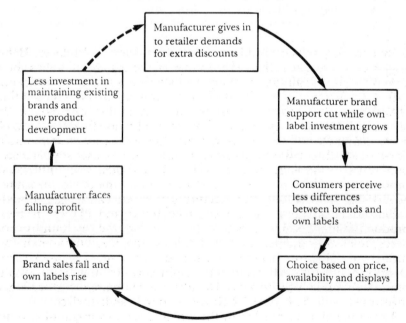

Figure 7.3   *The weakening manufacturer's brand*

From the vicious circle of deteriorating brand position, it can be appreciated that own labels are particularly strong in markets where there is:

- Excess manufacturing capacity.
- Products are perceived by consumers as commodities.
- Low levels of manufacturer investment are common.
- The production processes employ low technology.
- Brand advertising is not that significant.

Table 7.3 shows the top ten own label grocery product fields for 1989, all of which exhibit many of these characteristics.

Table 7.3 *The top 10 own label sectors in 1989*

Product field	Own label share
Packaged cheese	80
Kitchen rolls	61
Evaporated milk	59
Fruit juices	57
Instant milks	55
Frozen vegetables	54
Jam/cream-filled biscuits	54
Pre-packaged peas and beans	52
Cooking oils	51
Lards and compounds	50

(After Whitaker, 1990)

By contrast, strong brand manufacturers, such as Unilever, Heinz and Nestlé, realized that the future of strong brands lies in a commitment to maintaining unique added values and communicating these to consumers. They 'bit the bullet', realizing that to succeed they would have to support the trade, but not at the expense of the consumer. Instead, they invested both in production facilities for their current brands and in new brand development work. For example, Bernard Matthews, the Norfolk-based turkey group, uses sophisticated production technology unique to the UK and adamantly refuses to produce own labels. It has a strong commitment to consumer advertising. With strong manufacturers communicating their brands' values to consumers, these were recognized and choice in these product fields became more strongly influenced by quality and perceptions of brand personality. Retailers recognized these manufacturers' commitments behind their brands and wanted to stock them. Distribution increased through the right sorts of retailers, enabling brand sales and profits to grow. Healthy returns enabled further brand investment and, as Figure 7.4 shows, strong brands thrived.

The confectionery market in the UK is a good example of a sector where strong manufacturers' brands dominate. The major players,

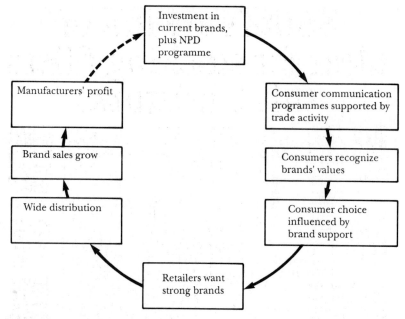

Figure 7.4 *Strong brand's response*

Mars, Nestlé and Cadbury control virtually three-quarters of this market, continually launching new brands and heavily advertising their presence. Interestingly, the power of multiple retailers is also dissipated by virtue of a third of sales going through confectioners, tobacconists and newsagents, with a further quarter through vending machines and garage forecourts.

Convenience versus non-convenience outlets

In the broadest terms, retail outlets can be classified as being convenience or non-convenience outlets, for which two different types of brand strategies are appropriate. Convenience outlets have a wide geographical coverage, making it easy for consumers to access them. The goods sold are not speciality items and consumers generally feel confident making brand selections. Consumers do not need detailed pack information to make a choice between alternatives. In convenience outlets, retailers strive for volume efficiencies. They typically include retailers of grocery and home improvement products.

In convenience outlets, manufacturers' brands will thrive only if they are strongly differentiated. This necessitates having added values that consumers appreciate, a strong promotional commitment and packaging that rapidly communicates brands' added values. Displaying a lot of information on the packaging may well be ineffective, since

Smith's are full of ideas for stocking fillers this Christmas.

There's more to discover at WH SMITH.

Exhibit 7.4   *W. H. Smith is a good example of a successful retailer integrating manufacturer brands into its own label range. (Courtesy W H Smith Ltd (advertiser) and DMB & B (agency))*

consumers want to make fast brand selections, with minimal search effort. Brand manufacturers need to ensure that they gain listings in retailers with the broadest coverage, ensuring minimal travel difficulties for consumers.

In non-convenience outlets, such as jewellers and electrical retailers, consumers will be more likely to seek more information and may well be prepared to spend time visiting a few retailers. To thrive in these outlets, manufacturers need to ensure that clear information is available at point of purchase. In particular, retailers' staff need to be fully aware of the brand's capabilities, since consumers often seek their advice. Unless sales assistants display a positive attitude about the brand and correctly explain its capabilities, they will not help it sell.

Retailers' own label expansion across Europe

With the removal of trade barriers opening access to 325 million European Community consumers, more retailers and manufacturers are moving into Europe. Consumers from different cultural backgrounds are experiencing new retail groups. These are either retailers who have joined an alliance, such as Argyll, Ahold and Casino, forming the European Retail Alliance, or foreign stores who have maintained their independence while crossing boarders, such as Tengelmann.

The advantages for retailers forming European alliances are many. It allows the sharing of marketing research, management information and experience amongst members. It facilitates the coordination of marketing, product development, distribution, logistics and information technology. It also offers significant economies through sourcing low cost suppliers and negotiating very large orders at favourable terms.

With pricing structures in the grocery trade being related to volume discounts, manufacturers are becoming increasingly worried about pan-European alliances. For example, when Ahold approached a computer manufacturer for a specially designed till, they were in a weak position asking for only 500 units. However, with their alliance partners, they were in a much stronger position, with an order for 55 000 tills. A further concern of manufacturers is that alliance members will discuss how much they are paying for the same manufacturer's products when different factories across Europe are being used. The indications are that retailers are going to become even more powerful in Europe.

Some retailers, such as Tesco, Aldi, Promodes and Delhaize 'Le Lion' have decided not to participate in European alliances. Their reasons include believing that they already have strong buying power, they are satisfied operating in their own domestic markets and they do not want to have their expansion plans subjected to debate by other retailers.

However, while a more open Europe may offer opportunities for own label expansion, it also creates problems. There does not yet appear to be a consensus view about how to position and name own labels. A true Euro-own label, if ever successfully developed, has to overcome the problem of finding a positioning that would appeal to consumers in cities as diverse as Leeds, Lisbon, Lausanne and La Rochelle. With strong cultural differences existing across Europe, it is unlikely that a homogeneous Euro-consumer will evolve immediately after 1992. However, with satellite television and the greater mobility of people, it is likely that a convergence of tastes and opinions will occur. This may well be accelerated by retailers' pan-European expansion.

Different retailers have followed diverse approaches to developing pan-European own labels. The Belgian GIB group, a member of the Euro-group alliance, has cooperated with its members to develop own labels with names that make them appear to be manufacturers' brands. For example, Le Bon Petit Diable biscuits and Star-Cat petfoods. While these can be carried across Europe, they lack the support of the retailers' names and are likely to be ignored by risk-averse consumers, who have never come across such names and are unable to recall any advertising.

By contrast, Asko Deutsche Kaufhaus is attempting to introduce a Euro-own label. They developed their own label range under the umbrella brand name of the fictitious character, Isabelle O'Lacy. This is internationally protected and was conceived to blend across different European cultures. This strategy assumes that the own label's personality will appeal to consumers from different countries. This is a brave assumption – if nothing else one has only to think of consumers' difficulties in pronouncing the name!

Manufacturer brands in Europe

The larger brand manufacturers are moving cautiously into Europe. Some are doing this by acquiring other firms. Examples of the more notable recent acquisitions were Grand Met buying Pillsbury, Philip Morris buying Jacobs Suchard and BSN buying RJR Nabisco, Galbani and HP Foods.

Other brand manufacturers are identifying product fields which are less subject to national taste differences, such as the confectionery and petfood product fields, for which they are developing pan-European strategies. Mars has changed the name of its confectionery bars Marathon to Snickers, as part of its pan-European approach and in the petfood sector, Cesar has replaced Mr. Dog.

Coca-Cola, Benetton, Kodak and Camel are good examples of strong brands gaining strength by taking advantage of more open markets. Brand positionings have been developed and fine tuned to appeal across Europe. For example, Coca-Cola is the drink for friends in any situation and Benetton represents the friend for any nation through its slogan 'The united colours of Benetton'. In the financial services sector, American Express has developed the positioning of being the known and trusted person with a pan-European campaign, 'You recognize me'.

To expand across Europe, brand manufacturers need to assess whether their brands will be used in the same way as they are in the UK. For example, United Biscuits recognized that in Italy, some consumers eat biscuits with milk at breakfast, just as British consumers eat breakfast cereals. With their Italian company, they reformulated one of their British brands and developed an advertising campaign positioning it more as a cereal.

Whether to become an own label supplier

Increasingly, manufacturers are faced with the decision about whether or not to accept invitations from retailers to produce an own label version of their brand. The short term attraction of extra sales needs to be weighed against long term issues – not least of which is creating their own competitor. Firms like Heinz and Kelloggs are not prepared to produce an own label. They believe they have very successful brands whose formulation others find difficult to emulate. They argue that they have such strong brand assets that they have little to gain in the long term from own label production. Mars is a particularly good example of this. Their experience of producing the world famous Mars Bar is such that no other company can emulate the quality of their brand at a cheaper, or similar price. In fact, one manufacturer's trials for a retailer indicated that a poor quality own label could only be produced with a price 50 per cent higher than the current Mars Bar!

One of the issues that needs considering is the economics of being a brand manufacturer versus an own label supplier. The firm needs to identify whether the payback in the long term from branding exceeds that from following an own label route. The analysis needs to identify all the activities involved in converting raw materials into final products and costs put against these. The first series of costs are those based on supplying an own label. The premium that the firm must pay for undertaking the extra work involved in branding then needs to be identified. Finally, the extra margin, if any, attributable to marketing a brand, rather than an own label, needs to be gauged. Providing the economics are sensible and any differential advantage can be sustained, as consumers recognize the quality difference over own labels, it would be wise to remain a brand manufacturer.

Production levels need to be evaluated. If there is 10 per cent excess capacity in the factory, and it is estimated that own label production will take 20 per cent of normal production, the manufacturer is faced with the problem of deciding which lines to limit.

If the brand's differential advantage is difficult to sustain – for example patents expire in a year's time, own label may be an attractive option. Before progressing down an own label route, however, the manufacturer needs to consider whether there is a lot of goodwill inherent in the brand's name which, in the short term, others may find difficult to overcome. If so, it is worth trading on this brand asset, rather than rushing into own label production.

It is necessary to question whether there is a commitment internally to investing in the future of brands. If a new director has recently been appointed, will he sway the board's views away from continually supporting brands? If the firm has recently been the subject of a takeover, will the new owners show the same concern about investment? To adopt a half-hearted approach may result in a secondary brand, which at best can look forward to a short lifespan as retailers employ systems such a Direct Product Profitability (DPP) to rationalize their range. As Figure 7.5 indicates, in its early days, a

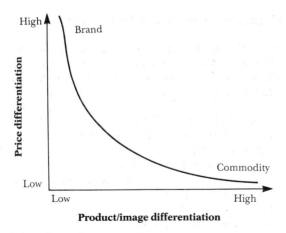

Figure 7.5 *Sliding down the commodity curve*

successful brand has well differentiated benefits which consumers appreciate and for which they are prepared to pay a price premium. Without investment, the point of difference will fade as more 'me-toos' appear, reducing the price premium once charged. As the brand slides deeper into the commodity domain, it is common for manufacturers to place more reliance on price cutting, further damaging the brand.

Some firms argue that if they do not supply own labels, their competitors will. This argument of 'blocking' competition was used by ICI with Wickes DIY group. To limit the sales of Crown paints, ICI persuaded Wickes to let them supply their own label. This forced Crown out, enabling ICI to supply both an own label, and also their Dulux range.

In some firms, there is a motivational issue involved in deciding whether to supply own label. Some managers think that they will have less contact with their advertising agencies or that they will have to change their style of always looking for the best, to one of finding the cheapest. They worry that if they subsequently stop supplying own label, the retailer will show their point of difference to one of their competitors. While previously they may have enjoyed negotiating from a position of strength, they may feel that they are becoming very dependent on the own label orders of a few, very large retailers.

Small manufacturers who underestimate sales potential may be particularly attracted by own label contracts. Taking a less than optimistic view of the future, they may short-sightedly see own label as their insurance. It would be far better if these firms evaluated the strength of their consumer franchise and assessed the potential for growing in a niche, selling their brand only through carefully selected retailers.

When managers argue for own labels because this helps build a closer working relationship with retailers, there are signs that they are not making the most of their current brands. There is no excuse for not maintaining regular contact with retailers through the existing portfolio of brands. This can be done through invitations to the manufacturer's sales conferences, to hospitality events, to hear about new product developments, etc. If anything, there is an argument that broadening the portfolio with own labels may well dilute the quality of discussions with retailers, since more lines need discussing at each meeting.

Retailers are unlikely to be equally interested in selling manufacturers' brands and their own labels, as some managers incorrectly argue. They view some lines as being particularly good for reinforcing their store image, or to generate store traffic or to boost profits. They place a different emphasis on different parts of their range and may well give the own labels better shelf positioning, at the expense of the original brands.

In some cases, own label can provide a basis for growth, particularly through expansionary retailers. However, against this must be weighed weak retailers who are ineffective in countering the encroachment of other retailers. They survive by adopting a policy of 'management by line of least resistance', giving prominence to those lines that sell best and putting little effort into slower moving lines. Producing own labels for these retailers is unlikely to lead to increasing profitability.

It is wrong to take the view that own labels can be used to cover overheads. The marketer needs to question why overheads are becoming significant and take action to resolve this problem. Launching an own label range for this reason may well be a short-term solution to a problem which will reappear. Retailers are likely to negotiate very low prices, probably giving the manufacturer a poorer rate of return for own labels than might otherwise be expected from brands.

How retailers select own label suppliers

With increasing demands for higher quality own labels, retailers are becoming more selective when choosing potential own label suppliers. Some of the considerations taken into account when assessing potential suppliers are:

- Can they produce the quality standards consistently?
- Are they financially sound?
- Do they have adequate capacity to meet the current targets and sufficient spare capacity to cope with increasingly successful own labels?
- Do they have the transport infrastructure to ensure reliable delivery?
- Is the production machinery up to date and well maintained?
- Do they have good labour relations?
- Will they be committed to the retailer?

- Do they have the flexibility to respond to short-term market fluctuations?
- Will they be able to hold adequate stock?
- Do they have a good trade marketing department that the retailer feels they can work with?
- Will the supplier maintain good communications with the retailer, regularly informing them of any relevant issues?
- Will the supplier agree to the retailer's payment terms?
- Would the retailer be proud to be associated with the supplier?

Prioritizing brand investment through different retailers

Even though retailer power is increasing, manufacturers, particularly those with strong brands, need to adopt an offensive, rather than a defensive, strategy when deciding where brand investment is needed. Ideally, manufacturers with strong brands always want to sell their brands through particularly attractive retailers. For some manufacturers, a retailer may be extremely attractive because of the high volume being sold, the retailer's image may be ideal for the brand and the retailer may well have a policy of strongly supporting the brand through good in-store positioning and rarely being out of stock. Such retailers need identifying and nurturing.

It is rare, however, for a firm to have a portfolio of brands that are all very strong brands. Likewise, it is rare for all possible retailers to be classified as highly attractive retailers.

To prioritize brand activity through different retailers, we have found a simple two-dimensional matrix to be particularly helpful. This is shown in Figure 7.6. Using the dimensions of brand strength and retailer attractiveness, it is possible to rank the order in which resources should be allocated.

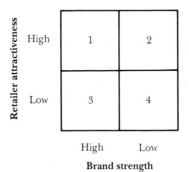

Figure 7.6 *Brand strength–retailer attractiveness matrix*

The first dimension of the matrix, *brand strength*, needs to be defined. A manufacturer's brand is a strong brand if it scores well on the factors critical for brand success. Brands thrive because their manufacturers have identified precisely what benefits consumers are seeking and have geared their firms to producing brands which meet these critical success factors. The critical success factors vary from market to market. For example, in the greetings card market, one of the more important critical success factors is a very varied range, while in the colour film market, trueness of colour and wide availability are important issues. To appreciate fully the strength of their brands in a particular market, the brand's team need to go through their consumer research data and extract the critical success factors. Normally, the list of critical success factors will be between five and seven attributes. In the hypothetical example shown in Table 7.4, five factors were identified as being crucial for brand success.

Some of the factors are more important than others, and the brand team could put a weighting against each of the factors to indicate their relative importance. In the example in Table 7.4, the brand team knew from market research that the camera's ability to produce life-like photographs was the most important issue, followed by ease of use. In a meeting, they came to the consensus view that a weighting of 0.35 should be assigned to 'produces life-like photographs' and a weighting of 0.25 for 'easy to use'. The weighting factors should total 1.00.

Table 7.4   *Calculating the strength of camera brand A*

Critical success factors	Scoring criteria			Weighting (W)	Brand A score (S)	S × W
	10	5	1			
Life-like photographs	High	Med.	Low	0.35	10	3.50
Easy to use	High	Med.	Low	0.25	5	1.25
Light to carry	High	Med.	Low	0.20	5	1.00
Makes consumer feel like professional	High	Med.	Low	0.15	1	0.15
Camera bodies come in a range of colours	High	Med.	Low	0.05	5	0.25
Total				1.00		6.15

A scoring criteria needs to be applied next. In our example, it was felt that brands should be rated as either 'high', 'medium' or 'low' on each of the critical success factors. Furthermore, the brand's team wanted to keep the exercise simple, so if a 'high' score was felt to be appropriate for a brand that met a particular attribute, it would be given a numerical score of 10. A medium score would be 5 and a low score 1.

The first camera brand, brand A, was evaluated on the brand strength dimension. For the most important attribute of being able to produce life-like photographs, the first brand was thought to be very good at meeting this attribute and was therefore given a score of 10. Its weighted score on this dimension is 10 × 0.35 = 3.50. On the next most important attribute, 'being easy to use', it was felt to be only quite easy to use and because of this it was scored '5'. Its weighted score on this attribute is $5 \times 0.25 = 1.25$. In a similar manner, the brand was assessed on the other three attributes. The five weighted scores for the brand were then aggregated and a total weighted score of 6.15 calculated. This brand strength score of 6.15 indicates a somewhat mediocre brand, since a score of 10 represents a very strong brand and 1 is a very weak brand.

For each of the other camera brands in the firm's portfolio which compete in this market, their brand strength scores need calculating.

The second dimension of the matrix, *retailer attractiveness*, then needs defining and applying to each current and potential camera retailer. The management team need to agree which are the few five or seven factors that characterize the attractiveness of retailers. For example, Table 7.5 shows the five key attributes that the team used to assess the attractiveness of camera retailers. Some of the attributes are more important than others and a weighting needs to be assigned to each attribute to reflect their importance. In the example in Table 7.5, the high volume of camera sales were thought to be particularly important and this factor was given a weighting of 0.40. As before, the weightings need to add to 1.00.

Table 7.5   *Calculating the attractiveness of retailer Z*

Attractiveness factors	Scoring criteria			Weighting (W)	Distributor score (S)	S × W
	10	5	1			
High volume of camera sales	High	Med.	Low	0.40	1	0.40
Quality image	High	Med.	Low	0.30	5	1.50
Strong supporter of our firm's brands	High	Med.	Low	0.15	1	0.15
Knowledgeable sales staff	High	Med.	Low	0.10	5	0.50
Wide geographical coverage	High	Med.	Low	0.05	5	0.25
Total				1.00		2.80

Using a similar scoring system to that previously described, each retailer then needs to be assessed on each attribute. For example, the team felt that retailer Z does not have a particularly high annual camera sales level. As such a score of 1 was given and a weighted score of $1 \times 0.40 = 0.40$, assigned. On the next most important attribute, 'having a quality image amongst consumers', retailer Z was felt to have a medium image. It was, therefore, given a score of 5 and its weighted score calculated as 5×0.3. In this way, retailer Z was assessed on each of the five attractiveness factors and by aggregating each of the weighted factor scores, it received an overall attractiveness score of 2.80. This low score indicates that retailer Z is not a particularly attractive retailer through which to distribute its brands.

Having calculated the scores for the strength of each brand and the attractiveness of each retailer through which the brand is sold, these scores can be plotted on the matrix shown in Figure 7.6.

Using this matrix, managers can prioritize their use of resources , in the order shown on the matrix. Resources should first be considered for strong brands being sold through highly attractive retailers. This is the ideal situation, with the brand and retailer perfectly matched. In the (probably unlikely) event of these retailers demanding better terms, the brand manufacturer is in an excellent position to counter such demands by clarifying the value of the brand.

From the manufacturer's perspective, after allocating resources to support those brands in quadrant 1, resources then need to be planned for brands which are not particularly strong, but which go through highly attractive retailers. This represents an opportunity to the manufacturer, since the change needed is one which is under their control and once completed, the strengthened brand can capitalize on the synergistic effects from trading with highly attractive retailers. The danger brands face in quadrant 2 is that retailers also regularly review their product mix and these brands would be regarded as under-performing. Corrective action for these brands can rapidly be diagnosed from the way that the brand scored on the different factors constituting the brand strength dimension.

After allocating resources for these two quadrants, attention should next be directed towards those brands in quadrant 3 – strong brands going through relatively unattractive retailers. The manufacturer needs to evaluate the strengths and weaknesses of these retailers, using the scores on the various factors of the retailer attractiveness dimension. They should also consider whether there are any other reasons which are not captured on the retailer attractiveness dimension indicating why strong brands are going through poor retailers. Once fully aware of the situation, the manufacturer then needs to decide whether to invest effort in improving the retailer (e.g. send in its own team of merchandizers on a more regular basis, etc.), or whether to cut brand support through that retailer (e.g. reduce the frequency of delivery, insisting on larger drop sizes, etc.).

Finally, after having supported brand activity in these three quadrants, the brand manufacturer needs to consider brands in quadrant 4 – weak brands being sold through unattractive retailers. The manufacturer should question why it is marketing brands which have *very* low brand strength scores which are available through *very* unattractive retailers. In such situations the most viable route may be divestment. By contrast, where mediocre brands are going through mediocre retailers, the manufacturer should consider whether investment would lead to a more equitable future.

Conclusions

An own label metamorphosis has occurred. They are now high quality retailer brands, backed by significant corporate promotional campaigns reinforcing clear personalities. Retailers are increasingly attentive to changing environmental circumstances, launching innovative own labels to capitalize on new consumer trends. Pricing policies position own labels as good-value lines, rather than cheap alternatives to manufacturers' brands. In view of these developments, we feel the term 'own label' is no longer appropriate. For too many managers this term is synonymous with a poor quality, cheap alternative to manufacturers' brands. As we enter the twenty-first century, with retailers likely to play an even more dominant marketing role, we believe it would be better to use the term 'retailer's brands'. This recognizes that the full repertoire of branding techniques is being employed by retailers, who are just as sophisticated in their strategic marketing as 'blue chip' brand manufacturers. Their rapid acceptance of information technology is but one example of their sophistication, enabling them to gain a further competitive edge.

There may well be scope for retailers to develop alternative types of own labels, such as 'lifestyle own labels', targeted at different consumer groups frequenting specific retailers. An essential ingredient for their success in such cases must be consumer-relevant added values – not just lower prices. As the generics experience has shown, it is only a minority of consumers who are prepared to trade off added values for low prices. Experienced consumers are no longer primarily motivated by low prices. When deciding between alternatives, price is often not a major consideration, and is not given a particularly high weighting when other added values are present.

Retailer dominance is likely to be a feature common to more markets as we move into the next millennium. More professional retail management will be better served by information technology, enabling retailers to make more rapid adjustments to their portfolio of brands, as new opportunities evolve. Manufacturers will succeed with their brands if they recognize the basis of their consumer franchise and continue to invest in this, rather than diverting their marketing budgets to buying shelf space.

Trade marketing will become increasingly more common, as manufacturers recognize the importance of their large customers. This function needs to show retailers the commitment they have to reinforcing their consumer franchise and should work with the trade to help consumers recognize the benefits of their brands.

As barriers to trading across Europe fall, more retailers are likely to expand their operations into new geographical areas. This will be either through forming retail alliances, or by maintaining their independence and growing organically across Europe. The problem that retailers are having to face is how to position their own labels so that they appeal to a significant proportion of consumers from different cultural backgrounds, with minimal fine tuning for each country. For those retailers who have entered into alliances, this problem is confounded by the need to make the Euro-own label equally appropriate for each of their members' stores.

As brand manufacturers are well aware, the problem of finding an appropriate pan-European positioning is not unique to retailers. However, it is clear from some of the current pan-European successes, such as Schweppes, Nescafé and Mercedes, that it is possible to persevere in developing an appropriate pan-European positioning.

Manufacturers can adopt a much more proactive approach to brand marketing in a retailer-dominated environment. They can assess the strengths and weaknesses of being an own label supplier by considering issues such as the economics of branding, the strength of their consumer franchise and the more effective use of production facilities. They can evaluate how well equipped they are to meet the needs of own label contracts. Furthermore, they can use the brand strength-retailer attractiveness matrix to prioritize brand investment programmes through different retailers.

Marketing action checklist

It is recommended that, after reading this chapter, marketers undertake the following exercises to test and refine their brand strategies.

1 On a two dimensional map for a specific market, with the axes representing price and quality, plot the position of your brand(s), your other branded competitors' brands and the own labels from the main retailers. Repeat the exercise, but do so thinking back ten years earlier. As a management team, consider why any changes have occurred and assess which factors have had a particularly strong impact on your brand.

2 Ten years ago, how did the leading retailers in your product field manage to sell their own labels cheaper than popular brands? Today, how are these own labels achieving their price advantage? What are the implications of this for your brands?

3 In the market where your brands compete, what propositions do each of the major retailers' own labels offer? Thinking back ten years, how have these propositions changed, if at all? What are the implications of these changes for your brands?

4 For any one of your markets where your brands compete against own labels, what are the differences between the leading retailer's own labels and your brand(s)? Where the retailer's own label has an advantage over your brand(s) evaluate how this advantage has been achieved and consider how you could better your brand on this attribute, if consumers would value such a change. Where your brand(s) has an advantage over the leading retailer's own labels, consider what is required to sustain this.

5 What proportion of your brand sales in a particular market go through multiple retailers? How does this compare against the situation five, ten, and fifteen years ago? What factors are giving rise to multiple retailer dominance? Will these factors continue to aid the growth of their power? How do you plan to compete in a market dominated by increasingly powerful retailers?

6 What personalities do consumers associate with your brands and

the own labels against which they compete? How clear are these personalities? Has your brand's personality become less distinctive over time, while retailers' own label personalities have become sharper? Do the personalities of the leading retailers' own labels mirror their stores' brand personalities? If there is any difference between the personality of a retailer's store and its own labels, evaluate why such a difference has occurred and what the implications are for your brands.

7 Are your brands sold through convenience or non-convenience outlets? Does your promotional strategy take into account the need for simple on-pack information through convenience outlets and the need to educate sales assistants in non-convenience outlets?

8 If you are currently involved in exporting, what will be the implications for your brands of the emergence of more European retailer alliances? What plans do you have to cope with increasing retailer dominance across Europe?

9 If you are thinking of taking your brand into Europe, what work have you done to check:

- Whether consumers can pronounce the brand name?
- What the current brand name is associated with in consumers' minds?
- Whether consumers in Europe will use the brand in the same way as in the UK?
- Whether the likely consumer profile in different European countries reflects that of the UK?
- Whether the current promotional campaign is appropriate for pan-European expansion?

10 Should you be debating whether to supply an own label version of one of your current brands, focus your decision by scoring the advantages against the issues:

- Others finding it difficult to emulate your brand.
- Whether there is a lot of goodwill tied up in the brand name.
- The economic implications of own labels and brands.
- Whether patents are soon to expire.
- The production implications in terms of existing capacity.
- Whether there will be continuing internal support for brand investment.
- What internal morale will be like if own label contracts are accepted.
- Whether own label production will help block competitors.
- The accuracy of sales forecasts for brands and own labels.

11 Should you wish to work on own label contracts, assess whether you will be in a strong or a weak negotiating position when pitching for this business by applying the audit questions in the section 'How retailers select own label suppliers'.

12 Evaluate the appropriateness of your priorities for brand support through different major accounts, by using the brand strength-retailer attractiveness matrix.

References and further reading

Anon (1991). Value of own label at Sainsbury. *The Grocer*, 6 July, p. 18.

British Business (1988). DTI retailing inquiry for 1986, *British Business*, 18 Mar., pp. 29–30.

Burnside A. (1990). Packaging and design. *Marketing*, 15 Feb., pp. 29–30.

Caulkin S. (1987). Retailers flex their muscles. *Marketing*, 7 May, pp. 37–40.

Davidson H. (1987). *Offensive Marketing*. Harmondsworth: Penguin.

Davis I. (1986). Does branding pay? *ADMAP*, **22**, (12), 44–8.

de Chernatony L. (1987). Consumers' Perceptions of the Competitive Tiers in Six Grocery Markets. Unpublished PhD Thesis. City University Business School.

de Chernatony L., Knox S. (1991). Consumers' abilities to correctly recall grocery prices. In *Proceedings of Marketing Education Group 1991 Conference* (Piercy N. *et al.*, eds). Cardiff Business School: MEG.

de Kare-Silver M. (1990). Brandflakes. *Management Today*, Nov., 19–22.

Economist Intelligence Unit (1971). The development of own brands in the grocery market. *Retail Business*, No. 166, (Dec.), 27–35.

Euromonitor (1989). *UK Own Brands*. London: Euromonitor.

The Grocer (1988). Multiple price pressure is blamed for the 'debasement' of ice cream. 23 Apr., p. 4.

The Grocer (1991). Why the squeeze was eased. 10 Aug., p. 10.

The Grocer (1991). The ultimate proposition? Money back and replacement pack. 16 Mar., p. 10.

Henley Centre for Forecasting (1982). *Manufacturing and Retailing in the 80s: A Zero Sum Game?* Henley: Henley Centre for Forecasting.

Liebling H. (1985). Wrapped up in themselves. *Marketing*, 7 Nov., pp. 41–2.

MacNeary T., Shriver D. (1991). *Food Retailing Alliances: strategic implications*. London: The Corporate Intelligence Group.

Macrae C. (1991). *World Class Brands*. Wokingham: Addison Wesley.

McGoldrick P. (1990). *Retail Marketing*. London: McGraw Hill.

Moss S. (1989). Own-goals. *Marketing*, 16 Feb., pp. 45–6.

Nielsen (1989). *The Retail Pocket Book*. Oxford: Nielsen.

Ohmae K. (1982). *The Mind of the Strategist*. Harmondsworth: Penguin.

Porter M. (1976). *Interbrand Choice, Strategy and Bilateral Market Power*. Cambridge: Harvard University Press.

Rapoport C. (1985). Brand leaders go to war. *Financial Times*, 16 Feb., p. 24.

Sambrook C. (1991). The top 500 brands. *Marketing*, 7 Mar., pp. 27–33.

Segal-Horn S., McGee J. (1989). Strategies to cope with retailer buying power. In *Retail and Marketing Channels* (Pellegrini L. and Reddy S., eds). London: Routledge.

Sheath K., McGoldrick P. (1981). Generics: their development in grocery retailing and the reactions of consumers. A report from the Department of Management Sciences, the University of Manchester Institute of Science and Technology.

Thompson-Noel M. (1981). Big time grocery brands – the beginning of the end? *Financial Times*, 9 Apr., p. 11.

Walters D., White D. (1987). *Retail Marketing Management*. Basingstoke: Macmillan.

Whitaker J. (1990). Single market – multiple opportunities. Paper presented at Private Label Manufacturers Association Conference.

8 Brand planning

Summary

This chapter considers some of the issues in brand planning. It opens by stressing that consumers welcome consistency and as such the brand's core values should not be tampered with. We show that consumers evaluate brands primarily by the extent to which they satisfy functional and representational needs. Through an appreciation of brands' functional and representational characteristics, we consider how best to invest in brands. We review some of the issues in developing and launching new brands and address the problems of managing brands during their growth and maturity phases. Finally, we look at ways of rejuvenating brands which may appear to be in decline.

Maintaining the brand's core values

In previous chapters, we have stressed the point that brands succeed because marketers have a good appreciation of the asset types constituting their brands. By recognizing which aspects of their brands are particularly valued by consumers, marketers have invested and protected these attributes, sustaining their value and maintaining consumer loyalty. Any pressures from accountants or factory managers to cut support for these core values have been strenuously resisted.

Over time, consumers learn to appreciate the core values of brands. They remain loyal to certain brands because their positioning has been consistently maintained. Unilever's approach to Persil is a classic example of the way a brand's core values have not been tampered with. This brand is not used as the training ground for a brand manager who is likely to move on after three or four years. Instead, only experienced

Exhibit 8.1   *With a well-established heritage, James Borrough Ltd have little intention of changing the core values of Beefeater Gin*

managers are allowed to work on it. They know that it is protected by the guardianship of an advertising agency with years of experience of the brand (J. Walter Thompson) and a group of very conservative senior Lever Brothers managers, the 'college of cardinals'. These senior managers were previous Persil brand managers who were responsible for nurturing the brand. Together, they have considerable experience and are always consulted before any major change can be made. The power to reject any proposed change is immense and it is only well-conceived changes which will be approved.

Exhibit 8.2   *Glenfiddich's added value is the connoisseur status perceived by the consumer. (Copyright William Grant & Sons Ltd, 1987)*

Persil as a brand has succeeded, partly because of the wealth of managerial experience that is brought to bear on it and also because it benefits from a consistently maintained positioning. It represents caring for whiteness, clothes, washing machines and mothers' reputations. When Ariel was launched as a biological washing powder, its positioning of washing strength was perceived by consumers as being harsh, particularly when Persil was being strongly advertised as a defence against the launch. Yet, during the 1980s, a decision was taken to introduce enzymes in Persil System 3. This went against the long-term positioning of gentle caring. As a result, confused consumers switched their brand allegiance. Corrective action saved the brand, helped in no small part by the long-term goodwill that had been built up between Persil and its consumers.

A characteristic of successful brands is the way that their position has been precisely defined and communicated internally. Any plans to cut back on the core values by production or financial management has been strenuously opposed by strong-willed marketers. Everyone working on a particular brand is regularly reminded of the brand's positioning and an integrated, committed approach is adopted, ensuring that the correct balance of resources is consistently applied. Any frills that do not support the brand's positioning are eliminated and regular value analysis exercises, rather than naive cost-cutting programmes, are undertaken to ensure the brand's positioning is being correctly delivered to consumers.

Successful brands are characterized by having their positioning clearly communicated to consumers through an approach that bridges their functional and psychological needs in a consistent manner. For example, Fairy Liquid has always been about a 'gentle' relationship, Colgate toothpaste about 'trusted' dental protection, Comfort fabric softener about 'loving' softness and Glenfiddich whisky about 'connoisseur' status. A role has been found for advertising which does not just communicate what the brand does, but also what the brand means. For example, the VW Golf advertising campaign, depicting a loser in Monte Carlo, doesn't just communicate the brand's functional reliability, but also the psychological reassurance that the driver needs.

Since a brand is the totality of thoughts, feelings and sensations evoked in consumers' minds, resources can only be effectively employed once an audit has been taken of the dimensions that define it in the consumer's mind. To appreciate this planned use of resources, it is therefore necessary to consider the dimensions that consumers use to assess brands.

Defining brand dimensions

When people choose brands, they are not solely concerned with one single characteristic, nor do they have the mental agility to evaluate a multitude of brand attributes. Instead, only a few key issues guide choice.

In some of the early classic brands papers, our attention is drawn to people buying brands to satisfy functional and emotional needs. One has only to consider everyday purchasing to appreciate this. For example, there is little difference between the physical characteristics of bottled mineral water. Yet, due to the way advertising has reinforced particular positionings, Perrier is bought more for its 'designer label' appeal, which enables consumers to express something about their upwardly mobile lifestyles. By contrast, Spa is bought more from a consideration of its healthy connotations. If consumers solely evaluated brands on their functional capabilities, then the Halifax and Abbey National Building Societies, with interest rates remarkably similar to other competitors, would not have the leading shares in the deposit savings sector. Yet, the different personalities represented by these building societies influence brand evaluation.

This idea of brands being characterized by two dimensions, the

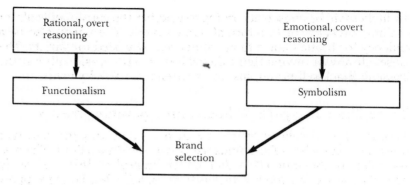

Figure 8.1 *Components of brand choice. (After Lannon and Cooper, 1983)*

rational function and the emotional symbolic, is encapsulated in the model of brand choice shown in Figure 8.1. When consumers choose between brands, they rationally consider practical issues about brands' functional capabilities. At the same time, they evaluate different brands' personalities, forming a view about which fits the image they wish to be associated with. As many writers have noted, consumers are not just functionally orientated; their behaviour is affected by their interpretation of brand symbolism, as was shown in Chapter 5. When two competing brands are perceived as being equally similar in terms of their physical capabilities, the brand that comes closest to enhancing the consumer's self-concept will be chosen.

In terms of the functional aspects of brand evaluation and choice, consumers assess the benefits they perceive from particular brands, along with preconceptions about efficacy, value for money, and availability. Through previous brand usage, they may well have built up a relationship with certain brands which they know can be trusted to satisfy their practical needs.

At a more emotional level, the symbolic value of the brand is considered. Here, consumers are concerned with the brand's abilities to help express something about themselves, to help them interpret the people they meet, to reinforce membership of a particular social group and to communicate how they feel. They evaluate brands in terms of intuitive likes and dislikes and continually seek reassurances from the advertising and design, that the chosen brand is the 'right' one for them.

This idea of brands being interpreted by consumers on the basis of a functional and an emotional dimension is supported by research in other areas, such as social psychology and attitude research. More recently, an American team looking at the way consumers make choices in over 200 product fields, again showed support for the importance of the two dimensions, functionalism and symbolism, in explaining brand choice. In this model of consumer choice, brands were chosen by consumers on the basis of how well they satisfied consumers' values in *specific situations*. For example, different brands of watches will be chosen according to whether the consumer is off for a sailing weekend, or to a formal dinner-dance. There may also be a tendency for brand choice to be influenced by a need for variety. The housewife always buying Heinz Baked Beans may occasionally buy the Crosse & Blackwell brand, just to experience its novelty value.

The de Chernatony–McWilliam brand planning matrix

There is a considerable amount of evidence supporting the view that consumers chose between brands using two key dimensions. The first dimension is the rational evaluation of brands' abilities to satisfy utilitarian needs. We refer to this as functionality. Marketing support is employed to associate specific physical attributes with particular brand names, facilitating consumers' decision making about primarily utilitarian needs such as, for example, quality, reliability and effectiveness. Brands satisfying primarily functional needs are Castrol GTX, Formica and Tipp-Ex. The second dimension is the emotional evaluation of brands' abilities to help consumers express something about themselves, be it for example their mood, or their membership of a particular social group, or their status. We call this dimension representationality. Brands are chosen on this dimension because they have values which exist over and above their physical values. For example, Yves St Laurent neck ties and Channel perfume are very effective brands for expressing particular personality types and roles, with a secondary benefit of inherent functional qualities.

These two dimensions of brands are independent of each other. Furthermore, consumers rarely select brands using just one of these two dimensions. Instead, they choose between competing brands according to the *degree* of functionality and representationality expressed by particular brands. As de Chernatony and McWilliam (1990) found it is possible to use these two dimensions to gain a good

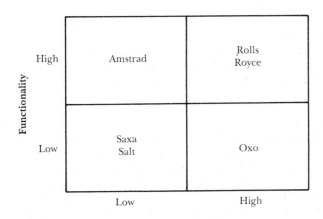

Figure 8.2 *An example of the de Chernatony–McWilliam matrix*

appreciation of the way consumers perceive competing brands. For example, Audi cars are perceived as being very effective brands for communicating status and personality issues, and at the same time also reassure consumers about design and engineering excellence.

Through qualitative market research techniques, it is possible to identify the consumer attributes reflecting the dimensions of functionality and representationality. By then incorporating these into a questionnaire, a large sample of consumers can be interviewed to gauge their views about the competing brands in a particular product field. Statistical analysis of these questionnaires enables the marketer to characterize each of the competing brands in terms of their functionality and representationality By knowing the scores of each brand on these two dimensions, a spatial display of the brands can be produced by plotting the brand scores on a matrix, whose two axes are functionality and representationality, as shown in Figure 8.2. From this matrix, the marketer is able to consider how resources could best be used to support their brand.

Strategies from the de Chernatony–McWilliam matrix

If the marketer is satisfied with the quadrant within which the brand is located, as would be Rolls Royce in the high representational–high functional quadrant, then the brand strategy needs reinforcing. If, however, the brand is not perceived by consumers in the quadrant desired by the marketer, a strategy appropriate to the desired quadrant should be enacted. To sustain the brand in a particular quadrant, the following strategies are felt to be particularly appropriate.

High representationality – high functionality
Brands in the top right quadrant of Figure 8.2 are perceived as providing functional excellence and, in the consumer's mind, are seen to be very good vehicles for non-verbal communication about themselves. Qualitative market research needs to be undertaken to appreciate the lifestyle that users wish to project through the brand and a positioning objective subsequently defined and satisfied through the appropriate marketing mix. A creative strategy that reinforces consumers' lifestyle requirements should be developed (e.g. using reference group endorsement, appropriate mood and tone of advertising, etc.) and communicated through selective media chan-nels. A continuous promotional presence is essential to reinforce users' brand choice and to communicate symbolic meaning to those in contact with brand users. The quality of the brand needs to be maintained through high standards of quality control and continuous product development. Regular consumer surveys need to assess users' views on product performance and any negative comments investi-gated. Availability of the brand should be restricted to quality distributors. A strict audit of the way distributors interact with the brand is required and they would need to be dissuaded from any activities which may undermine the brand's value.

**AIRPACK. THE EASY WAY
TO FLY GIFTS STRAIGHT TO THE HEART.**

No paper, no string, no stamps and no queuing to have it weighed.
An Airpack is a one piece package that only needs sealing with a kiss to
speed it on its way.

It is pre-paid to allow you to send a whole half kilo to Europe
for only £2.25, or £4.99 to anywhere else in the world.

An Airpack is an ideal way to send your gifts abroad. And the
convenience will allow you to save your energies for choosing the gift,
as the only string you'll pull is a heartstring.

Exhibit 8.3 *On the de Chernatony–McWilliam matrix, Royal Mail Airpack
would appear to be positioned as high representationality–high functionality*

Low representationality – high functionality
These brands are in the top left quadrant of Figure 8.2. They are sought
by consumers because of a high utilitarian need and a less pressing
drive to communicate something about themselves. Product superiority needs to be maintained. Continuous investment in product

development is particularly necessary here, since it will be vitally important for the company to maintain functional advantage over the competition. 'Me-tooism' will always be a potential threat to these products. Promotional support is important in communicating the functional benefits of the brand. The creative strategy would probably focus upon 'product as hero' in the advertising and a notable presence would be required

JURA. THE FLAVOUR OF AN ISLAND.

ISLE OF JURA

SINGLE MALT SCOTCH WHISKY

Since the 17th Century our island has made
just one single malt Scotch Whisky.
Naturally it's called Isle of Jura.
For this is a dram which takes after its homeland.
It is light and fresh with a dry character.
And has only the most delicate hint of peat,
complemented by the invigorating tang of the sea.
It is matured to perfection.
Isle of Jura.
An island that truly is a joy to discover.

FROM INVERGORDON DISTILLERS GROUP

Exhibit 8.4   *On the de Chernatony–McWilliam matrix, Isle of Jura Single Malt Whisky is positioned as high on functional excellence, with a small amount of representationality supported by the image aroused from the topographical advertisement*

Exhibit 8.5   *On the de Chernatony–McWilliam matrix Seiko would appear to be positioned as low representationality–high functionality*

High representationality–low functionality
Consumers are primarily concerned about using brands in the bottom right quadrant of Figure 8.2 as symbolic devices and are less concerned about satisfying functional needs. They would probably recognize that there are small differences between brands in product performance, but they would believe that the representational issues are of more importance. The role of advertising for these brands is either to gain their acceptability as 'part of the culture' (e.g. The Oxo Family), or to reinforce a lifestyle (e.g. Martini). A continuous advertising presence would be needed here. Product development issues would be less crucial compared with those brands which satisfy high functional needs. The product's strategy, however, must ensure a coherent approach to satisfy the positioning objective. More reliance needs to be placed upon the results of branded, rather than blind product-testing against competition.

Low representationality–low functionality
Brands in the bottom left quadrant of Figure 8.2 are bought by customers when they are not particularly concerned about functional needs. The development of Spar as a 'convenience store' epitomizes this type of brand – a limited range of groceries that satisfy consumers who realize they have run out of a grocery product and whose sole concern is replacing the product regardless of brand availability. In general, brands in this quadrant must have wide distribution and be very price competitive. To be able to fight on price, the producer needs to strive for cost-leadership in the industry. This entails being an efficient producer, avoiding marginal customer accounts, having long production runs and continually monitoring overhead costs. Brands in this quadrant are vulnerable to delisting and to succeed, the supplier must be able to justify an attractive price proposition to the distributor and consumer. It is quite possible for manufacturers to deliberately launch 'fighting brands' into this sector, the purpose of which, for example, would be to complete a range of products or as an offensive attack against a particular competitor, or as part of a segmented approach to their market.

Managing brands over their life cycles

So far, this chapter has focused on clarifying what combination of marketing resources best support a particular type of brand, *at a given point in time*. It needs to be appreciated, however, that the returns from brands depend on where they are in their life cycle. Different types of marketing activities are needed according to whether the brand is new to the market, or is a mature player in the market. In this section, we go through the main stages in brands' life cycles and consider some of the implications for marketing activity.

Developing and launching new brands

Traditional marketing theory, particularly that practised by large, fast-moving consumer goods companies, argues for a well-researched new product development process. When new brands are launched, they arrive in a naked form, without a clear personality to act as a point of differentiation. Some brands are born being able to capitalize on the firm's umbrella name, but even then they have to fight to establish their own unique personality. As such, in their early days, brands are more likely to succeed if they have a genuine functional advantage; there is no inherent goodwill, or strong brand personality, to act as a point of differentiation. One of the problems with the innovative excellence of Sir Clive Sinclair was that his new technological brands came to market without sufficient bench testing or anticipation of consumer usage. Several of his brands could not deliver on the functional benefit claimed by the promotional support. Miniature televisions stopped working after twenty minutes, due to overheating, and the batteries in the Sinclair digital watches only lasted for about a month, due to the number of times users wanted a time display.

New brand launches are very risky commercial propositions. The well-documented reviews of new brand launches show that less than 10 per cent of new launches prove successful. To reduce the chances of a new brand not meeting its goals, many firms rightly undertake marketing research studies to evaluate each stage of the brand's development amongst the target market. Sometimes, however, excessively sophisticated techniques are employed, lengthening the time before the new brand is launched. While such procedures do reduce the chances of failures, they introduce unnecessary delays, which often cannot be financially justified. It is particularly important that delays in the development programmes for technological brands are kept to a minimum. For example, it was calculated that if a new generation of laser printers has a life cycle of five years and assuming a market growth rate of 20 per cent per annum, with prices falling 12 per cent per annum, delaying the launch of the new brand by only six months would reduce the new brand's cumulative profits by a third.

Marketers launching new technological brands need to adopt a far more practical approach, balancing the risk from only doing pragmatic, essential marketing research, against the financial penalties of delaying a launch. The Japanese are the ultimate masters at reducing risks with new technology launches, with their so-called 'second fast strategy'. They are only too aware of the cost of delays and once a competitor has a new brand on the market, if it is thought to have potential, they will rapidly develop a comparable brand. In June 1989, Sony launched the very successful CCD TR55 camcorder. This weighed 800 grams and had 2200 components shrunk into a space which was a quarter of that of the conventional camcorder. Within six months, JVC had an even lighter version, soon followed by Sanyo, Canon, Ricoh and Hitachi. In the 35 mm single-lens-reflex camera market, Minolta launched the first autofocus model. Realizing the potential in this new development, Canon underwent a crash research programme and shortly afterwards launched an improved model, which halved the autofocusing time.

It is less common for Japanese companies to test new brand ideas through marketing research to the extent seen in Western Europe. For example, one report estimated that approximately 1000 new soft drinks brands were launched one year in Japan, with 99 per cent failing. In both low and medium cost goods, more emphasis is placed on testing through selling. In part, this reflects the Japanese philosophy of not just passively listening to the customer, but more actively in leading them. Few purchasers have the ability to envisage futuristic new products such as the NEC dream of the telephone that can translate different languages or Motorola's desire for telephone numbers attached to people rather than places. The greater emphasis on testing new products through selling also reflects the Japanese view that this enables their managers to get much more experience of new markets much faster. Failures are not seen as a hunt for a scapegoat. Instead analysis is undertaken to learn from the failures and these results rapidly feed back to better the next generation of products.

The benefits from being first to launch a new brand in a new sector are considerable. First, technological leapfrogging cuts brands' life-expectancies. For example, electromechanical brands of typewriters had fifteen years of sales before electric ones replaced them, albeit with only seven years sales before first generation word processors became popular.

Secondly, being first with a new brand that proves successful, presents opportunities to reduce costs. This is due to issues such as economies of scale and the experience effect – every time cumulative production is doubled, costs per unit item fall by a finite amount. The pharmaceutical industry is a good example of innovative brands being particularly profitable due to economies of scale. Empirical analysis of new launches showed that over a four-year period, the pioneering brands achieved a return on investment of about 23 per cent, the early follower 21 per cent and the late entrant 17 per cent.

Thirdly, being first, and strongly supporting the brand, can result in strong consumer loyalty. Almost without thinking about it, they ask for the brand which has become generic for the product field. Xerox copiers have been so well supported with their innovative developments, that they've become part of everyday terminology.

Fourthly, being the first with a new brand sets habits which are difficult to change. For example, in the drugs industry, GPs prefer to prescribe medication with which they've become confident. To listen to a sales representative talking about a 'me-too' version takes time and introduces uncertainty about efficacy in the GP's mind.

When launching new brands in technological markets, marketers are only too aware of the high costs they are likely to incur. As such, the successful firms look at launching a new technology into several product sectors. For example, Honda's development work on multivalve cylinder heads with self-adjusting valves, was extended across motorcycles, cars, lawn-mowers and power-generation equipment.

New technological brands succeed because the firm emphasizes coordination, rather than functional skills. Project teams are set up, integrating a variety of functional competencies. In 1985, Hewlett-Packard put together a team of researchers, engineers and marketers to look at developing a new laser printer which, while slower than the standard printer, would be sold for less than half the price. With clear objectives, they learnt about customers' needs and evaluated the weaknesses of existing low cost printers. Once a technological solution was identified, manufacturing engineers joined the team to develop the concept of a new print head. When this was shown to be feasible, a formal marketing plan was prepared and agreed. A prototype was then developed and tested. Once this goal was achieved, the project team grew to include specialists in component sourcing, mechanical design and control software. As further prototypes were being developed and tested with customers, production facilities were built and marketing programmes were refined. In February 1988, twenty six-months after the idea was first discussed, the Hewlett-Packard Deskjet printer was successfully launched. Most of the original team were subsequently transferred to other projects within the firm. The remainder became attentive to customer comments and in a similar way worked to launch a faster, cheaper version by April 1989.

One of the nagging doubts marketers have when launching a new brand is that of the sustainability of the competitive advantage inherent in the new brand. The 'fast-follower' may quickly emulate the new brand and reduce its profitability by launching a lower-priced brand. In the very early days of the new brand the ways that competitors might copy the new brand are through:

- Design issues, such as, colour, shape, size.
- Physical performance issues, such as quality, reliability, durability.
- Product service issues, such as, for example, guarantees, installation, after-sales service.
- Pricing.
- Availability through different channels.
- Promotions.
- Image of the producer.

If the new brand is the result of the firm's commitment to functional superiority, the design and performance characteristics probably give the brand a clear differential advantage, but this will soon be surpassed. For example, in areas like consumer electronics, a competitive lead of only six months is not unusual. Product service issues can sometimes be a more effective barrier. For example, BMW installed a software chip in their engines that senses, according to the individual's driving style, when the car needs servicing. Only BMW garages have the ability to reset the service indicator on their cars' dashboards. Price is an easy variable to copy, particularly if the follower is a large company with a range of brands that they can use to support a short-term loss from pricing low. British Airways overcame the challenge from Laker on the trans-Atlantic route by cutting prices on this route, and using the rest of their routes to subsidise this action. Unless the manufacturer has particularly good relationships with distributors that only stock his brand, which is not that common, distribution does not present a barrier to imitators.

Finally, if the firm is prepared to give the new brand promotional support, they can take advantage of the halo effect from any positive associations through the firm's image and generally develop a strong brand personality. Promotional support helps communicate the new brand's point of difference and can sustain its competitive edge.

Managing brands during the growth phase

Once a firm has developed a new brand, it needs to ensure that it has a view about how the brand's image will be managed over time. The brand image is the consumers' perceptions of who the brand is and what it stands for – it reflects the extent to which it satisfies consumers' functional and representational needs. A lot has been written about appropriate strategies for managing a product or service over its life cycle, but there are few references about how to manage the brand's image over time.

At the launch, there must be a clear statement about the extent to which the brand will satisfy functional and representational needs. For example, Lego building bricks, when originally launched in 1960, were positioned as an unbreakable, safe toy, enabling children to enjoy creativity in designing and building. Using the earlier brands matrix, this brand was positioned as high on functionality and low on representationality.

As sales rise, the brand's image needs to be protected against inferior, competitive, look alikes. The functional component of the brand can now be reinforced, either through a problem-solving specialization strategy, or a problem-solving generalization strategy. If the specialization strategy were to have been followed, Lego would have been positioned solely for educational purposes. It would have been targeted at infant and primary school teachers. The problem with this strategy is that in the long term, competitors may develop a brand that meets a much broader variety of needs. By following a product-solving generalization strategy, the brand is positioned to be effective across a variety of usage situations. This was the route that Lego actually followed.

The original approach to supporting the representational component of the brand needs to be maintained as sales rise. For example, for those brands that are bought predominantly to enable consumers to say something about themselves, it is important to maintain the self-concept and group membership associations. By communicating the brand's positioning to both the target and non-target segments, but selectively working with distributors to make it difficult for the non-targeted segment to buy the brand, its positioning will be strengthened.

Managing brands during the maturity phase

In the maturity part of the life cycle, the brand will be under considerable pressure. Numerous competitors will all be trying to win greater consumer loyalty and more trade interest. One option is to extend the brand's meaning to new products. A single image is then used to unite all the individual brand images. This strategy was successfully employed by Polycell. It established an image of DIY simplicity and reliability with its original range of wallpaper paste, then extended this across such products as fillers, double glazing and home security. When following this strategy in the maturity stage, the firm must continually question whether a new addition to the product range will enhance the total brand image. If the individual line would dilute the original positioning, the new line should be rejected.

Where the brand primarily satisfies consumers' functional needs, these functional requirements should be identified and any further brand extensions evaluated against this list to see if there is any similarity between the needs that the new brands will meet and those being satisfied by an existing brand. Where there is a link between the needs being satisfied by the existing brand and the new needs fulfilled by a new brand, this represents an appropriate brand extension. For example, Black & Decker's proposition is that of making DIY jobs easier with the use of high-performance, electrically powered tools. Their extension from hand-held electrical drills, to lawn-mowers, to car vacuum cleaners, was entirely consistent with their original brand image. By contrast, when the brand primarily satisfies representational needs, these should be assessed and taken as an essential criteria for future brand extensions. For example, the quality Gucci range of fashion wear and accessories says a lot about the chic and discerning tastes of a sophisticated person. Their range is successfully expanding by building on this representational dimension, showing how the consumer's lifestyle is more complete with further Gucci brands.

Managing brands during the decline phase

As brand sales begin to decline, firms need to carefully evaluate the two main strategic options of recycling their brand or coping with decline.

When the brand is recycled the marketer needs to find new uses for the brand, either through the functional dimension, or the representational dimension. A good example of functional brand recycling is the Boeing 727 aircraft. In the late 1960s rising oil prices made this aircraft less attractive to airline companies and sales fell. Boeing refused to let this brand die and redesigned the 727, making it more economical on fuel. Sales of the brand recovered between 1971 and 1979 with this functional improvement. Guinness is a classic example of how a brand was repositioned to capitalize on demographic change, with marketing activity focusing on representationality. Spearheaded by a novel promotional campaign, Guinness was repositioned to appeal to younger drinkers.

Should the firm feel there is little scope for functional or representational brand changes, it still needs to manage its brands in the decline stage. If the firm is committed to frequent new brand launches, it does not want distributors rejecting new brands because part of the firm's portfolio is selling too slowly. A decision needs to be taken about whether the brand should be quickly withdrawn, for example, by cutting prices, or whether it can gradually die, enabling the firm to reap higher profits through cutting marketing support.

Financial implications of brands during their life cycle

According to the stage in the brand's life cycle, so it needs to be managed for long-term profitability. In the early stages of its life, the brand will need financial support, while in the maturity stage it should generate cash. The matrix in Figure 8.3 shows these financial implications.

In its introduction stage, the new brand will be fighting for awareness amongst consumers and will depend heavily on the skills of the salesforce to win the trade's interest and so stock the new brand. Company executives must resist the temptation to try to recoup the large R&D brand investment by saving on promotional support; all this will do is to prolong the period of slow sales. On the matrix in Figure 8.3, the very early days of the brand are represented by quadrant A, where there is a need for large cash resources, with only a small market share resulting. At this stage, the new brand is a drain on company resources.

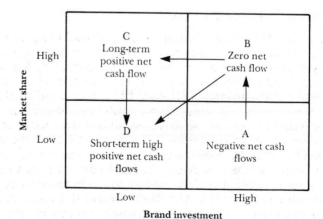

Figure 8.3   *Financial management of brands. (After Ward et al., 1989)*

brands, according to the consensus view about how well each brand satisfies consumers' functional needs. Do this on a scale where 10 represents 'excellent satisfier of consumers' functional needs' and 1 represents 'extremely poor satisfier of consumers' functional needs'. What could be done to improve your brand's positioning on this dimension? What is the brand leader doing particularly well on the functional dimension?

With those colleagues who have been with your firm for some time, repeat the exercise, but this time for a period twelve months ago. Compare the historical and current scores for all the brands on the functional dimension and evaluate why these movements took place.

4 Amongst your colleagues, form a consensus view about what consumers are trying to say about themselves when they buy brands in your product field. Identify no more than five attributes describing this representational dimension. Score your brand and competitors' brands according to the consensus view about how well each brand satisfies consumers' representational needs. Do this on a scale where 10 stands for 'excellent satisfier of consumers' representational needs' and 1 represents 'extremely poor satisfier of consumers' representational needs'. Are there any improvements that will help your brand's positioning on this dimension? What is the brand leader doing particularly well on the representational dimension?

With long-serving colleagues, repeat the exercise for a period twelve months ago. Compare the historical and current scores for the brands on the representational dimension and evaluate why these movements took place.

5 Undertake an audit of all the new brands which your firm has launched in the past five years. Focusing on those brands that have since been withdrawn, and those which are regarded as doing badly, identify the reason for their poor performance. Does any one reason continually appear?

6 For any one of your more recently launched new brands, get your marketing research department to produce a timetable detailing the amount of time taken for each piece of marketing research. Does any one piece of marketing research appear to have consumed a lot of time? Are there any reasons why this took so long? How much time elapsed between the completion of fieldwork for each project and the presentation of results? How long could it have taken to a brief 'top line' finding, where only the results on each question are presented, without any detailed cross-analysis and without any written report? Are there any implications about how time can be saved on future marketing research reports?

7 Are there any product fields where one of your new brands could augment the operating characteristics of one of these products, extending the product's lifespan and increasing sales of your new brand?

8 How effective is your firm at bringing together groups of people from different functional backgrounds to form a new brand project team? Are there any barriers within your firm that impede the formation of new project teams?

9 Do your brand plans consider how each brand's image will be protected as they pass through their life cycles?

10 For any recent brand extensions, evaluate whether there is a natural link between the functional, or representational, needs satisfied by the brand extension and the original brand. Where there is only a weak link, it is worth considering severing any association between the two brands.

11 Using the matrix shown in Figure 8.3, plot where each of your brands currently resides. If there are no brands in quadrant C you should question what has to be done to secure your firm's future over the next three years.

12 For each of your established brands, identify any social, economic, technological, political, competitive and channel changes that have occurred since they were launched. In view of these changes, is the current presentation of each brand relevant to the new marketing environment? If any brand is in need of a change to make it more relevant for the current environment, use the flow chart in Figure 8.4 to identify appropriate actions.

References and further reading

Alcock G., Batten C. (1986). Judging the worth of brand values. *Marketing Week*, 25 Apr., pp. 58–61.

Anon. (1991). What makes Yoshio invent. *The Economist*, 12 Jan., p. 75.

Berry N. (1988). Revitalising brands. *Journal of Consumer Marketing*, **5**, (3), 15–20.

Buzzell R., Gale B. (1987). *The PIMS Principles – linking strategy to performance*. New York: The Free Press.

Clifford D., Cavanagh R. (1985). *The Winning Performance: how America's high growth midsize companies succeed*. London: Sidgwick and Jackson.

Connor B. (1986). How oldies go for black. *Marketing*, 20 Feb., pp. 39–43.

Cooper R. (1987). *Winning at New Products*. Agincourt, Ontario: Gage.

de Chernatony L., McWilliam G. (1990). Appreciating brands as assets through using a two dimensional model. *International Journal of Advertising*, **9**, (2), 111–19.

Gardner B., Levy S. (1955). The product and the brand. *Harvard Business Review*, **33**, (Mar.–Apr.), 35–41.

Hamel G., Prahalad C. (1991). Corporate imagination and expeditionary marketing. *Harvard Business Review*, **69**, (Jul.–Aug.), 81–92.

Hoggan K. (1988). Back to life. *Marketing*, 3 Mar., pp. 20–2.

Interbrand (1990). *Brands – an international review*. London: Mercury Books.

Jones J. P. (1986). *Whats in a Name?* Lexington: Lexington Books.

Katz D. (1960). The functional approach to the study of attitudes. *Public Opinion Quarterly*, **24**, (Summer), 163–204.

Kim P. (1990). A perspective on brands. *Journal of Consumer Marketing*, **7**, (4), 63–7.

Landon E. (1974). Self concept, ideal self concept and consumer purchase intentions. *Journal of Consumer Research*, **1**, (Sept.), 44–51.

Lannon J., Cooper P. (1983). Humanistic advertising. *International Journal of Advertising*, **2**, 195–213.

Lawless M., Fisher R. (1990). Sources of durable competitive advantage in new products. *Journal of Product Innovation Management*, **7**, (1), 35–44.

Munson J., Spivey W. (1981). Product and brand user stereotypes among social classes. In: *Advances in Consumer Research* (Monroe K., ed.) vol. 8. Ann Arbor: Association for Consumer Research, pp. 696–701.

Nevens T., Summe G., Uttal B. (1990). Commercializing technology: what the best companies do. *Harvard Business Review*, **68**, (May–June), 154–63.

Olshavsky R., Granbois D. (1979). Consumer decision making – fact or fiction? *Journal of Consumer Research*, **6**, (Sept.), 93–100.

Park C., Jaworski B., MacInnis D. (1986). Strategic brand concept image management. *Journal of Marketing*, **50**, (Oct.), 135–45.

Saporito B. (1986). Has-been brands go back to work. *Fortune*, 28 Apr., pp. 97–8.

Sheth J., Newman B., Gross B. (1991). Why we buy what we buy: a theory of consumption values. *Journal of Business Research*, **22**, (2), 159–70.

Solomon M. (1983). The role of products as social stimuli: a symbolic interactionism perspective. *Journal of Consumer Research*, **10**, (Dec.), 319–29.

Urban G., Star S. (1991). *Advanced Marketing Strategy*. Englewood Cliffs: Prentice Hall.

Ward K., Srikanthan S., Neal R. (1989). Life-cycle costing in the financial evaluation and control of products and brands. *Quarterly Review of Marketing*, (Autumn), pp. 1–7.

Weitz B., Wensley R. (1988). *Readings in Strategic Marketing*. Chicago: Dryden Press.

Wicks A. (1989). Advertising research – an eclectic view from the UK. *Journal of the Market Research Society*, **31**, (4), 527–35.

9 Competitive considerations in branding

Summary

The purpose of this chapter is to review the diverse ways of positioning and sustaining brands against competitors. It explores the two broad types of brand competitive advantage – being cost driven or value added – and considers how value chain analysis can help identify the sources of competitive advantage. In considering the competitive scope of brands, strategies to develop different brands are reviewed. Methods of sustaining competitive advantage are described within a context of clarifying who are competitors and how their responses can be anticipated. The strategic implications from a knowledge of brand share are presented. Characteristics of winning brands are presented, along with findings about advertising activity. Issues about building or buying brands are raised and a structured approach to brand extensions is described.

Brands as strategic devices

In Chapter 2, we showed that firms interpret brands in different ways and as a consequence they place different emphasis on the resources they use to support their brands. For example, some firms believe that brands are primarily differentiating devices and as such they put a lot of emphasis on finding a prominent name. Others view brands as being functional devices and their marketing programmes emphasize excellence of performance. Our research has shown, however, that the really successful companies adopt a holistic perspective by regarding their brands as strategic devices. In other words, they analyse the forces that can influence the profitability of their brand, identify a position for their brand that majors on the brand's unique advantages and defend this position against competitive look-alikes. By adopting this perspective, the marketer does not just emphasize design, or advertising, but instead coherently employs all the company's resources to sustain the brand's advantage over competitors.

A lot of time and effort will have been devoted to developing added values for a brand that purchasers appreciate. Once confident about their relevance to purchasers, brand plans will be developed and followed through to ensure that the brand's differential advantage is sustained. At this point, it is worthwhile repeating our definition of a brand from Chapter 2, which encapsulates all these points

A successful brand is an identifiable product, service, person or place, augmented in such a way that the buyer or user perceives relevant, unique added values which match their needs most closely. Furthermore, its success results from being able to sustain these added values in the face of competition.

The strategist subscribing to this holistic view of branding recognizes that the key to success lies in finding a competitive advantage that others find difficult to copy. Unless the brand has a sustainable competitive advantage, it will rarely succeed in the long run. Brands such as Frigidaire fridges, Sinclair Spectrum computers, and Double Diamond ale disappeared because they were unable to sustain their added values against more innovative competitors, who were attentive and responsive to changing consumer needs.

In the market for overnight delivery of letters and parcels there are many competent brands to choose from, yet none match the positioning that Federal Express boasts in its advertising, 'When it absolutely, positively has to be there overnight'.

Federal Express's ability to sustain, particularly in the USA, its competitive advantage of rapid delivery is due to their efficiency in integrating a variety of supporting issues. All of their employees are carefully selected and trained to deliver superior customer service. Everyone is committed to the dictum, 'satisfied customers stay loyal to my firm' and individuals are encouraged to be independent, resourceful and creative in helping to meet customers' requests. Logistics planning and investment in physical distribution enable the firm to have the infrastructure to provide timely delivery. Supporting systems have been carefully designed and installed to ensure total customer satisfaction. For example, microprocessor technology enables any enquirer to be rapidly informed as to the location of their parcel. By integrating all of these issues within a clearly communicated strategy, Federal Express has gone from strength to strength.

In the industrial sector, Snap-on Tool's competitive advantage of superior service enables it to sell its tools successfully at a higher price than competitors – and sustain this position. Dealers regularly call on customers, mainly garages, with well stocked vans. Call schedules are designed so their customers know when to expect visits. Typically, on each visit, the salesperson goes in with new products, allowing customers to try them out. Very thoroughly trained salespeople learn to understand each of their customers and are able to offer attractive credit terms. With life-time guarantees and the reputation of the salespeople, the firm stays away from competing on price.

Both of these examples show brands succeeding through having a competitive advantage and a strategy to ensure that competitors cannot easily share this position.

The first stage in developing a competitive advantage is to analyse the environment in which the brand will compete. One of the most helpful ways of doing this is to use the framework shown in Figure 2.3 in Chapter 2. This logically enables the marketer to consider the opportunities and threats facing the brand from within his own organization, distributors, consumers, competitors and the wider marketing environment. Fully aware of the forces that the brand must face, the strategist can then start to find the most appropriate positioning for the brand.

Value-added or cost-driven brands?

Brands succeed because they are positioned to capitalize on their unique characteristics, which others find difficult to emulate – their competitive advantages. This positioning is a coherent, total positioning, since it is backed by every functional department in the firm. Everyone should be aware of what the brand stands for and they all need to be committed to contributing to its success.

A brand's competitive advantage gives it a basis for outperforming competitors because of the value that the firm is able to create for consumers. Consumers perceive value in brands when:

- it costs less to buy them than competing brands offering similar benefits, i.e. 'cost-driven brands'.
  and, or
- when they have unique benefits which offset their premium prices, i.e. 'value-added brands'.

Cost-driven brands

The advertisement in early 1990 for the Mazda 626GLX Executive is a good example of a cost-driven brand. The advertisement is making the point that if the consumer is mainly concerned about luxurious car fittings, this car offers as standard the same features as those on a BMW 735iL and a Mercedes 560SEC, but at a price which is at least £26 000 cheaper. Those consumers to whom this advertisement is targeted, are likely to perceive value in the Mazda brand because it offers high specifications at a lower price.

Cost-driven brands thrive because action is continually being taken to curtail costs. As Figure 9.1 shows, compared against the industry average, their total costs are always lower. A profit margin at least equivalent to that of other competitors can then be added, and yet still result in a selling price lower than the average competitor.

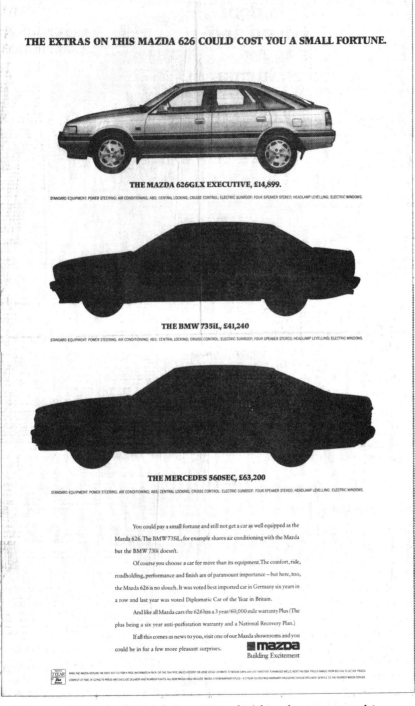

Exhibit 9.1   *Strategically Mazda is positioned in this advert as a cost-driven brand. (Reproduced with kind permission of Mazda Cars (UK) Ltd)*

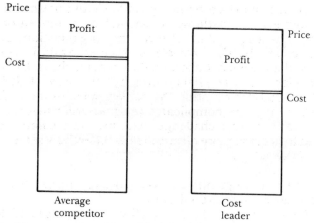

Figure 9.1   *The economics of cost-driven brands*

Some marketers shun the idea of cost-driven brands since they equate low cost with low quality. In some cases, of course, they are justified. Reducing quality standards, however, is only one way of reducing costs, but is not the recommended route to follow since it can cause consumer dissatisfaction. Some of the other ways of cutting costs are through economies of scale, gaining more experience faster than competitors, more selective raw materials sourcing, dealing only with large order customers, introducing new technology in production and streamlining the product range. By understanding precisely what the target market wants, unnecessary frills can be eliminated and an attractively priced proposition developed. For example, in grocery retailing, Kwik Save strives for the lowest cost position, as do its competitors Aldi and Netto, not by cutting back on quality, but by eliminating frills and services not relevant to the target market. Its low cost competitive advantage is achieved by:

- Not price marking individual items.
- Not having 'free' bags.
- Not accepting credit cards and their handling fees.
- Having a small number of lines.
- Not stocking own labels and thus being able to negotiate better discounts from manufacturers.
- Having small stores that typically cost £1m to open, compared with anything up to £50m for superstores.
- Being able to open their stores in a shorter time than Superstores.
- Taking advantage of information technology.

Likewise in the motel sector, some of the ways that Travelodge are able to offer budget prices for comfortable, clean rooms to travellers are:

- Making the most of spare land next to Little Chefs.
- Being well located close to main routes.
- Not having to provide dining facilities in the motels.

Following a cost-driven branding route should not mean demotivating employees. If anything, it can act as a motivator through presenting challenges that stretch the organization and allow individual creativity. For example, to succeed against Xerox in the personal copier business, Canon set its engineers the task of designing a home copier to sell at $1000 – over half the price of their current range. By literally reinventing the copier, substituting a disposable cartridge for the more complicated image-transfer mechanism, they were able to meet this challenge. Without the resources of Xerox, Canon had to become more creative in cost effectively selling its range. This was achieved by:

- Distributing through office-product dealers rather than meeting head-on Xerox's massive salesforce.
- Designing reliability and serviceability into its range and delegating servicing to its dealers rather than setting up service networks.
- Selling rather than leasing their machines, thus not having to administer leasing facilities.

Cost-driven brands succeed when everyone in the firm knows that each day they have to become more independent and more creative in curtailing the costs of good quality brands. Any newly launched competitor brands are subjected to careful scrutiny to see if further cost improvements can be made. Cost advantages are not just sought from one source, but from many areas.

In common with all strategies, there are risks in developing cost-driven brands. R&D activity may result in lower cost, superior brands as a result of new technology, whilst some firms may have short-sighted views about the sustainability of the current technology. For example, NEC's objective of building a core competence in semiconductors resulted in over 100 strategic alliances by 1987. Another danger is that marketers fail to foresee marketing changes because of their blinkered attention to costs. In the 1920s, Ford was busy improving production efficiency and achieving lower costs on models whose sales were falling since General Motors had started to offer a wider range of cars, better enabling drivers to express their individuality. The days of 'Any car, provided it's black' were not to last that long.

Before following a cost-driven brand strategy, the marketer needs to consider how appropriate this is. For example:

- Is the price-sensitive segment sufficiently large and likely to grow?
- How will buyers respond when competitors launch low price alternatives?
- How fast can experience be gained to reduce costs?
- Is the culture of the firm geared to reducing costs?

Should there be doubts about this route, the alternative of value-added brands needs assessing.

Value-added brands

Value added brands are those that offer more benefits than competitors' brands, for which a premium price is charged. Cray Research supercomputers have the competitive advantages of huge data processing capabilities and are able to interface with any other computer equipment. They operate with software written in any language and are supported by an ever-expanding software library. There is an on-site support team that ensures users know how to use the machines effectively and which maintains virtually 99 per cent problem-free running time. At over $15m for each computer, this brand represents the computing dream of most engineers and scientists.

Value-added brands do not just succeed through functional excellence; a strong image can also be a powerful competitive advantage. For example, both the Toyota Supra Turbo and the Porsche Carrera have an acceleration of 0–60 mph in 6.1 seconds and both have approximately the same top speed of 150 mph. Yet, the Porsche image, created by years of advertising, helps contribute to this car's price of approximately £38 000 compared with £23 000 for the Toyota.

To produce and market a value-added brand, the firm usually incurs greater costs than the average competitor in that sector. There is something special about the brand that necessitates more work to make it stand out. By making the brand different, it is likely that consumers will notice this and, for relevant added values, they will be prepared to pay a higher price. In such a situation, the marketer is able to anticipate a higher margin than his competitors and set a price which fully reflects the benefits being sold. The resulting economics of value-added brands is shown in Figure 9.2.

In the grocery retailing sector, Harrods Food Hall is a good example of a value-added brand. Consumers recognize that they are always certain of high quality produce, backed by a no-quibble guarantee. They enjoy the tastefully designed environment and appreciate being served by knowledgeable staff. Furthermore, the image surrounding

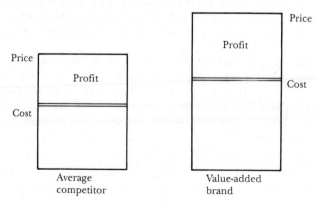

Figure 9.2   *The economics of value-added brands*

the well-known brand of Harrods adds further value to the grocery shopping experience and justifies the price premium.

In the potato market, Marks & Spencer has transformed a cheap commodity into a value-added brand through innovative marketing. They developed a value-added brand by only accepting a certain size of potato, washing its skin, cutting it, placing cheese in it, aesthetically wrapping it and proudly giving it a prominent shelf position in their stores. Through this value-adding process, they were able to charge a price considerable higher than the cost of the raw materials.

Ideally, value-added brands differentiate themselves using a variety of attributes, as can be appreciated from the way that Citibank managed to increase its business in the hostile Japanese retail banking sector. Its six branches operated in a cartelized sector, where all banks were required by the Ministry of Finance to pay the same interest on yen investments. In 1985, it had no automated teller machines, while many of its competitors each had over a thousand. After undertaking a situation analysis, it developed its retail banking operation into a value-added brand through a series of actions.

1 *It competed on the basis of foreign yield* The regulations forbid offering competitive rates on yen investments, but said little about foreign currency deposits. By offering virtually double the interest on deposits in American dollars, they attracted a significant number of new customers.
2 *It advertised aggressively* Breaking the traditional Japanese pro-motional approach of not having comparative advertising, they aggressively advertised the higher rates on American dollar deposits.
3 *It redefined service* It was common for customers to have to wait to be served in banks. As such, the Japanese made their banks comfortable places to wait in. By launching a telephone banking service Citibank changed the rules of engagement by not making customers wait.
4 *It defined an image and targeted customers* Citibank stressed its international, sophisticated image and targeted itself at clearly defined groups who travelled abroad a lot and were likely to have considerable liquid assets. These included expatriates, business executives and, following their service orientation, professionals who have little time to queue.
5 *It widened distribution* An agreement was made with a bank in Tokyo which has a significant number of automated teller machines (ATMs) allowing Citibank customers to use their ATMs to make cash withdrawals.
6 *It expanded the product portfolio* High interest deposit accounts were developed for other foreign currencies, as well as gold deposits.

Developing value-added brands, however, also has its risks. The price differential between the value-added brand and its lower cost competitors may widen to such an extent that consumers may no longer be prepared to pay the extra cost, particularly when there is little promotional activity justifying the brand's more exclusive positioning. Another threat is that of competitive imitations. If the technology supporting the added value benefits is not that difficult to copy, 'look-alikes' will soon appear, at a lower price. Alternatively, as we outlined in Chapter 6, buyers become more sophisticated as they repeatedly buy brands in the same product field and they start to take for granted the most recent added value change, expecting more from the brand.

Value-added brands with cost-driven characteristics

It should not be thought that brands can only have the competitive advantage of being *either* cost-driven *or* value-added. These two scenarios represent extreme cases. Instead, it is more realistic to think of the extent to which brands have a cost-driven component as well as a value-added component. By considering which of these two components is more dominant, the marketer is able to think in terms of having a brand which is predominantly cost-driven or predominantly value-added.

By considering the contribution of cost driven and value added elements of branding, it is possible to classify brand types and identify appropriate strategies. In Figure 9.3, we have presented a matrix that shows the classification of brands on a strategic basis. This model of strategic brands can best be appreciated through examples of different brands of travel agents.

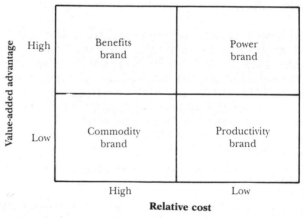

Figure 9.3   *Classifying brands on a strategic basis*

An example of a *commodity brand* would be a travel agent in a small market town, probably without any other competitors in that town and dangerously unaware of much more competitive and customer-orientated travel agents in the nearby towns. It is likely to be a small, independently run business with small offices and a cramped display in its front window. Inside the agency, there is probably a small open

The tastiest savings come from Sainsbury's.

Sainsbury's Frozen
British Grade 'A' Chicken
(Up to 4lb 8oz) 58p

39p per lb

When it comes to value, Sainsbury's lead the pecking order.
Our quality is consistently high and our prices consistently low.
Good food costs less at Sainsbury's.

SPECIAL OFFERS VALID UNTIL 24TH AUGUST 1991. ALL MERCHANDISE SUBJECT TO AVAILABILITY. SOME LINES AVAILABLE AT LARGER BRANCHES ONLY. **PRODUCTS ALSO AVAILABLE AT SAVACENTRE** THE SAINSBURY'S HYPERMARKET

Exhibit 9.2   *Attracting a lot of consumers through a range of quality goods,*
Sainsbury's is able to offer competitive prices and is categorized as a power brand

plan office, with a brochure stand restricted to only the leading travel operators. The office would be open during the weekdays from 9.00 to 5.30 and would be closed on Wednesday afternoons. It would only open on Saturdays from 9.00 to 12.00, without the full complement of staff. The staff inside the office see their role as being that of solely ensuring brochures are on display and taking customers' orders. Their ability to help customers choose a holiday is restricted to their own limited travel experience. With limited training, they are unable to advise customers about anything other than the brochures for standard package holidays. Questions about cheap flights, or visits to far away obscure foreign cities, or hotels with special facilities, cannot be competently and rapidly answered. Facilities for arranging foreign currency rarely exist and there is no service to arrange special visas. No discounts are offered. This commodity brand offers consumers an inferior service compared with other travel agents and its chances of surviving are not that good – particularly when a new agency opens.

A *benefits brand* is one which is not able to offer significant cost savings, but instead offers a particularly good service. Typical benefits brands are travel agents specializing in business travel. They have developed computerized systems to cope with requests, often at very short notice, to book complex itineraries for executives, arrange hotel accommodation along with taxis to and from all airports, advise and arrange visas, provide insurance and arrange foreign currency. The staff are well trained and regularly receive information about new developments in global travel. They spend a lot of time ensuring that they have as wide a portfolio of contacts as possible with airlines, shipping firms and hotel booking agents. These travel agents tend to target their services at organizations where there is a continual demand for 'stress free' executive travel. Unless there is a sole agency agreement, they do not offer any discounts.

A good example of *productivity brands* are those 'bucket shop' operations specializing in cheap travel arrangements. They are continually scouring the market to learn where the best travel bargains are to be found. Their shop windows and press advertisements have a simple theme – low price tickets. The larger operators sell cheap travel tickets to a wide variety of destinations, however the smaller firms service a narrower range of destinations. Very few services are provided by this type of operator.

Power brands are those successful brands that offer consumers many relevant added values. As a consequence of high consumer satisfaction, they have a high relative share of the market, enabling them to take advantage of economies of scale and the experience effect. By passing on some of these cost savings to consumers in the form of lower prices, they are able to give their brands a price advantage over competitors and maintain a virtuous brand marketing circle. Thomas Cook, as a leading travel agent, is a prime example of a power brand. It offers consumers very knowledgeable staff, a wide range of holidays to numerous destinations, long opening hours and foreign currency facilities. Its staff are well versed in their wide portfolio of holidays and can provide advice about the most appropriate destination/hotel for the concerned client. They provide attractive terms for arranging travel insurance and competitive rates when arranging currency/travellers cheques.

Commodity brands offer no advantages over any other brand and they are not particularly good value for money. Before F.W. Woolworth in the UK became part of the Storehouse group, it was a commodity brand in retailing. It was unsuccessfully trying to appeal to everyone and its lack of focus resulted in a fuzzy image. It had too wide a product range, which put excessive demands on management time and tied up capital in high stocks of slow-moving lines. History has shown that the commodity brand domain is an area to be avoided.

Benefits brands succeed because they are targeted at a specific segment, with a company-wide commitment for a process which delivers added values which consumers particularly appreciate. It is essential for these brands that the firm maintains regular contact with its market to assess satisfaction with the brand continually and identify ways that it could be improved. The firm should constantly be looking at how the brand can be improved and investment will continually be made in R&D, production, logistics and marketing to ensure that the brand remains the best. Any cost-saving programme which might have an adverse impact on the brand's quality must be resisted.

Productivity brands need to be supported by a company-wide mission that stresses the need for each individual to be continually questioning 'why do we have to do it this way?'. These brands' cost advantages can only be sustained if all aspects of the business system are continually subjected to tight cost controls. Wherever possible standardization and narrowing of the product mix need to be encouraged. Potential segments which fall below a critical size must be ignored.

Power brands like Coca-Cola, Kodak, American Express, Sony and Nescafé thrive through being very responsive to changing market needs and continually trying to improve their brands, while at the same time looking for cost advantages. While North America shrugged off the appearance of small Japanese motorcycles as an event unlikely to succeed, they failed to recognize the significance of much larger Japanese motorcycles being raced on European circuits. The racing experience provided valuable learning about designing and producing larger motorcycles. While building up a volume production and selling capability in small motorcycles this quickly resulted in a cost advantage, enabling the returns to be used to invest in widening the portfolio and adding value through attractively priced larger motorcycles.

Identifying brands' sources of competitive advantage

When managers are faced with the problem of identifying their brands' competitive advantages, Porter's Value Chain can be a very useful tool. An example of this is shown in Figure 9.4. A flow chart first needs to be constructed showing all those actions involved in transforming raw material into profitable sales – the value-creating processes. This is divided into the stages:

- In-bound logistics, for example, materials handling, stock control, receiving goods.

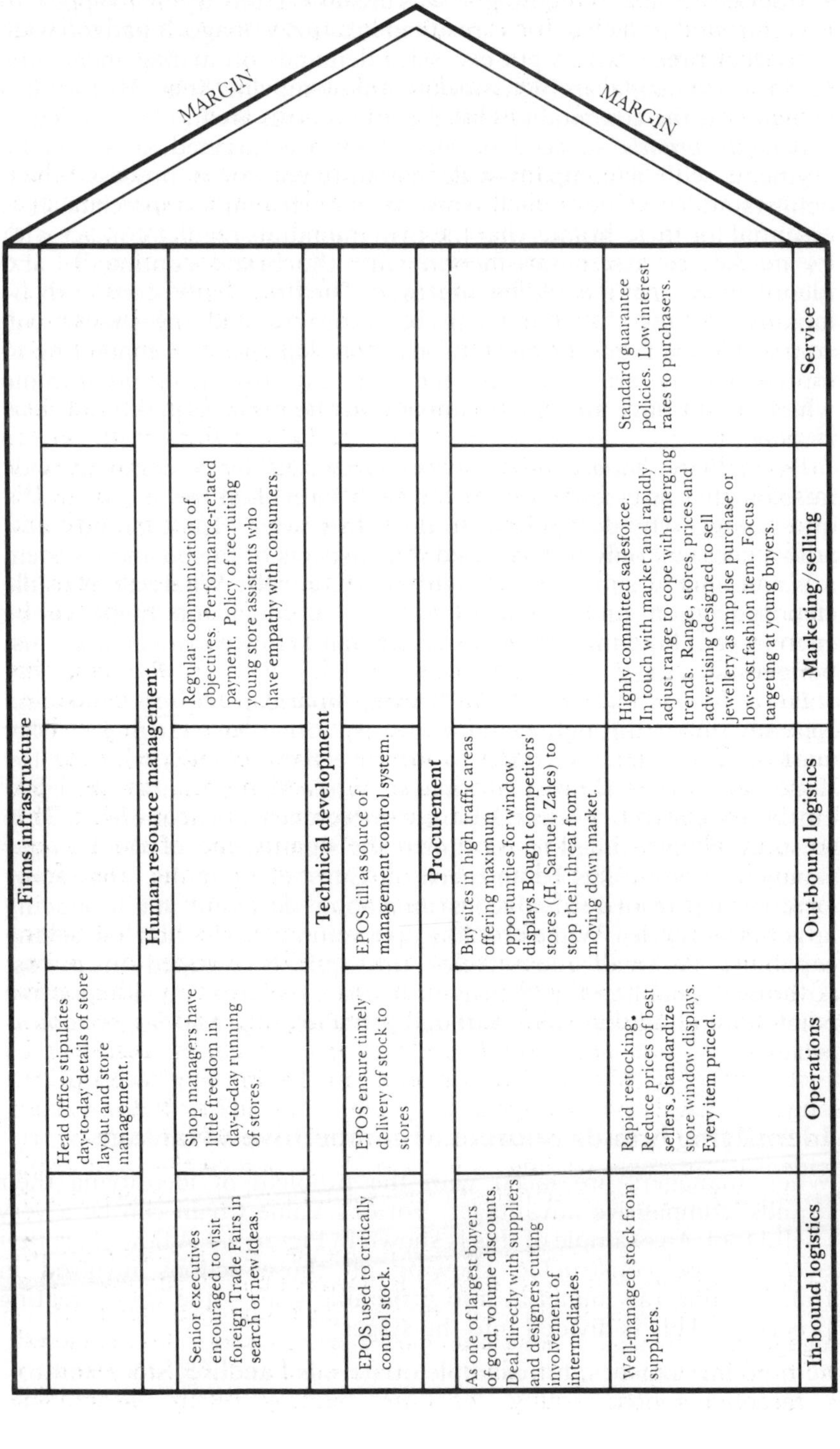

MARGIN

Firms infrastructure

Human resource management

Technical development

Procurement

	In-bound logistics	Operations	Out-bound logistics	Marketing/selling	Service
Firms infrastructure	Senior executives encouraged to visit foreign Trade Fairs in search of new ideas.	Head office stipulates day-to-day details of store layout and store management.			
Human resource management		Shop managers have little freedom in day-to-day running of stores.		Regular communication of objectives. Performance-related payment. Policy of recruiting young store assistants who have empathy with consumers.	
Technical development	EPOS used to critically control stock.	EPOS ensure timely delivery of stock to stores	EPOS till as source of management control system.		
Procurement	As one of largest buyers of gold, volume discounts. Deal directly with suppliers and designers cutting involvement of intermediaries.		Buy sites in high traffic areas offering maximum opportunities for window displays. Bought competitors' stores (H. Samuel, Zales) to stop their threat from moving down market.		
	Well-managed stock from suppliers.	Rapid restocking. Reduce prices of best sellers. Standardize store window displays. Every item priced.		Highly committed salesforce. In touch with market and rapidly adjust range to cope with emerging trends. Range, stores, prices and advertising designed to sell jewellery as impulse purchase or low-cost fashion item. Focus targeting at young buyers.	Standard guarantee policies. Low interest rates to purchasers.

Figure 9.4   Ratner's value chain

- Operations, for example, production, quality control, packing.
- Out-bound logistics, for example, storing finished goods, delivery, order processing.
- Marketing and sales, for example, pricing, promoting.
- Service, for example, installing, training, repairing.

The services supporting these activities are categorized into purchasing (procurement), technical development, human resource management and infrastructure. These are presented in the format shown in Figure 9.4, since each of these services can support many of the value-creating processes. For example, different departments within the firm may be buying raw materials, the skills of industrious employees, delivery lorries, creative advertisements and an after-sales support unit.

Benchmarking itself against its competitors, the firm should then identify those activities that its managers believe they do better, or cheaper. As competitive advantage is a relative concept, it is important that the key competitors are identified for that particular segment. If a firm has a brand competing in several distinct segments, it should produce value chains for each segment.

Within the template of the value chain, managers can start to identify their brands' competitive advantages. This may be better appreciated using the example of Ratners, the jewellers.

Since Gerald Ratner took over as Chairman of Ratners, this organization has grown to the extent that in 1991 it controlled approximately 2500 outlets, with a 31 per cent share of the jewellery market. The group operates under a series of names, such as H. Samuel, Ernest Jones, Watches of Switzerland and, in the USA, Kay. A not insignificant part of its growth came from acquisition. This not only allowed its expansion into the quality end of the market, having bought H. Samuel and Zales, but also stopped the threat from these retailers moving down into its low cost stronghold.

Its size has enabled it to capitalize on economies of scale that cannot be achieved by the large number of small jewellery competitors. As one of the world's largest gold buyers, it can negotiate very competitive prices and in the diamond market, by dealing direct with loose stone polishers, it cuts out several levels of intermediaries, resulting in further savings. With a clear vision about having the lowest-priced range of jewellery to appeal to young consumers, Ratners have developed a portfolio of cost-driven brands which are particularly evident in its stores trading as Ratners. Each part of the value chain has been successfully managed in these Ratner stores to drive costs down.

Many executives are sceptical about whether Ratners has gone too far down the low cost route, debasing the value buyers perceive. What they fail to appreciate is that Ratners have changed the rules of engagement. Instead of positioning jewellery as a seriously considered, life-time investment, normally for middle-aged and wealthy people, it is targeted at the young consumer seeking highly fashionable accessories to match their clothing and moods. They buy on impulse, not after a lengthy period of deliberation.

In the quest for low prices, Ratners have invested in information technology and a highly efficient logistics system. Through the use of scanning systems or Electronic Point of Sale (EPOS) at the cash registers, order processing systems are effectively managed, as well as rapid replacement of in-store stock. Linking each of the stores' EPOS tills with the central management information system, provides decision-makers with rapid and accurate information about sales activity. This enables them to identify the fast selling lines, which are discounted more than slower moving lines in aggressive consumer price reductions. The argument behind this selective extra discounting is that these lines are particularly responsive to price cuts. All items are clearly price marked.

The costs of the sales force are to some extent controlled by paying a basic wage, plus a bonus related to increases in turnover. Store managers spend a significant proportion of their time at the front of the shops selling, rather than at the back of the shops taking care of store administration. This is due in part to the effective use of information technology and the management control from head office stipulating details about how each individual store will be run. All stores follow a standardized layout format dictated by mock-up photographs issued on a regular basis from head office. Not only does the use of young employees enable young consumers to establish a relationship quickly during the brief sales transaction, but yet again, it contains labour costs.

Another way that Ratners are able to offer fashion jewellery at low prices is by getting their designers to work to a low price objective. For example, rather than using solid gold in a necklace, they have hollow gold. As their consumers want to be fashionable, they value being able to replace or add to their jewellery accessories regularly.

Ratners has set its sights on always being a fashion leader, and is able to respond quickly to changing tastes. Its internal operations have been structured to capitalize rapidly on new opportunities. For example, there was a great deal of interest about the type of engagement ring Princess Diana would have. As soon as the press had a photograph, this was rushed to their suppliers, who immediately set to work producing a look-alike. Four days later on Friday, stock was dispatched to their stores and by Saturday, they had sold approximately 10 000 pieces at £28.50 each. The original ring was estimated to be worth £30 000.

Unfortunately, to liven up his afternoon presentation at a conference, early in 1991, Gerald Ratner lightheartedly referred to his sherry decanter, retailing at £4.95, as 'crap'. The considerable media coverage that then ensued did little to help Ratners. In fact, after establishing a good profit record, when Ratner declared a loss of £17.7m in September 1991 there were comments that some of this was due to the ill-considered comment. The goodwill that had been built up over the years had been tarnished and some consumers changed their allegiance to other jewellery retailers.

While Ratners once stood out as being a successful low cost branding operation, it did not anticipate the severity of the recession during 1991 and 1992. In January 1992, following a 15 per cent fall in UK jewellery sales in the important six weeks before Christmas, Ratners forecast that they would only break even in the year to 1 February, but interest payments and exceptional costs would pull it into a loss.

Gerald Ratner's skills were in spotting market opportunities and driving his brands with low overhead costs. The problem was that he overstretched the organization in his acquisition programme, continually appealing to the City for more cash. This £800m acquisition programme proved a strain on the firm which, combined with the severe recession and a deterioration in consumer goodwill after his rather rash comment, resulted in a lack of confidence in the Stock Market. In a year, Ratners' share price fell from over 200p to approximately 20p in January 1992. Jim McAdam subsequently accepted Chairmanship from Gerald Ratner in an attempt to refuel City and consumer confidence, as well as implementing a rationalization plan with stringent cost controls. It's one thing to successfully change the competitive rules of engagement from 'don't come in unless you're knowledgeable and want to buy something' to 'everyone, including budget shoppers, is welcome'. However, it's another matter managing a growth programme that doesn't belittle the consumer or the City.

Besides acting as a guiding framework to help managers identify *how* brands achieve a competitive advantage, the value chain also helps managers check *whether* they are reinforcing and capitalizing on their competitive advantages. This is done by considering how well linked each of the activities are. For example, if the managers believe that the brand achieves its low cost competitive advantage because of its unique production process, this may well be protected by buying higher priced, but better quality, raw materials. As a consequence, less time and lower costs could result from not needing such significant quality control procedures at the goods-in stage, from smoother running of the production process and from less wastage at the finished-goods stage. Coordinating internal activities should ensure that all of the processes in the value chain are optimized to give the brand the best chance of capitalizing on its competitive advantages. For example, at Disney, which prides itself on its excellence of customer service, telephones are discreetly located in its theme parks, so that employees can quickly have access to advice and, if needs be, extra resources, when they spot a problem occurring.

Overlooking the linkages between any of the activities in the value chain can harm a brand. In its attempt to respond to an increasingly hostile competitive environment, EMI Medical, which had been developing different body scanners, was persuaded to let its North American company undertake the development research for a new generation of CT scanner. The problem was that they paid little attention to the five-hour time-lag and 2000-mile distance between the new R&D location and its Central Research Laboratory in England, where a wealth of technical expertise had developed earlier models. Communication between the two centres impeded progress and after two years, many UK scientists and technologists had to be transferred to America to make up time on the much-delayed programme. This was but one of the factors contributing to the demise of EMI's CT body scanner.

When considering linkages between activities, firms should not take a myopic perspective and solely consider their internal linkages. Instead, they should also identify advantages by linking their value chain back to their suppliers, or forward to their customers. For example, Xerox gives its suppliers access to its computerized manufacturing schedules, enabling them to schedule production more efficiently and ensures parts are available only when needed. Similarly, British Home Stores allows its suppliers access to parts of its computerized information system. Clearly the better a supplier understands how his industrial customer will use his product, the more scope he has for adding value by designing his value chain to integrate better with that of his buyers.

The value chain, however, has one major disadvantage. To be used effectively, managers need to have a good data base describing the processes and economics of each aspect of every competitor's value chain. It is rare to have such a rich data base. Trade journals, industry reports, salesmens' reports, distributors' comments and Monopolies and Mergers Commission reports can help to build a data base, but any remaining gaps will have to be filled by management's judgement. Clearly if there are a lot of gaps in competitor analysis and if the wrong assumptions are made, any comparative analysis may well be flawed.

Focusing brands' competitive advantages

So far, we have concentrated on strategic brands in terms of the two broad competitive advantages of value added and cost driven. But, beside the *type* of competitive advantage, the marketer also has a choice about the *scope* of the market he wishes his brand to appeal to. Again, drawing on the work of Porter, marketers are able to refine their brand strategies further by considering whether a cost-driven or value-added competitive advantage should support their brand for either a narrow or a broad target market. The four possible generic strategies are shown in Figure 9.5.

Amstrad personal computers (pc) is a good example of a brand that has followed a *focus cost* generic strategy. In the early days of pcs, Alan Sugar, Chairman of Amstrad, set his design and production engineers the task of building a pc to sell for £399 – a figure significantly lower than anything available. The new brand was targeted at small businesses and householders with an interest in computers. At the time of its launch, it aroused a lot of interest amongst this narrowly

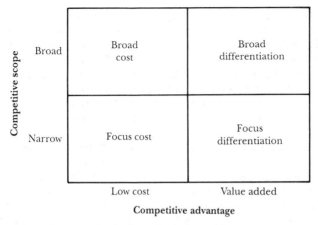

Figure 9.5   *Generic strategies for brands. (Adapted from Porter, 1985)*

defined target market, because it represented very good value for money. While the features offered were rather limited, it none the less enabled the target market to acquire basic computing capabilities, easing the administrative problems in their small businesses or homes. Brands succeed in this quadrant because they solely focus on a clearly defined group of purchasers who have very apparent needs, often less than the much broader needs of other groups. Any temptations to add new features which may appeal to a closely related group are resisted, since the marginal volume gains incur significant costs.

By contrast, Fujitsu, the world's second largest computer manufacturer, has followed a *broad cost branding* strategy. Its good quality computers appeal to a broad range of industries, and, as a global competitor, it is able to gain significant economies of scale. It markets a wide range of computers, which, while not having the subtle extras of some brands, are seen as providing a more than capable facility for most users.

IBM has built its brands following a *broad differentiation* strategy. It has developed a range of highly respected computers that appeal to virtually all industries. Not only does it have a significant R&D investment, giving it a basis for functional excellence, but it has also developed an image that is the envy of many of its competitors. The IBM brand name is synonymous with the ultimate guarantee of a computing capability that will reliably solve users' problems. The recent campaign, 'I think, therefore IBM', further reinforces this positioning. Having created respect in the market for its machines and a belief amongst buyers about function excellence, they are able to charge a price premium. Broad differentiators succeed by creating value for buyers and communicating this. A heavy cost is incurred achieving a value-added positioning and, while attempts are made to hold down costs, through, for example, information technology, the higher price is used positively to reinforce the quality positioning.

Cray Research computers have been following a very successful focus differentiation strategy with their supercomputers. Offering the most powerful computers in the industry, backed by an R&D investment of virtually 15 per cent of annual revenue, the philosophy at Cray Research is to focus only on customers for supercomputers. Even with the advent of mini supercomputers, Cray refuses to be drawn into this related market, arguing that it would dilute its total effort and jeopardize its number one position. For a carefully targeted, small number of customers, they have created a unique brand with many added values, for which a significant price premium has been charged.

Sustaining a competitive advantage

Having identified the sources of the brand's competitive advantages, and positioned it with the most appropriate generic strategy, the marketer is then faced with the problem of sustaining the brand's uniqueness. If the brand is successful, competitors usually work hard to understand the basis of this success and then rapidly develop and launch their own version – often with an improvement. The time before competitors develop their own improved versions of a new brand is shrinking, due in no small part to companies' understanding and appreciation of technology. For example, the 64K RAM, which first appeared in 1981, had virtually four and a half years before being superseded by the 256K RAM. By contrast, this had only two and a half years before the arrival of the one megabyte RAM.

The challenge facing the marketer is how to sustain the brand's competitive advantage. This is a particularly difficult problem in the services sector, where competitive responses can very quickly appear. One study proves particularly illuminating. It analysed thirty-six successful new services that competitors had difficulties in copying. Interviews with managers associated with these brands indicated ten factors that impeded rapid competitive responses. Table 9.1 shows

Table 9.1   *Factors inhibiting competitive copies*

Factor	Contribution to competitive positioning
Company reputation	4.3
Effective branding	3.9
New software introduced	3.4
Linking into existing network	3.4
Administrative and learning barriers	3.2
Access to users	3.1
New hardware introduced	2.9
Hardware already available	2.6
Software already available	2.6
Development of new network	2.1

Scores based on 5 = major contribution to competitive positioning and 1 = no contribution.

Based on Easingwood, 1990.

their views about which factors were particularly effective at slowing competitors' responses.

The company's reputation was regarded as presenting the most effective barrier to rapid competitor 'me-too' brands. In consumers' minds, the Automobile Association is strongly associated with services for cars and the launch of its new credit card for car-related expenditure was instantly accepted. Were the card to have come from a financial institution, it is thought that it would have had a lot more resistance to overcome.

The next most effective inhibitor was effective branding – logically extending the brand into a related area with the same positioning. For example, Little Chef took advantage of space adjacent to its road-side restaurants and built Little Chef Lodges, offering low rate overnight rooms.

The next most important factors impeding competitor responses were 'new software' and 'linking into existing networks'. To enhance its position as a power brand, Thomas Cook developed software which, amongst other things, controlled the stock of foreign currency each outlet had and set currency rates. Other travel agents were impressed by the system and leased the software rather than devising their own version. Having a well-established distribution network enabled The National Express Bus Company to develop a new service by using its network to launch its Express Rapide coach service.

The fifth most effective blocker was felt to be the administrative and learning barriers associated with the brand. For example, one airline company which launched a service based on collecting passengers from their homes or offices, driving them to the airport and offering the same facilities after the plane had landed, had to spend a lot of time understanding and planning with the appropriate airport authorities. They argued that it would take any competitor time to learn how to replicate this service.

Other authors argue that customer service is one of the major contributors to sustaining a brand's positioning. The type of service associated with a brand is strongly influenced by the people working on it. As company employees, they share a unique company culture with distinctive values and attitudes. Disney, British Airways, Federal Express and McDonald's are all legendary in the way that they have developed training programmes to ensure that their employees give a unique type of customer service. Provided that the employees are sufficiently briefed about new brands, their contribution to sustaining its added values can inhibit competitor responses.

One way of helping the brand remain competitive is to be the first into a market. Being the first to exploit a market opportunity leads to the cost advantages of economies of scale, and the learning curve effect. If the firm has a policy of not allowing its employees to present case studies at trade conferences, any learning is proprietary and competitors find it hard to appreciate how to gain from 'sitting on the side' and observing brand developments. There is evidence that being a pioneer can lead to above average returns on investment, but being first to a market does not automatically mean the brand will be far more profitable. It does, however, offer scope for gaining an advantage through opportunistic marketing.

Anticipating competitor response

One of the ways that firms and financial analysts in stock brokers evaluate brand strength is on the basis of their market share. Strong brands tend to be market leaders who have capitalized on the opportunities from economies of scale and experience effect. Likewise, the brand strategist is concerned with evaluating his brand's performance against key competitors. He will normally have a clear view about who are his prime and secondary competitors. As he formulates brand strategy, he will consider how he can group his competitors according to their characteristics. For example, two authors have suggested that the strategic grouping of firms in the brewing industry can be characterized by their degree of diversification and whether they are local, regional or national marketers. By modelling the competitive environment into clusters of competitors based on the degree of similarity between members of the strategic groups, the strategist is better able to evaluate competitors' strategies and anticipate responses to his brand activity. For example, one author reported that in the early 1980s, two strategic groups could be identified amongst RAM manufacturers. The first strategic group, predominantly containing Japanese firms, was characterized by:

- Being technological followers.
- Having a commitment to quality, reliability and low cost.
- Being diversified firms with large computer divisions.

The second strategic group, with firms such as Motorola and Texas Instruments, were:

- Technological innovators.
- Leaders in process innovation.
- Mainly semiconductor firms.

With such clear appreciation of the similarities of firms' strategies, it becomes easier to plan against known competitors.

Yet, while economists have historically conceived of an industry as a clearly defined group of competitors, evidence is beginning to mount showing that managers in a particular industry do *not* have similar perceptions about who the main competitors are. As part of a major research programme being sponsored by the Economic and Social Research Council to evaluate managers' perceptions of strategic groupings, de Chernatony and Johnson interviewed the senior managers of an industrial organization and found differences between members of the same management team concerning who their competitors were and the basis that they were using to form strategic groupings. While there was commonality between managers concerning many competitors, several competitors were not mentioned by all the managers. After debriefing the team about their views on who are the competitors and what bases they were using to formulate their strategic grouping, the team were better able to appreciate how each member was formulating his strategy.

If companies are going to become more effective at formulating competitive brand strategies, managers in the same firm will need to discuss more openly amongst themselves who they perceive as their competitive brand strategies, managers in the same firm will need to discuss more openly amongst themselves who they perceive as their competitors and what criteria they are using to group competitors.

After all those working on the brand have debated who they perceive their competitors to be and what the bases for strategic groupings are, they then need to evaluate which competitors are likely to respond fastest and in the most aggressive manner as a result of the firm's changes to its brand strategy. For example, the emotional commitment of the Showering family to the Babycham brand was overlooked by Seagram's when they launched Crocodillo. A significant defensive barrier was built around the Babycham brand with an investment that financial analysts might argue exceeded the value of the brand.

Attitudes can be an indicator of likely competitor response. For example, Mars, Unilever and Procter & Gamble have always striven to be leaders in their particular markets. It goes against their corporate cultures to accept that a newcomer to their market can go unchallenged in its quest to rob them of their brand shares. History may be another pointer to competitive responses. For example, in some firms, there may be a deep resentment against a particular market, or type of product, because the firm tried and failed to succeed with its brand. It does not want to re-open old wounds and may well take no action when a new competitor appears to be succeeding. Alternatively, the size of investment in plant may indicate what response to anticipate. In the packaging market, Metal Box has a considerable investment in machinery to produce high volume runs of standard size containers. It cannot afford to let its lines run slowly and any new competitor brand launches are quickly evaluated and challenged.

The brand strategist needs to consider how important the market is to each of his competitors and what their degree of commitment is. Particularly when competitors have a wide variety of brands across many different markets, their interest and commitment to protecting their brands is likely to vary. For example, commitment to part of the range might be particularly high because these markets are regarded as having significant growth potential, and have historically enabled their brands to achieve healthy returns, as well as enabling them to be highly visible players, gaining spin-offs for some of their other brands. In the UK breakfast cereals market, Kellogg's, with its wide range of brands, would never let its flagship brand, Kellogg's Corn Flakes, fall against other competitors. For too many consumers, this particular brand *is* the firm. Any weakening on this brand might be read as a weakening of the Kellogg's firm and, by inference, a deterioration of the rest of its range.

A considerable amount of *data* may well be held on competitors about such things as their plant capacities, labour rates, organizational structure, discount structures and suppliers used. However, we would question whether sufficient *information* is available on their brand strategy. To position a brand and anticipate competitors' responses, marketers should either know, or be able to gauge for each competitor:

- Its main brands, their size, profitability, growth and importance of each brand to that firm and its commitment to that brand.
- Its brand objectives and the strategy being followed. For example, are they trying to enter, improve, maintain, harvest or leave the market?
- Its brands' strengths and weaknesses.
- The competitive position of each brand, in terms of having either a leadership, strong, favourable, tenable or weak position.

The meaning of brand share

When marketers try to outflank competitors' brands with their own brands, they use market share data to track their performance. Unfortunately, all too often, market share is used predominantly as a monitoring device, rather than as a further aid to brand strategy formulation. Kenichi Ohmae's considerable experience of strategy consulting throws a lot more light on the way that brand share can help strategic thinking. Figure 9.6 shows the strategic meaning of brand share.

When a firm has achieved a presence in a market, its share of the market reflects the extent to which its brand is meeting consumers' needs better than other brands. Particularly with a high brand share, marketers are prone to complacency and, short-sightedly, do not consider the two components of market share. One element is those consumers actively competed for and won – area D in Figure 9.6. This can be regarded as *active brand marketing*. An often overlooked constituent of the brand's market share, however, is represented by area E in Figure 9.6 – those consumers buying the brand who were not competed for. This component, resulting from *passive brand marketing*, may well be those consumers, for example, intent on buying Heinz Baked Beans. When doing their grocery shopping, they discover that this particular brand is out of stock and, rather than go to another store, they choose an alternative brand. The more successful the brand, the closer the ratio D:E approaches 1. Marketing research can help identify this ratio by asking buyers just before the purchase what brand they intended buying and then recording the brand actually bought. By questioning those who bought a different brand from the one intended and why they did this, marketers can develop ways of marketing their own brands more effectively.

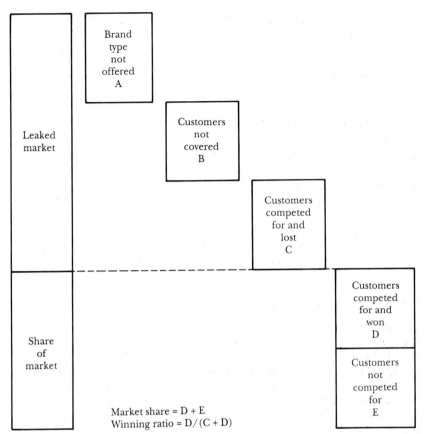

Figure 9.6 *The strategic meaning of market share. (Based on Ohmae, 1982)*

We believe the model in Figure 9.6 can be further developed. Those customers competed for and won, shown in area D, could be broken down into four further groups:

- *D1* Customers who are satisfied with the brand and who will actively select the same brand on the next occasion, regardless of competitive activity.
- *D2* Customers who are satisfied with the brand, but who can be enticed to a competitor's brand on the next occasion, if there is an attractive incentive, such as a price discount.
- *D3* Customers who regard the brand as being adequate, but not fully satisfying their needs. They stay with the brand since it is inconvenient to switch to a different brand. An example of such inconvenience might be changing bank accounts, where all the standing orders have to be changed.
- *D4* Customers who have tried the brand, but on the next purchase occasion will switch to an alternative brand, even though this may involve more effort on their behalf.

Customers D1, the 'loyalists', need to be nurtured and frequently consulted about their views on the brand. Any dissatisfaction needs to be quickly resolved.

Customers D2, the 'swingers', exist in all markets. The trade-offs they are making when choosing a particular brand need to be understood and incorporated as a further factor to consider when formulating brand strategy.

Customers D3, the 'apathetic', are offering the brand a chance for survival. If the marketer can evaluate what aspects of the brand need fine tuning to satisfy this group, he is then better able to consider implementing corrective action rapidly. Otherwise, a competitor will find a way of taking care of consumers' perceptions of inconvenience and encourage them to switch brands. For example, some building societies marketing cheque accounts, offer to take care of notifying the new consumers' employer as well as arranging to take care of the smooth transfer of standing order arrangements from their previous bank/building society account.

Customers D4, the 'doubters' gave the brand a chance and are sceptical about whether it could be changed to meet their needs. Their perceptions about what the brand could do for them, or say about them, was not realized. The reasons for these perceptions need to be assessed and, if possible, changes considered.

Area C in Figure 9.6 (customers competed for and lost) was an important part of Sir John Egan's strategy when trying to halt the decline of Jaguar cars in the mid 1980s. Market research studies with previous Jaguar owners who had switched to a different marque indicated problems with Jaguar's quality and reliability. Changes were made to improve quality and reliability and these were communicated in a new promotional campaign.

Some brands do not fully capitalize on their capabilities, since they are not available to all of the potential market, as represented by area B in Figure 9.6. This may require a more intensive distribution push to cover new areas.

Area A represents a brand opportunity, since there is a group of consumers who share needs similar to those of the core market. However, they are looking for something extra, which the brand is not yet offering. For example, the novice sailor gains basic sailing skills from the stable Topper dinghy, but then switches to the more finely balanced Laser dinghy, offering greater scope for racing. The challenge here is being able to develop new variants which capitalize on the core brand's heritage, yet which do not damage the image of the core brand.

Characterizing winning brands

The core of a successful brand is that it offers benefits to consumers in a way that other brands are unable to meet. However, profitability doesn't only result from a brand's unique competitive advantages, as research has shown.

Profitable brands are leaders

A research project was instigated in 1972 to evaluate which dimensions of strategy affect profitability. This resulted in the highly respected PIMS data base. Information from approximately 3000 business units has been analysed and one of the key findings is that large share brands are much more profitable than small share brands. On average, number one brands achieve pre-tax returns on investment three times that of brands in the fifth and lower ranked position. There are many reasons why leading brands are more profitable.

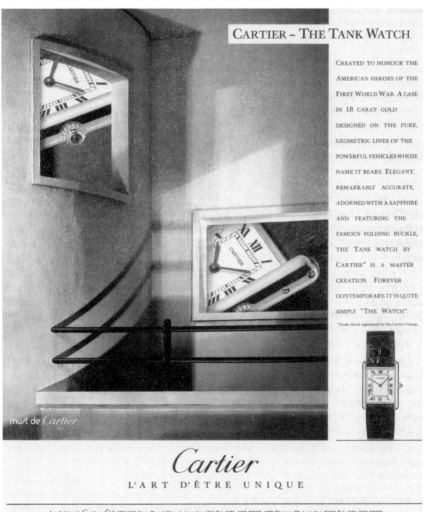

Exhibit 9.3 *Prized for its quality excellence, Cartier commands a price premium, reinforcing perceptions of quality*

Leading brands have lower costs than followers. Economies of scale are one way that costs are reduced. For example, one source estimates that a 90 million ton oil refinery costs only one and a half times as much to build as a 45 million ton refinery. Running costs per unit of output are also lower for larger production processes. The larger refinery needs less than double the number of employees of the smaller refinery. Production efficiencies are achieved with some techniques once a critical volume level is exceeded.

The learning curve presents a further opportunity for leading brands to curtail costs. For example, production managers soon learn the best way of configuring their employees on the production line and engineers soon begin to appreciate how to better harness the new technology. Taken together, economies of scale and the experience effect cause a constant reduction in costs each time cumulative production is doubled.

Leading brands instil more confidence in risk-averse consumers. They also attract higher quality employees, who are proud to be associated with a winning brand and willing to stretch their own involvement with the brand so that it maintains its dominant position.

Profitable brands are committed to high quality

The PIMS data base has shown that those brands which offer superior perceived quality relative to competitors' brands are far more profitable. Having a brand which consumers perceive to be of superior quality than other brands makes it easier for the marketer to charge a price premium. Part of the extra revenue should be used for R&D investment to sustain the quality positioning for future earnings. Also by committing everyone in the organization to doing their job in the best possible way, there is a greater conformance to standards, which results in less rejection, fewer brand recalls, less re-working and, ultimately, greater profitability. Higher quality results in higher brand shares and all the benefits that this brings.

Two points need to be stressed. The first is that it is *perceived* rather than *actual* quality which counts. Engineering may well set internal specifications for others to follow, but, ultimately, consumers decide whether the quality meets their expectations. Furthermore, consumers are often unable to evaluate the quality of a brand and they use clues to assess its performance. For example, the size of stereo speakers may be taken as an indication of their performance, or the price of a brand of wine as to its taste. In some product fields, they take the core benefit for granted and assess quality by the way the brand has been augmented. Nowadays, consumers automatically accept that any airline will safely transport them to their destination. They assess quality through issues such as the politeness of the staff, the in-flight entertainment, choice on the menu, etc.

The second point is that quality is assessed by consumers on a relative basis. They assess brands against other brands. The way they do this might not necessarily be the way that the marketer would expect. For example, even though McDonald's sees Burger King as a competitor in the hamburger market, to the consumer, McDonald's may well be competing against Pizzaland, since their interest lies in places serving fast meals.

For these and many other reasons, consumers should be interviewed regularly to enable us to understand who they see a particular brand competing against and what criteria they use to assess relative quality. Only consumer-relevant attributes should guide quality improvement initiatives. Employees should be encouraged to go out and listen to consumers' views about their brands. A corporate culture, such as that at Honda, which encourages employees to challenge existing procedures and make improvements, can raise consumers' perceptions of quality.

Having achieved a reputation amongst consumers for being a quality brand, marketers need to continuously work to improve this. Over time, there is a danger of the quality positioning eroding. As markets become more mature, competitors try harder to emulate the leader. Some organizations become complacent and underestimate the potential of new competitors. Others fail to protect their quality image and do not invest in product enhancement.

Profitable brands capitalize on their environment

The PIMS data base shows that different market characteristics offer different levels of profitability for brands. By actively seeking markets that have the right characteristics, the marketer can more successfully utilize resources to nurture a profitable brand. Some of the factors which have an impact on brand profitability are:

- Market evolution. Brand profitability is highest in fast growing markets and lowest in declining ones.
- Markets with a high level of exports are more profitable than those with a significant import element.
- Markets with frequent new product launches are subject to lower returns on investment, although this is less so in the services and distribution sector.

Winning brands are memorable

Brands win the minds of consumers because they are distinctive and stand out as having relevant added values. In other words, it is not just because they are heard above the noise of competitors, but because they are making the *right* noises. A brand could be scoring well on awareness, but if consumers abhor its brashness, it will not succeed.

Communicating a brand's added values is an essential component contributing to long-term success. A communication strategy, however, needs to be carefully devised. It is wrong to assume automatically that advertising is the prime route to follow. For example, Marks & Spencer have traditionally made little use of advertising, since they have correctly recognized that there are many other appropriate ways for brand communication. Consumers assess the Marks & Spencer brand from the locations where their stores are sited, from their store designs, store layout, quality of goods, the way they are treated by staff, their prices and the way they handle customer complaints.

Winning brands have a supporting communication strategy which results from a deep understanding of the myriad of clues that consumers use to interpret them. For those brands differentiating themselves primarily through their unique image, advertising is invaluable. It reinforces the essential images amongst consumers and their peer group alike. By establishing the brand on a unique and highly valued pedestal, the marketer is yet again able to charge a premium price.

Levels of promotional support

The relationship between advertising spend and brand share is a complex domain, not least because the quality of advertisements and competitors' activity are but two of many other variables that influence the equation. There is a lot of evidence to show that leading brands are committed to significant advertising spends. For example, an analysis was undertaken of the top seventy-five brands in twenty-five packaged grocery markets for 1978. The results, in Table 9.2, show that the advertising shares of the leading brands exceeded their sterling sales shares.

Table 9.2   *Advertising and sales data for 25 grocery markets*

	Sterling sales share %	Advertising share %	Advertising to sales ratio %
Brand leader	30	35	6
Number 2 brand	17	21	7
Number 3 brand	11	13	8

After Broadbent, 1979.

To compensate for the fact that big brands tend to spend more on advertising than smaller brands, the advertising to sales ratios provide further insight. Table 9.2 shows brand leaders spending less on advertising as a proportion of sales revenue than the number two or three brands. The inference is that promotional budgets are more effective for the leading brand, than for the close followers. One of the reasons for this is advertising economies of scale. The causes of this are not yet fully understood, but are probably related to an aspect of consumer behaviour in respect of leading brands which leads to above-average purchase frequencies – what one researcher has referred to as the 'penetration supercharge phenomena'.

More recently, the WPP Group has been further analysing the PIMS data base. Reassuringly, the findings from the late 1970s still held true. Also, high market share brands still have larger advertising spends than competitors. Their findings are shown in Table 9.3.

Table 9.3 *Advertising analysis using PIMS data*

Advertising to sales ratio versus direct competitors	Average share of market (%)	Average return on investment (%)
Much less	14	17
Less	20	22
Equal	25	22
More	26	25
Much more	32	32

After Biel, 1990.

It would seem that consistently having an advertising to sales ratio greater than competitors is associated with a higher brand share, which in turn enhances the probability of better profitability.

The problem facing the marketer, is to decide the optimum advertising spend to maximize brand profitability in the long run. Normally, one would expect that a brand's share of market approximates to its share of voice, that is its advertising share. In an analysis of data collected in 1987 for 1096 J. W. Thompson advertised brands from 23 countries, these were categorized as being:

- Profit-taking brands, or underspenders, whose share of voice is the same as or below their share of market.
- Investment brands, or overspenders, whose share of voice exceeds their share of market.

Over half (56 per cent) of the brands were categorized as investment brands. In other words, their owners were taking a long-term view about the benefits of advertising.

It would, however, be wrong to assume that, by increasing advertising spend on a quality brand to the extent that share of voice considerably exceeded short-term share of market, would automatically lead to brand success. Without understanding the other brands' market shares and their shares of voice, this could bankrupt the brand.

To help appreciate what broad levels of advertising are appropriate for different brands, the matrix in Figure 9.7 is of value.

In quadrant A, there is an opportunity to increase brand share when competitors' advertising spend is low and they are slow to respond. The challenging brand must exceed competitors' advertising spending and should have a favourable cost structure to enable it to sustain continued advertising.

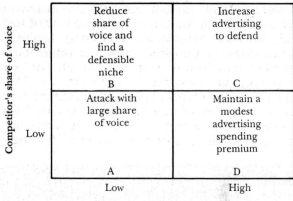

Figure 9.7   *Evaluating appropriate advertising levels. (After Schroer, 1990)*

In quadrant **B**, the small brand is under attack from a competitor with a much more noticeable share of voice. With its higher costs, the brand cannot realistically sustain an advertising war and it would do better by finding a niche that it can defend.

By contrast, in quadrant **C**, the brand leader is more likely to have a cost advantage, because of its size, and it should increase its advertising activity to defend its position.

In quadrant **D**, the smaller competitor has accepted the status quo and has a low share of voice. In this situation, it is wise to aim for a small advertising spend premium, thereby maintaining the brand's higher market share.

Should a company build brands or buy brands?

Some have argued that the rising cost of advertising during the 1980s caused many marketers to shift their attention towards buying other firms' brands, rather than building their own. Particularly for those new brands that needed a continuous advertising presence, the time that could be afforded on television began to shrink dramatically.

Another reason for the surge in brand buying during the 1980s was the ability to extend brand leverage throughout the European Community. Where a multinational felt it to be strategically appropriate to have a particular range in each major country, it was not unusual to find a team evaluating different brand purchases, and, hopefully, also assessing how easily the new brands could be integrated.

A brand acquisition is particularly attractive when the brand has built up a considerable amount of goodwill and when its value is not included on the balance sheet. With the increasing interest of accountants in brand valuations, however, it is likely to become increasingly more difficult to find companies who have not made some attempt at estimating the value of the goodwill of their brands.

Brand acquisitions are often seen as a quick way of gaining entrance to a new market. However, the difficulty of integrating the new brand into the company's structure is often overlooked. Furthermore, the potential for synergy can sometimes be overestimated. The take-over of the American Howard Johnson hotel and restaurant chain in 1980 by the Imperial Group floundered because Imperial's knowledge of consumer markets was irrelevant to the American hotel and fast food market. This unsuccessful acquisition was sold off five years later.

Exhibit 9.4   *With videos and satellite receivers being companion products, Amstrad have logically extended their brand*

By contrast, brands which are acquired in product or services sectors closely related to the firm's current expertise stand a greater chance of succeeding under the new owner than those in sectors where the owner has little expertise. There are many stories of firms unsuccessfully diversifying this way. For example, BP bought its way into the coal minerals and information technology sectors, all of which are markedly different from their core competence in oil exploration, transportation, refining and distribution. It soon recognized the problems of this diversification route and sold off these interests.

Extending brands

If the firm finds that it is unable to penetrate the market further with its current brands, it may consider moving into a related market. It could argue that the best way to overcome consumer apathy and competitive resistance would be to stretch its existing name. While the inherent goodwill and awareness from the original brand name may help the new brand's development, however, there is also the danger that it could dilute the strength of the original brand and convey the wrong perceptions with a consequent detrimental effect on the original brand.

The economics of establishing new brands are pushing companies more towards stretching their existing names into new markets. Daunted by the heavy R&D costs, and more aware of the statistics about failure rates for new brands, marketers are increasingly taking their established names into new product fields. For example, Persil moved into washing up liquid. One study reported that in America, by 1984, virtually two fifths of new launches in supermarkets were extensions.

A researcher by the name of Tauber reviewed a sample of 276 brand extensions to evaluate the different ways of extending brands and concluded that there are seven types of brand extensions:

- *Same product in a different form*   For example, Mars Bars extending into Mars Bars ice cream.
- *Distinctive taste, ingredient or component*   An ingredient or component of the current brand is used to make a new item in a different category. For example, Kraft extended the distinctive taste of their Philadelphia cream cheese into Philadelphia Cream Cheese Salad Dressing.
- *Companion product*   Where some products are used with others, these lend themselves to brand extensions. For example, Duracell batteries in Duracell torches.
- *Same customer franchise*   Marketers develop different brands to sell to their loyal customers. For example, the AA is primarily known for its roadside assistance service to motorists, yet it markets a variety of AA products, such as books, to its customers.
- *Expertise*   Brands are extended into areas where consumers believe the original brand has connotations of special knowledge or

experience. For example, Canon's perceived expertise in optics was extended into photocopiers.

- *Unique benefit, attribute or feature owned by the brand* Some brands stand out for their uniqueness on a particular attribute, which is extended into a related field. For example, the makers of Sunkist orange drink launched Sunkist Vitamin C tablets.
- *Designer image or status* Some consumers feel that their Saab cars have a higher status by knowing that Saab also work in jet aircraft.

When considering extending the original brand name into a new sector, the benefits that come from stretching the name must be weighed against any negative connotations with the original name and any damage that may be done to the core brand. Looking at each of these three areas in more detail, using a checklist adapted from a researcher called Aaker, should enable marketers to decide whether it is wise to extend the brand name.

A Possible benefits from extending the brand name

1 *Awareness* Are consumers aware of the brand name? Whirlpool, the white goods manufacturer entered into a joint venture with Philips in 1989, as part of its expansion programme into Europe. Philips was not prepared to sell its well-known name and Whirlpool employed a dual-branding policy, knowing that by 1999 they must drop the Philips name.
2 *Brand associations* Will the consumer consider the extension to be a credible move? Does the name bring the right sorts of associations to mind? Cadburys use of its name in the liqueur market brings to mind automatically an expectation about a certain type of taste.
3 *Quality associations* Will the name stretch to give the correct perception of quality? IBM is able to use its name whenever it launches small or large systems, in part because of quality perceptions.
4 *Encourage trial purchase* Will the name give the needed reassurance to the risk-averse consumer?

B Possible weaknesses from the core brand name

1 *No value added* Will the name add value to the new line? Some would argue that the designer label status from the name Pierre Cardin adds little to its line extensions – particularly when it marketed bathroom tiles in Spain.
2 *Negative associations* Will the wrong associations result? For example, Levi Strauss were known and respected for their jeans. The extension into Levi Tailored Classics suits failed because of the wrong associations.
3 *Name confusion* Does the name imply the type of product about to marketed? With Audits of Great Britain offering a much wider range of market research services than just continuous research, its other divisions trade under the initials of AGB.

C *Possible damage to the core brand*

1 *Undesirable associations* Will the image of the core brand be damaged? Black & Decker's acquisition of the small appliances range from General Electric caused much internal debate. It was questioned if the heavy duty image that Black & Decker had would be weakened by stretching their name across the new range.
2 *Perceived quality deteriorates* Will the perceived quality of the core brand fall? With its acquisition of holiday companies, Thompson's kept the original names, such as Horizon, so protecting the Thompson Holiday brand.
3 *What about disasters?* Will an unforseen threat damage the core brand? When Persil launched Persil System 3, it did not anticipate dermatological problems and the resulting short-term market resistance.

Besides these three broad areas of questioning, it may well be wise for the marketer to address two further questions that focus on the economics of brand extensions. Are there limitations on the size of the marketing budget? If the brand marketer is constrained by company cut backs, brand extensions may be the only viable route. However, of more importance may be the question of cannibalization. The presence of the core brand name may result in sales of the new brand coming not just from new consumers, but also from those who used to buy the core brand. While it is inevitable that some cannibalization will occur, the marketer needs to anticipate the likely extent of this.

Recently researchers investigated the extent to which brands which stress functional or prestigious connotations can be extended. For example, consumers regarded Timex watches as being more associated with functional benefits, while Rolex watches have more prestigious associations. They found that a brand name which is strongly associated with functional benefits can be more easily extended into product areas bought mainly for their functional benefits. So, for example, a branded wrist watch, positioned primarily as offering functional excellence, could stretch its name, with little difficulty, into stopwatches. By contrast, they found that if the original brand name majored on the dimension of prestige, it could be more easily extended into a product field known for its prestige, rather than its functionality. In other words the Rolex name could more likely be extended to grandfather clocks than into stopwatches.

It was also reported that when consumers perceived a brand being extended into a product field that many firms would find relatively easy to produce, the brand extension would not be accepted. This may be because consumers felt that in the new product field there was little difference between competing brands and that the new entrant was going to do little more than use its image to charge an unnecessary price premium. On a more positive note, where consumers perceive

- The original and extended product classes to be complementary, and

- The firm is viewed as being able to transfer its skills and resources in making the extension,

then there is a greater likelihood of the brand extension being accepted.

Conclusions

By analysing environmental opportunities and threats, as well as thoroughly appreciating the nature of the brand's competitive advantage, marketers are able to develop strategies that position their brands to achieve the best return, while being protected from competitive attacks. The lifespan of brands will depend on the sustainability of their competitive advantage.

The two broad competitive advantages inherent in successful brands are based on either delivering similar benefits cheaper than competitors (i.e. cost-driven brands), and/or delivering superior benefits than competitors at a price premium (i.e. value-added brands). It is crucial that a decision is taken about the strategic path that the brand will follow, and that everyone is informed of this. Each of these two routes makes different demands on employees, resources and processes. With everyone in the firm aware of the branding route being followed, they can all contribute by being vigilant in cost-curtailing activities and by being creative in devising added value. Strategies appropriate for each type of brand need developing, avoiding at all costs the commodity brand domain, characterized by little added value and, frequently, no cost advantage.

A useful device for identifying the competitive advantages of brands is Porter's Value Chain. This helps managers to consider the processes and supporting services involved in transforming commodities into highly respected brands. It also acts as a check as to whether the competitive advantages of brands are being reinforced, by considering the linkages in each part of the value adding process.

A more sophisticated way of developing brand strategy is to consider both the type of competitive advantage inherent in the brand, and the competitive scope of the market it will be targeted at, i.e. a narrow or broad group of consumers. From the resulting matrix, four generic strategies can be documented.

Having identified the brand's competitive advantage, and the strategic direction to be followed, the marketer then needs to anticipate competitors' responses and develop ways of sustaining the brand's advantage. An important issue is agreeing as a brand team who the competitors are and using the concept of market share to evaluate future opportunities.

Winning brands focus on adopting leadership positions in specific markets, offering superior perceived quality than competitors, taking advantage of environmental opportunities and being memorable. It is not unusual for their share of advertising spend to exceed their market share.

More recently, high advertising costs have forced many firms to look more favourably at buying, rather than building brands from scratch. Another way that marketers can save costs is by extending the core brand's name into new markets. The dangers inherent in this strategy, however, need to be carefully evaluated.

Marketing action checklist

It is recommended that, after reading this chapter, marketers undertake the following exercises to test and refine their brand strategies.

1 Write down what you believe to be the reasons why consumers buy your brand and your competitors' brands. For each of these reasons, evaluate which of the brands comes closest to satisfying consumers needs. If this information is already available from an accurate marketing research study, it should be used instead of management judgement. On a separate sheet of paper, summarize these findings by stating for each brand which attributes it best satisfies. This is one way of identifying each brand's competitive advantage(s). Those brands which do not have any 'success attributes' are unlikely to succeed for long.

2 How easy is it for your competitors to copy any of your brands' competitive advantages? What actions are you taking to sustain your brands' competitive advantages?

3 For each of your brands separately, use the matrix of value-added advantage versus cost-driven advantage in Figure 9.3, to plot your brand and those of your competitors. Whichever quadrant your brand occupies, ask how appropriate your current strategies are. Those competitors' brands falling in the same quadrant as your brand represent potentially the greatest threat. What are you doing to protect your brand against these?

4 Using the example of the value chain in Figure 9.4, identify all those activities you undertake in transforming low value goods or services into high value, finished goods or services. Which of these activities do you believe you do, or could do, better than competitors? How do these 'doing better or cheaper' activities relate to the competitive advantages identified in 1 above? Try to assess what proportion of costs can be allocated to each part of the value chain for a particular brand. How do these cost components compare with competitors? How well linked are each of the processes and support activities on the value chain?

5 For each of your brands separately, use the matrix of competitive scope versus competitive advantage in Figure 9.5, to plot your brand and those of your competitors. Whichever quadrant your brand occupies, check the appropriateness of your current strategy. Which competitive brands fall in the same quadrant as your brand? How appropriate are their current strategies? What plans have you to protect your brand against those brands in the same quadrant?

6 For any of your brands which compete in services markets, evaluate which of the ten factors in Table 9.1 are most appropriate for sustaining their competitive advantages.

7 As individuals (rather than in a team) select a brand and write down which competitors it competes against. Then, as individuals, group competitors together into discrete clusters such that those competitors grouped together show a similarity in terms of the strategy being followed. Then meet as a management team and discuss your rationale for the named competitors and the different basis for strategic groupings.

8 From 7, which competitors did the management team identify as following a similar strategy to your brand? How much relevant information do you hold about these competitors – consult the section at the end of 'Anticipating competitor response'.

9 Using Figure 9.6, which shows the components of brand share, what marketing research data do you hold to evaluate the volume of sales that is, or could be made to customers in the blocks A to E? In terms of those customers competed for and won in block D, what proportion of customers fall into the categories D1, D2, D3 and D4? What actions could be taken to maximize the number of customers in category D1?

10 What marketing research data is held about consumers' perceptions of the quality of your brand and those of competitors? From qualitative research, are you able to establish accurately how consumers evaluate the quality of your brand and competitors' brands? Based on these marketing research reports, what actions are needed to improve consumers' perceptions of your quality?

11 This question is only applicable if advertising is appropriate for your brands. Produce a table for your brand, and those brands against which it competes, showing each brand's share of market and share of voice, as well as each brand's advertising to sales ratio. For the brand that you believe your brand competes most against, use the matrix of competitor's share of voice against your share of market, Figure 9.7, to assess the most appropriate level of advertising activity.

12 On the last occasion that you followed a policy of using an existing brand name for a new addition to your range, evaluate:

- The strengths of using the core brand name.
- The advantages for the new line by carrying the core brand name.
- The effect the new line had on the core brand.

Taking all of these points into consideration, was it wise to have followed a brand extension policy?

References and further reading

Aaker D. (1988). *Strategic Market Management*. New York: Wiley.
Aaker D. (1990). Brand extensions: the good, the bad and the ugly. *Sloan Management Review*, **31**, (4), 47–56.

Aaker D. (1991). *Managing Brand Equity*. New York: The Free Press.

Aaker D., Keller K. (1990). Consumer evaluations of brand extensions. *Journal of Marketing*, **54**, (Jan.), 27–41.

Abell D., J. Hammond (1979). *Strategic Marketing Planning*. Englewood Cliffs: Prentice Hall.

Biel A. (1990). Strong brand, high spend. *ADMAP*, (Nov.) 35–40.

Broadbent S. (1979). What makes a top brand? *The Nielsen Researcher*. No. 3.

Buday T. (1989). Capitalizing on brand extensions. *Journal of Consumer Marketing*, **6**, (4), 27–30.

Buzzell R., Gale B. (1987). *The PIMS Principles*. London: Collier Macmillan.

Christopher M., Majaro S., McDonald M. (1987). *Strategy search*. Aldershot: Gower.

Clifford D., Cavanagh R. (1985). *The Winning Performance: how America's high growth midsize companies succeed*. London: Sidgwick and Jackson.

Davidson H. (1987). *Offensive Marketing*. Harmondsworth: Penguin.

de Chernatony L. (1991). Formulating brand strategy. *European Management Journal*, **9**, (2), 194–200.

Doyle P. (1989). Building successful brands: the strategic options. *Journal of Marketing Management*, **5**, (1), 77–95.

Easingwood C. (1990). Hard to copy services. In *Marketing Educators Group Proceedings* (Pendlebury A., Watkins T., eds). Oxford: MEG, pp. 325–336.

Easton G. (1988). Competition and marketing strategy. *European Journal of Marketing*, **27**, (2), 31–49.

Grossberg K. (1989). How Citibank created a retail niche for itself in Japan. *Planning Review*, (Sept.–Oct.), 14–17, 48.

Hamel G., Prahalad C. (1989). Strategic intent. *Harvard Business Review*, (May–June), 63–76.

Johnson G., Scholes K. (1989). *Exploring Corporate Strategy*. Hemel Hempstead: Prentice Hall.

Jones B., Ramsden R. (1991). The global brand age. *Management Today*, Sept., 78–83.

Jones J. (1990). Ad spending: maintaining market share. *Harvard Business Review*, (Jan.–Feb.), 38–42.

Karakaya F., Stahl M. (1989). Barriers to entry and market entry decisions in consumer and industrial goods markets. *Journal of Marketing*, **53**, (Apr.), 80–91.

Karel J. (1991). Brand strategy positions products worldwide. *Journal of Business Strategy*, (May-June), 16–19.

Kelley B. (1991). Making it different. *Sales & Marketing Management*, (May), 52–55, 60.

Lex (1991). Ratners. *The Financial Times*, 17 September, p. 22.

Lorenz C. (1988). Unrelated takeovers spell trouble. *The Financial Times*, 4 March, p. 22.

Ohmae K. (1982). *The Mind of the Strategist*. Harmondsworth: Penguin.

Park C. W., Milberg S., Lawson R. (1991). Evaluation of brand extension: the role of product feature similarity and brand concept consistency. *Journal of Consumer Research*, **18**, (Sept.), 185–193.

Peters T., Waterman R. (1982). *In Search of Excellence*. New York: Harper & Row.

Porac J., Thomas H. (1990). Taxonomic mental models in competitor definition. *Academy of Management Review*, **15**, (2), 224–40.

Porter M. (1979). How competitive forces shape strategy. *Harvard Business Review*, (Mar.–Apr.), 137–145.

Porter M. (1980). *Competitive Strategy*. New York: The Free Press.

Porter M. (1985). *Competitive Advantage*. New York: The Free Press.

Porter M. (1988). *Michael Porter on Competitive Strategy*. Harvard Business School Video Series. Boston: Nathan/Tyler.

Prahalad C., Hamel G. (1990). The core competences of the corporation. *Harvard Business Review*, (May-June), 79–91.

Schroer J. (1990). Ad spending: growing market share. *Harvard Business Review* (Jan.–Feb.), 44–8.

Tauber E. (1988). Brand leverage: strategy for growth in a cost control world. *Journal of Advertising Research*, (Aug.–Sept.), 26–30.

Thornhill J. (1992). Jewellery innovator and the textile veteran. *The Financial Times. Weekend*. 11/12 January, p. 6. See also p. 1 and p. 22.

Urban G., Star S. (1991). *Advanced Marketing Strategy*. Englewood Cliffs: Prentice Hall.

Wachman R., Fairbairn S. (1992). Ratner steps down as sales slump. *London Evening Standard*. 10 January, p. 5.

Woodward S. (1991). Competitive marketing. In *Understanding Brands* (Cowley D., ed.). London: Kogan Page.

Zeithmal V., Parasuraman A., Berry L. (1985). Problems and strategies in services marketing. *Journal of Marketing*, **44**, (Spring), 33–46.

Index